# Events and Semantic Architecture

# Events and Semantic Architecture

PAUL M. PIETROSKI

OXFORD

UNIVERSITY PRESS

# OXFORD

UNIVERSITY PRESS

Great Clarendon Street, Oxford OX2 6DP

Oxford University Press is a department of the University of Oxford.
It furthers the University's objective of excellence in research, scholarship,
and education by publishing worldwide in

Oxford New York

Auckland Cape Town Dar es Salaam Hong Kong Karachi
Kuala Lumpur Madrid Melbourne Mexico City Nairobi
New Delhi Shanghai Taipei Toronto

With offices in

Argentina Austria Brazil Chile Czech Republic France Greece
Guatemala Hungary Italy Japan Poland Portugal Singapore
South Korea Switzerland Thailand Turkey Ukraine Vietnam

Oxford is a registered trade mark of Oxford University Press
in the UK and in certain other countries

Published in the United States
by Oxford University Press Inc., New York

British Library Cataloguing in Publication Data

Data available

Library of Congress Cataloging in Publication Data

Data available

Typeset by Newgen Imaging Systems (P) Ltd., Chennai, India
Printed and bound in Great Britain
on acid-free paper by
Biddles Ltd., King's Lynn

ISBN 0–19–924430–8   978–0–19–924430–0
ISBN 0–19–924431–6 (Pbk.)   978–0–19–924431–7 (Pbk.)

1 3 5 7 9 10 8 6 4 2

# Preface

In my first week as a graduate student, I was introduced to Frege's logic via George Boolos, and to the subject of linguistics via Noam Chomsky. In retrospect, that seems to have been a formative experience, from which I have since been trying to recover—with lots of help, beginning with teachers like George and Noam and Richard Larson, who were willing to encourage ill-prepared students.

For better or worse, I never doubted that Frege's toolkit could be fruitfully applied to the study of natural language, or that logic, linguistics, and the philosophy of language are continuous enterprises. Such thoughts, once formed, seemed obviously true. But a little inquiry brings ignorance into focus. And the need for a dissertation, followed by life as an assistant professor advertised as a philosopher of mind, pushed me towards other topics. A counterveiling force, Jim McGilvray, kept nudging me back to issues concerning linguistic meaning and innate constraints on human thought. Jim also forced me to confront various respects in which Frege's technical apparatus is ill-suited to natural language, as stressed by Frege and Chomsky themselves. One of my goals in writing this book—and another in the works—has been to get free of some assumptions that I had absorbed in spite of my first teachers: in particular, that a semantic theory for a natural language will associate predicates with *sets* and sentences with *truth*-values.

Jim also started a reading group at McGill University, focused mainly on issues at the cusp of linguistics and philosophy. This proved enormously important for me. My thanks to the members of that group, and especially Mark Baker, who provided many tutorials that helped me understand the power and beauty of a severely constrained universal grammar. Mark has continued to be an invaluable resource. And because of Ernie Lepore, whose reputation for mentoring is entirely deserved, I have been part of another group of philosophers and linguists (including Mark) who have prompted or shaped most of my work for the last five years. Thanks to all the participants, especially Peter Ludlow, Richard Larson, Roger Schwartzschild, Jason Stanley, Zoltan Szabo, Jeff King, Mark Richard, Delia Graff, Rob Stainton, and of course, Ernie.

While in Montreal, I met Norbert Hornstein when he was on leave. This prompted me to spend part of my first sabbatical in Maryland, co-teaching a course with Norbert and learning about minimalism. One thing led to another, and I now benefit from Norbert's intellectual enthusiasm on a regular basis. He has been wonderfully supportive of this project. Moving to Maryland also led to very productive collaborations with Stephen Crain and Juan Uriagereka. Thanks to them, and my other colleagues, for creating and inviting me into an especially good space for the study of language and mind. Georges Rey, Peter Carruthers, Dan Blair, Susan Dwyer, and Jeff Horty provided sympathetic yet not uncritical ears, along with sound advice. Students in several seminars, along with colleagues in many audiences, provided useful comments and challenges. For help with earlier versions of this material, I thank Norbert, Juan, an anonymous referee for the press, Elena Herburger, Utpahl Lahiri, and Jim Higginbotham—another teacher whose broader influence will, I hope, be clear. Barry Schein commented extensively on an early incarnation of the manuscript, providing help at many levels of detail. Barry too has been influential in ways not fully conveyed with references.

A book like this one would have been published sooner, with a serious error in the treatment of quantification, if not for Tim Williamson. The remaining errors do not include the one Tim spotted at the Logic and Language conference in March 2003. Conversation with him and Barry Smith, whose generous commentary at the conference helped clarify my project, provided a starting point for the newer treatment. I am (now) grateful for what turned out to be an impetus to massive revision of a manuscript I thought was nearly finished. On a related note, thanks to John Davey for editorial patience, encouragement from the beginning, and consistently helpful suggestions. Readers should be grateful, as I am, for Susan Dwyer's input at various stages. Sue also provided more important support, in making life good.

# Contents

# Introduction

Here is the idea, shorn of all the qualifications and supplementations: each complex expression of natural language is the concatenation of two simpler expressions; these two constituents, together with the meaning of concatenation, determine the meaning of the complex expression; constituents are understood as monadic *predicates*, and concatenation signifies *conjunction*. So, from a semantic perspective, every complex expression is a conjunction of predicates.

If this is correct, then core aspects of linguistic meaning are quite simple, though quite different from how they are standardly depicted. Defending the idea requires qualification, supplementation, and more than one book. But the guiding thought is that phrases like 'red ball' provide semantic paradigms: a red ball is something that satisfies the condition imposed by 'red' *and* the condition imposed by 'ball'. In light of Davidson's (1967b, 1985) proposals and subsequent developments, it is also plausible that the meaning of (1) is given roughly by (2).

(1)  Pat hugged Chris quickly
(2)  there was something such that
     it was done by Pat, *and* it was a hugging, *and* it happened to Chris, *and* it was quick.

On this view, the subsentential expressions in (1) indicate conjuncts of a complex monadic predicate; where a conjunct may be logically complex, and a sentence reflects existential closure of a predicate.

I argue that many constructions—involving quantification, plurality, 'that'-clauses, and causal verbs—can and should be analyzed in this fashion. This does not yet establish the general thesis, according to which (2) reveals fundamental principles of semantic composition in natural language, since the meaning of concatenation may not be uniform across *all* complex expressions. Though as we shall see, there are reasons for assuming uniformity, absent evidence to the contrary. Some of the arguments provided here are new. But in defending the proposed conception of how natural language syntax contributes to meaning, I draw on work by many theorists.[1]

# 1. Overview

According to many linguists and philosophers, sentence (1) means roughly that something had the following properties: Pat did it, it was an event of hugging, Chris underwent it, and it was quick. Using formal notation, and ignoring tense, the suggestion is that the meaning of (1) is given by (1M),

(1M)   $\exists x[\text{Agent}(x, \text{Pat}) \ \& \ \text{Hugging}(x) \ \& \ \text{Theme}(x, \text{Chris}) \ \& \ \text{Quick}(x)]$

where 'Agent' and 'Theme' express relations between events and *participants* in those events. From this perspective, each word in (1) corresponds to a predicate of events, but the syntactic arguments of the verb—the subject 'Pat' and direct object 'Chris'—are also associated with "thematic roles". I'll argue that (1M) is indeed the right way to specify the meaning of (1), that the conjunctive aspects of (1M) reflect the *combinatorial structure* of (1), and that this is an instance of a far more general pattern.

## 1.1. *Concatenation Signifies Conjunction*

As a first approximation, we can regard (1) as the result of concatenating 'hugged' with 'Chris', adding 'quickly', and then

---

[1] Especially important and discussed below are Davidson (1967*b*, 1985), Castañeda (1967), Higginbotham (1983, 1985, 1986), Taylor (1985), Parsons (1990), Schein (1993), Larson and Segal (1995). There are also points of contact with Chomsky's (1995, 2000*b*) minimalist program in syntax.

combining that phrase with 'Pat'. The result can be represented in many ways.

```
        / \
  Pat / \            Pat^((hugged^Chris)^quickly)
      / \ quickly    [Pat [[hugged Chris] quickly]]
  hugged  Chris
```

If each word corresponds to a predicate of events, as suggested by (1M), perhaps the branching structure itself contributes to the meaning of (1). Clearly, the sentence doesn't mean that something had the following property: Pat did it, *or* it was a hugging, *or* Chris underwent it, *or* it was quick. In my view, this is because the semantic correlate of concatenation is conjunction, as opposed to disjunction or anything else. The ampersands in (1M) reflect a semantic contribution of syntax.

Of course, even if this is correct, one wants to know how thematic notions like 'Agent' and 'Theme' come to be involved in sentential meanings. But suppose the *grammatical* structure of (1) reflects the fact that 'Pat' and 'Chris' are arguments of the predicate 'hugged', while 'hugged Chris' and 'hugged Chris quickly' are complex predicates that take one argument, as shown in (1G);

(1G)   [Pat$_\alpha$ [[hugged$_{\Pi^*}$ Chris$_\alpha$]$_\Pi$ quickly]$_\Pi$]

where the subscripts '$\alpha$' and '$\Pi$' indicate grammatical arguments and predicates, respectively, and '$\Pi^*$' indicates a (two-place) predicate that combines with an argument to form a (one-place) predicate.[2] Then a natural thought is that subjects of "action verbs" represent things *as* Agents, while objects of such verbs represent things *as* Themes. Perhaps when speakers hear (1), 'Pat' is understood as the eventish predicate 'Agent(x, Pat)' because 'Pat' is the subject of 'hugged', and

---

[2]  One can interpret the subscripts in (1G) as follows: 'Pat' is an $\alpha$ (an argument), 'hugged' is a $\Pi^*$ (a predicate that combines with an $\alpha$ to form a $\Pi$, which is a unary predicate), and so on; see Chomsky (1957, 1965) on the theoretical role and interpretation of labels. One can, if one likes, replace '$\alpha$' and '$\Pi$' with 'NP' (or 'DP') and 'V'. But I want to be as neutral as possible with regard to which syntactic labels (if any) are semantically important; cf. Collins (2001). For now, I am also

'Chris' is understood as the eventish predicate 'Theme(x, Chris)' because 'Chris' is the object of 'hugged'. If so, then appeal to thematic roles provides a way of describing a certain relation between grammatical structure and meaning: at least for purposes of semantic combination, verbs and their syntactic arguments are interpreted as monadic predicates, which may have thematic structure.

Precisely because appeals to thematic roles figure prominently on this view, I am *not* denying that natural language meanings involve relations. But if the arguments of action verbs are interpreted as monadic predicates, this invites the thought that many other expressions are interpreted similarly. Since (1) can be paraphrased with 'There was a hugging of Chris by Pat', an obvious thought is that the prepositions 'of' and 'by' indicate thematic roles, with 'of Chris' and 'by Pat' understood like the subject and object of (1); see Gruber (1965, 1976), Fillmore (1968), Jackendoff (1972, 1987), Chomsky (1981). Maybe semantic relationality in natural language is due to a relatively small stock of relations, largely associated with certain grammatical configurations or "functional" expressions (like prepositions).

Still, *sentences* are not merely predicates. Declarative sentences, at least when they are used, can typically be evaluated for truth or falsity. So one wants to hear more about the source of the existential quantification in (1M). Why does (1) mean that *there was something* of a certain sort? One might also wonder how concatenation could possibly correspond to conjunction in sentences like (3–4)

(3)   Chris sang or Pat did not dance
(4)   No dancer hugged every linguist

These issues will be addressed in due course. But as we'll see, one can maintain that concatenation signifies conjunction of (monadic)

---

abstracting from various issues concerning the label (if any) of 'quickly', how to label sentences, the meaning of thematic predicates, and the possibility that hugged$_{\Pi*}$ is a complex expression formed by combining a $\Pi$ with a covert element. More on all this below. But whatever the details, the proposal is that a structure like (1G)—in current terminology, an LF—is mapped to a semantic structure or "logical form" like (1M).

predicates, even in sentences like (3–4). And this hypothesis about natural language turns out to be better than a standard alternative.

It is widely held that if concatenation signifies anything, it signifies *function-application*. On this view, a complex expression like 'Chris sang' means what it does because: the syntactic predicate ('sang') is semantically associated with some function; the syntactic argument ('Chris') is associated with some entity in the domain of that function; and concatenating a predicate with an appropriate argument yields an expression associated with *the value of* the relevant function as *applied to* the relevant entity.[3] The trick is to specify the functions and entities in a plausible way; and this can be done for a significant range of cases, including sentences like (3–4). But I think "Functionism" is ultimately unsatisfactory. The plan is to show that "Conjunctivism" is theoretically viable, and to provide some arguments for adopting it. So of necessity, much of the book is devoted to showing that Conjunctivists can do what Functionists have done. (And in the hope that comparing these approaches may help novices think about the empirical content of each, I have tried to err on the side of explicitness, at the risk of boring specialists.)

One might think that Functionism is truistic: a consequence of the only plausible notational scheme for semantics, as opposed to an empirical hypothesis that might be compared with an alternative. So in Chapter 1, I begin with a general discussion of how the two approaches—and a third "mixed" view—differ, while still sharing some foundational assumptions about how to construct semantic theories that accommodate a certain range of elementary facts. I also review some old arguments for the claim that sentences like (1) involve covert quantification over events. This claim is compatible with several views about the semantic correlate of concatenation. Though by the end of Chapter 2, which is primarily concerned with quantification and its relation to plurality,

---

[3] If 'sang' is associated with function S, and 'Chris' is associated with entity c, then 'Chris'^'sang' is associated with S(c)—i.e., the value of S given c as the (semantic) argument to S. See Ch. 1.

we will have an attractive Conjunctivist semantics for sentences like (1–4) and many other textbook cases. Indeed, the resulting account is preferable in several respects to a Functionist account.

In Chapter 3, I extend this positive case, arguing for a Conjunctivist approach to various causal constructions and to verbs (like 'said') that take sentential arguments. A running theme will be that Conjunctivism is better than Functionism even with regard to many cases of predicates combining with arguments—in particular, cases involving *plural* arguments, *causal* verbs, speech-act verbs with *sentential* complements, and even *determiners* (like 'every') that take predicates (like 'bottle' and 'fell') as arguments. This is important, since the initial attractions of Functionism lie with its treatment of predicate–argument combinations. Cases of adjunction, like 'red ball' and 'sang loudly' (in which a noun or verb combines with a modifier) favor Conjunctivism. So if Conjunctivism provides a better account of theoretically interesting predicate–argument combinations, that is bad news for Functionism. It also tells against the mixed view that concatenation of *predicates with arguments* signifies function-application, while concatenation of *predicates with adjuncts* signifies predicate-conjunction.

My plan is to motivate Conjunctivism by showing its virtues across a variety of constructions. But no discussion of any construction type is offered as anything like a full treatment of its topic. (Experts on serial verbs, for example, will note that Chapter 3 describes only the tip of their iceberg.) Along the way, I sketch replies to some potential objections; though unsurprisingly, I do not provide a complete Conjunctivist semantics for English, much less every natural language. And for reasons hinted at in the final chapter, evaluating potential counterexamples quickly leads to large questions about how meaning is related to truth. Nonetheless, I hope to show that Conjunctivism is an attractive thesis that is preferable to more familiar alternatives.

## 1.2. *Form and Meaning*

Let me conclude this overview by locating the main issues in a slightly different context. For any sentence of a natural language, we can ask the following questions: what is its grammatical structure; what does it mean; and how is its structure related to its meaning? The structure of a sentence clearly bears on how it is understood by speakers of the relevant language. Sentences like (5) and (6)

(5)   Pat hugged Chris
(6)   Chris hugged Pat

differ in meaning, presumably, because the subject–object distinction matters semantically. Similarly, 'lawyer who needed a doctor' and 'doctor who needed a lawyer' have analogous but different meanings. But even for sentences like (5), we don't really know *how* grammatical form is related to meaning.

Upon reflection, this is unsurprising. Semantics is difficult, in part because it calls for the solution of an equation with three variables (see Higginbotham, 1985, 1986). Given a linguistic expression, we need theoretically perspicuous representations of its grammatical and semantic properties, in order to ask how these (perhaps overlapping) properties are related. So even given a tentative view about the structure of a given expression, two relevant aspects of linguistic reality remain unknown. One cannot formulate a clear proposal about how form is related to meaning without representing the latter. And while the meanings of expressions may in some sense be "transparent" to competent speakers, *explaining* semantic facts typically requires nontrivial representations of—i.e., substantive hypotheses about—those facts. Specific representations may suggest proposals about how grammatical and semantic properties are related. But any such proposal must be evaluated in light of all the available evidence.

For example, suppose the grammatical structure of (5) is as shown in (5G),

(5G)   $[\text{Pat}_\alpha \ [\text{hugged}_{\Pi^*} \ \text{Chris}_\alpha]_\Pi]$

on the model of (1G) above. There are many features of (5) that (5G) does not capture, and some of these features may well be semantically relevant. Still, (5G) is presumably correct as far as it goes. It is less clear how we should represent the meaning of (5). As any speaker of English can tell you, it means that Pat hugged Chris. But the question is how to represent this meaning for purposes of doing semantics. We can—by stipulation, if necessary—denote the meaning of (5) with 'that Pat hugged Chris'. But this does not yet begin to characterize the theoretically important properties of this sentential meaning. For reasons reviewed below, I assume that sentential meanings are structured. This raises questions about *how* they are structured, and how the meanings of complex expressions are related to natural language grammar.[4]

Jumping ahead a bit, consider three hypotheses about the "semantic structure" of (5).

$(5a)$  $H_2(p, c)$
$(5b)$  $\exists x[H_3(x, p, c)]$
$(5c)$  $\exists x[\text{Agent}(x, p) \ \& \ H_1(x) \ \& \ \text{Theme}(x, c)]$

Here, 'p' and 'c' are labels for individuals in some domain; '$H_2$' is a binary predicate satisfied by certain ordered pairs of individuals; '$H_3$' is a ternary predicate satisfied by certain ordered triples, with 'x' ranging over events; and '$H_1$' is a unary predicate satisfied by events. If $(5a-c)$ reflect importantly different proposals about the meaning of (5), and I argue that they do, we want to know which one figures in the best explanations of the semantic facts. The answer is not obvious.

Correlatively, it is initially unclear *how* the meaning of (5) is related to the meanings of its constituents, if only because there are several available hypotheses about the semantic contribution of verbs. Setting $(5b)$ aside for now, should theorists represent the semantic contribution of a verb like 'hugged' with a predicate satisfied by ordered pairs of individuals, or with a predicate satisfied by certain events? As we'll see, the first suggestion fits naturally with the idea that combining expressions indicates function-application; the second fits naturally with the idea that combining expressions

---

[4] We also want to know *why* grammatical form is related to meaning in certain ways. I return, in particular, to the question of why being the subject or object of a verb has *thematic* significance.

indicates predicate-conjunction. And *many* considerations are relevant to evaluating these alternative hypotheses.

Interpretations of semantic theories can also be tendentious. Though in my view, claims about our theoretical formalism can and should be guided by relevant empirical facts, just like claims about the semantic significance of concatenation. In Chapter 2, I focus on the need for theories that employ *second-order* quantification. This raises questions about how to interpret such quantification as it appears in our metalanguage, given facts about plural noun-phrases like 'three linguists', 'most philosophers', and 'the students'. Indeed, part of my argument for a Conjunctivist account of such expressions relies on a nonstandard but empirically attractive conception of second-order quantification.[5]

The concluding chapter briefly addresses a large question that I discuss elsewhere; see Pietroski (2003*d*, forthcoming, in progress). Do declarative sentences of natural language have *truth*-conditions, perhaps relative to contexts? It is widely held that they do, and that facts about truth-conditions are the primary explananda for semantic theories. For most of the book, I adopt this view as an idealization. Though following Chomsky (1977, 2000*a*), I suspect that semantic theories are really theories about intrinsic features of linguistic expressions; where these features constrain *but do not determine* truth-conditions, not even relative to contexts. This bears indirectly on the main issue, since counterexamples to overly simple views about how meaning is related to truth can look like counterexamples to otherwise plausible views about how syntax contributes to meaning; and Conjunctivism is a thesis about meaning, not a thesis about truth *per se*. But we can delay debates about *how* meaning constrains truth, since at least initially, they are orthogonal to the main issue here.

Let me stress, however, that the difference between Functionism and Conjunctivism is intramural. Both are proposals about how to

---

[5] Here, I will draw on Boolos (1998) and Schein (1993). It turns out that (5) is an especially simple sentence that does not force us to consider second-order quantification over potentially many events with potentially many participants. Other sentences do.

apply a certain theoretical framework—deriving from Frege, Tarski, and others—to the study of natural language. I take it as given that formal tools can be fruitfully applied to questions about how the meaning of a complex expression, like 'quickly found the red ball that most philosophers saw', depends on the relevant word meanings and how the words are combined into phrases. The issue concerns the relative merits of different hypotheses about the semantic role of forming a phrase by combining expressions. Does concatenation signify function-application, or predicate-conjunction, sometimes one and sometimes the other, or none of the above? In posing this question, I assume that (i) complex expressions of natural language have semantic properties determined by their parts and how those parts are arranged, and (ii) theorists can defend specific hypotheses, couched in a formal idiom, about these properties. I cannot here defend these presuppositions in a way that fully responds to skeptics.[6] But the rest of this introduction, which indicates the kinds of facts I think a theory of meaning should account for, may at least motivate the assumptions for newcomers. This is a backdrop against which we can ask more specific questions about the semantic significance of concatenation.

## 2. A Plethora of Semantic Explananda

A speaker of a natural (spoken) language, like English or French, can reliably associate sounds of the language with meanings. This striking fact calls for explanation.

Speakers of French hear 'neige' *as* a sound with a certain meaning. Speakers of English hear 'snow' as a sound with a (presumably similar) meaning, while associating the sounds of 'child' and 'every' with quite different meanings. For a monolingual speaker of

---

[6] For useful discussion that does not presuppose Functionism, see Higginbotham (1985, 1986), Larson and Segal (1995). For formulations of more standard views, see also Heim and Kratzer (1998), Chierchia and McConnell-Ginet (2000). But for reasons hinted at in the previous paragraph, I am not assuming that there are compositional theories of *truth* for natural languages.

English, the sound of 'neige' is meaningless, while the sound of 'bank' has several meanings. Speakers of English can also identify certain strings of words—like 'every child', 'sang loudly' and 'every child sang loudly'—as meaningful complex expressions. Indeed, such a person can hear 'Every child sang loudly' as meaning that every child sang loudly; and she can hear 'Pat found the hiker with a map' as having two different meanings.[7] A speaker of Japanese may lack such capacities, but she can hear 'Masaaki-ga migete-o ageta' as meaning that Masaaki raised his right hand. To repeat: such facts call for explanation. One can declare it definitional, and in this sense trivial, that speakers of English can understand English. But it is far from trivial that certain human beings have certain linguistic capacities, especially since these capacities are *unbounded* and *systematically related* in several respects.

## 2.1. *Unboundedness*

If you know English, you can understand (9) as soon as you hear it.

> (9)   The orange duck went to his office, proved two theorems, and hired a very tall architect

If someone utters (9), you might wonder why. But that is because you would hear the utterance *as* a bizarre claim about a mathematically gifted waterfowl who employed someone of unusual

---

[7] Here the ambiguity seems to be *structural*—i.e., due to different ways of combining the words (not the ambiguity of a word-sound.) Using structural descriptions of expressions, we can say: [Pat [found [the [hiker [with a map]]]]] means that Pat found the hiker who had a map [Pat [[found [the hiker]] [with a map]]] means that Pat found the hiker by using a map. Similar remarks apply to examples like 'Chris saw the man with binoculars'. There are at least sixteen readings of 'I can duck and hide when visiting relatives may scare me', and sixteen semantic facts about what the sound can mean (relative to a grammatical way of arranging the words). This suggests that the semantic facts *far* outstrip any facts that could be reported in a "homophonic" or "disquotational" way. So I see no reason to assume that theorists should (even try to) formulate theories whose theorems are homophonic or disquotational—*pace* suggestions to the contrary by Davidson (1984) and others. Why should ordinary language provide the resources needed for semantic theorizing?

height. And this would be so, even if you had never encountered (9) before. By contrast, (10) is word salad.

> (10)   Tall a went the proved his orange two to duck theorems hired very architect office and

Yet (11) is another meaningful rearrangement of the words in (9).

> (11)   The architect went to his orange office, hired two very tall ducks, and proved a theorem

There seems to be no upper bound to the number of novel sounds, corresponding to strings of known words, that a speaker can understand. This suggests that when a speaker is presented with the sound of a sentence, in a language she knows, the speaker can somehow figure out the associated meaning(s) by virtue of: knowing which meanings are associated with the component word-sounds; and knowing how, in general, the meaning of a complex expression $\Sigma$ is determined by the structure of $\Sigma$ and the (semantic properties of) the components of $\Sigma$.

It is worth noting that there are different kinds of unboundedness, since the differences will be important later. Sentential connectives, like 'or' and 'and', introduce unboundedness of the sort also exhibited by the propositional calculus. The result of connecting any two sentences (as in 'Pat sang or Chris danced') is a sentence, which can be joined with any sentence to form a still longer sentence; and so on. Or putting the focus on speakers, as opposed to expressions, speakers of English can (in principle) understand endlessly many "connected-sentence" sounds. We can also understand 'Pat sang or Chris danced and Sam laughed' in two ways, associating the relevant sound with two meanings that can be distinguished with different bracketing, as indicated below.

> {[(Pat sang) or (Chris danced)] and (Sam laughed)}
>
> {(Pat sang) or [(Chris danced) and (Sam laughed)]}

But it's hard to get very excited about this. Slightly more interesting is the fact that a declarative sentence can be extended by prefixing it with 'It seems that' or 'Someone said that'. Speakers of English can understand 'Someone said that Chris danced', 'It seems that someone said that Chris danced', etc. Though by itself, this is still only moderately impressive. If there were just a few sentential prefixes and finitely many "basic" sentences, a speaker might be able to understand endlessly many sentences by learning the meaning of each basic sentence and mastering a few principles like the following: for each sentence S, 'Someone said that'$^\wedge$S means that someone produced an utterance with the meaning of S; and for each pair of sentences, $S_1$ and $S_2$, $S_1{}^\wedge$'or'$^\wedge S_2$ means that either $S_1$ is true or $S_2$ is true.

Speakers of a natural language can, however, understand a *lot* of sentences that include neither connectives like 'or' nor prefixes like 'someone said that'. Consider (12).

(12)   This is the mouse that lived in the red brick house that Jack, who disliked mice ever since one ate some very expensive Gruyere, built on the first Tuesday after the first Monday in November of the year when the rent on Jack's spacious downtown apartment skyrocketed.

Nouns like 'apartment' can be modified with adjectives *ad nauseam*; and one can use an entire sentence, like 'Jack built the house', to create a phrase with a relative clause as in 'the house that Jack built'. Similarly, a verb like 'built' can be extended via modifiers like 'on the first Tuesday after the first Monday in November'; and adverbial phrases can have sentential constituents, as in 'when the rent skyrocketed'. So there are endlessly many such sentences of English, each of which speakers of English can (in principle) understand. Indeed, I think we should view *adjuncts*—adjectives, adverbs, and relative clauses—as the paradigm sources of linguistic unboundedness.[8]

In any case, such unboundedness raises the question of how we are able to understand so much, given our limited experience and brains. Focusing on expressions, there are endlessly many sound-meaning

---

[8] Much more on this below. But note that each adjunct *adds* content. A house that Jack built is both a house and built by Jack. A spacious downtown apartment is an apartment that is downtown and spacious—or at least spacious for a downtown apartment. (I return to the caveat in Ch. 2.)

pairings. But how could there *be* so many semantic facts unless they somehow follow from finitely many "core" semantic facts? Speakers don't invent meanings for novel sentences; understanding a novel sentence is not a matter of guesswork. The meaning of a novel sentence is somehow determined prior to its use. This seems to be a precondition of systematic communication. Of course, figuring out *why* a speaker said what he did is often hard. And figuring out *what a speaker said,* as opposed to *what the sentence means,* can be hard. It may not be obvious what the speaker was talking about, or what the speaker intended (the audience to think he intended) to communicate with regard to the topic of conversation. But if we hear a sentence spoken, we typically grasp its meaning—we have the experience of hearing (an utterance of) a sentence with a certain meaning—even if we would prefer not to. This is the sense of understanding that I focus on in what follows.

## 2.2. *Semantic Relations*

The meanings of expressions in a natural language are also *related* in ways that go beyond the part–whole relations exhibited within complex expressions. Distinct expressions can be synonymous, or at least close paraphrases, as with 'lawyer who needed a doctor' and 'attorney who needed a physician' (in American dialect). Similarly, 'Pat hugged Chris' and 'there was a hugging of Chris by Pat' are roughly synonymous. And even setting aside such cases, pairs of expressions often exhibit *systematic* semantic relations. Or putting the focus back on people, hearers understand spoken language in systematic ways.

Intuitively, the meanings of 'Pat sang' and 'Chris danced' are closely related to the meanings of 'Pat danced' and 'Chris sang'. If a child knows enough English to understand the first two sentences, she can also understand the last two. Speakers who can comprehend these sentences and 'someone hugged Sam' can also comprehend 'someone sang', 'someone danced', 'someone hugged Chris', 'Pat hugged someone', and so on. As such examples suggest, we don't acquire the capacity to discern meanings one sentence at a time.

When we learn a new word, we acquire the capacity to understand a host of complex expressions in which the word appears.[9] This bolsters the idea that meaning and comprehension are compositional, and that a semantic theory should help explain this.

Sentences also seem to exhibit patterns of *implication*. Consider (13–16).

(13)  Someone sang
(14)  Pat sang
(15)  Pat sang loudly
(16)  Pat sang and Chris danced

Speakers of English know that such sentences are related in a special way. We can begin to characterize this relation by saying that speakers know that (13) is true if (14) is, and that (14) is true if either (15) or (16) is. This knowledge seems to be different in kind from knowledge of other (necessary) conditional facts. Sophisticates may know that Pat drank some $H_2O$ if Pat drank some water, or that the axioms of set theory are consistent with the Continuum Hypothesis if these axioms are consistent. But one can be a fully competent speaker of English without knowing such things; whereas it seems that any competent speaker of English will know that someone sang if Pat sang. Or put another way, one can *comprehend without endorsing* many conditionals that turn out to be (necessary) truths. But this gap between grasping the meaning of a sentence and seeing that (an utterance of) it is bound to be true, seems absent—or at least greatly diminished in a way that calls for explanation—with regard to sentences like (17–18).

(17)  Someone sang if Pat sang
(18)  Pat sang if Pat sang loudly

Such conditionals seem to be risk-free in a way that other conditionals are not. I think talk of analyticity is appropriate here.

---

[9] See Evans's (1982) discussion of the "Generality Constraint"; see also Davidson (1984), Davies (1981). Fodor and Lepore (2002) also discuss "reverse" compositionality: the idea that anyone who understands a complex expression understands the parts.

Speakers know, by virtue of understanding sentences like (17–18), that such sentences are *bound to be true*.[10] One can try to argue that the appearance of analyticity is an illusion. But presumably, speakers judge that conditionals like (17) and (18) are risk-free because such conditionals *share parts* in certain ways. So one might well hope for a semantic theory from which it follows that certain sentences—like (14) and (15), or 'Pat is a linguist' and 'Pat is a tall linguist'—are analytically related in the following sense: given how the meaning of a complex expression is determined in natural language, and given some minimal assumptions about how meaning constrains truth, it follows that the first sentence is true if the second sentence is true.

Of course, speakers might all know something because they all share some nonlinguistic knowledge. In a community of English speakers who are brilliant mathematicians, conditionals like (19)

(19)   Set theory plus the Continuum Hypothesis is consistent if set theory is consistent

might seem obviously true, much as '3 + 4 = 7' seems obviously true to us. Similarly, one might suggest, any English speaker with basic logical competence would find (17) and (18) obvious. One still needs a semantic theory that says enough about the meanings of sentences to make it clear why and how logical competence is relevant; see §1.1 chapter 1. But perhaps all (actual) speakers of English have basic logical competence by virtue of their non-linguistic cognitive capacities; and perhaps "intuitions of implication" reflect more than just knowledge of meaning. This is, as it seems, an empirical question: do the very capacities that speakers employ in systematically discerning the meanings of novel complex expressions give rise to their knowledge that conditionals like (17–18) are sure to be true? Or put another way, does the semantics of English ensure that certain pairs of expressions are semantically *related* so that certain conditionals are sure to be true come what may?

[10] Cf. Quine (1951, 1960). Though if semantic theories are primarily concerned with intrinsic features of sentences, analyticity (as understood here) may be relatively innocuous; and the sense in which (17–18) are "bound to be true" may be philosophically boring. Moreover, perhaps as Chomsky (2000a) suggests,

Let me stress (mainly for philosophers) that this question is worth asking, even if the resulting notions of analytic truth/knowledge/etc. do not tell us much about (language-independent) truth or knowledge. For if the semantic architecture of natural language gives rise to "spandrels" in the form of analyticities, investigation of the spandrels may reveal something about the underlying architecture. Semantic implication may be of interest mainly because of what it reveals about human language, as opposed to truth or knowledge. Moreover, while logical acumen varies across speakers, many implications are recognized by all competent speakers. So absent an independently plausible theory of "Universal Logic" that explains why speakers find obvious the conditionals they do find obvious, one should welcome an independently motivated theory that diagnoses the truistic character of such conditionals as by-products of how speakers understand the expressions in question.[11]

we should think of analyticity (and semantic features) on analogy with rhyme and alliteration. Speakers know that sentences like 'Clever clowns clap' and 'Nervous ninjas nap' have certain properties. A theory of linguistic sounds might explain this in terms of hypothesized phonological features of expressions.

[11] I'll return to this point, once we have some explanations on the table. But declaring in advance that there can't be—or must be—analytic truths seems like a bad way to conduct inquiry. My view is not that language or psychology is responsible for *the conditional fact* that someone hugged Chris if Pat hugged Chris. This fact, like the fact that rocks fall when dropped, is independent of how we represent the world. Though while semanticists should try to explain why our sentences mean what they do, explaining the truth of our claims (that are not claims *about* meaning) is less clearly part of the job. That said, speakers can *recognize* sentences like (17–18) as truisms. And I think this psychological/epistemological fact is importantly related to meaning and understanding in ways that good semantic theories will reveal.

There may also be normative facts, concerning how speakers *ought* to infer, that go beyond (or perhaps even conflict with) the facts that ordinary competent speakers can discern. And one can define 'semantics' so that such normative facts are—or are among—the primary semantic explananda. But I think this conflates the study of linguistic meaning with the study of good inference, to the detriment of both; see §2.5 below. If someone provides a *theory* of the alleged normative facts that also accounts for the descriptive facts—say, by characterizing a clear and explanatory sense in which

## 2.3. *Context-Sensitivity*

Some sentences have meanings that can be reported, correctly if uninformatively, by "disquotation". For example, 'Seven is a prime number' means that seven is a prime number. But sentences like (20–21)

(20)   I sang
(21)   This is bigger than that

have meanings that resist disquotational reports. Nobody's utterance of (22)

(22)   'I sang' means that I sang

captures the meaning of (20), which has nothing to do with any particular speaker. Anyone who utters (22) says, incorrectly, that the meaning of (20) has something to do with *her*. Correspondingly, the claim you make by using (20) differs from the claim anyone else makes by using (20). By constrast, different speakers make the same claim whenever they use 'Seven is a prime number', at least if we ignore any tense associated with 'is'. In this sense, the meaning of (20) is *context-sensitive*: it follows from the meaning of the sentence that it cannot be evaluated for truth or falsity, except relative to a context that somehow "includes" the relevant speaker. Similarly, it follows from the meaning of (21) that it cannot be evaluated for truth or falsity, except relative to a context that includes some things a speaker could demonstrate with 'this' and 'that'.

This leaves it open whether contexts are conversational situations (whatever *they* are), ordered n-tuples of things corresponding to grammatically indicated *aspects of* conversational situations, or something else. For now, the important point is just that similar

speakers "imperfectly grasp" the relevant norms—such a theory will merit serious consideration. But until then, it seems reasonable for those interested in natural language to focus on the kinds of facts discussed in the text, and to construe the enterprise of natural language semantics as an attempt to explain such facts.

expressions can, by virtue of their meaning, differ with regard to context-sensitivity. Suppose we introduce 'Zyx', stipulating that it is a name for the author of *Events and Semantic Architecture*. Then 'Zyx', 'I', and 'He' are all simple nominal expressions. But any utterance of 'Zyx sang' implies that the author of *Events and Semantic Architecture* sang; whereas an utterance of 'I sang' implies that the speaker, whoever it is, sang; and an utterance of 'He sang' implies that the person demonstrated by the speaker (when using 'He') sang. Thus, 'Zyx' is context-insensitive in a way that 'I' and 'He' are not, while 'I' and 'He' are context-sensitive in different ways. A semantic theory should reflect such facts.[12]

## 2.4. *Negative Facts and Displacement*

In addition to the facts about (speakers' knowledge concerning) how sounds are related to meanings, there are also endlessly many facts about how sounds *aren't* related to meanings. Consider again (7),

(7)   Pat hugged Chris

which *doesn't* mean that dogs barked. Nor does it mean that there was a hugging of Pat by Chris—or that for some x, Pat did x *or* x was a hugging *or* Chris underwent x, etc. The sound of (23)

(23)   The prince attacked the duke from Gloucester

is associated with two meanings: the prince attacked the duke *who was from Gloucester*; or the prince attacked the duke *and the attack was from Gloucester*. But speakers of English can't hear (23) as meaning the prince *who was from Gloucester* attacked the duke. Correspondingly, (23) has a meaning on which it implies (24) and a

---

[12] See Kaplan (1989). This will be especially important in Ch. 2. In addition to pronouns and demonstratives, there are time-sensitive and place-sensitive words ('now', 'here'). In fact, given tense, it is hard to find sentences of natural language with *no* context-sensitive elements. Compare 'Seven is prime, but seven was not prime yesterday' with 'Seven is prime, but seven is not prime'.

meaning on which it implies (25), but no meaning on which it implies (26).

(24)    The prince attacked the duke, and the duke was from Gloucester

(25)    The prince attacked the duke, and the attack was from Gloucester

(26)    The prince attacked the duke, and the prince was from Gloucester

Upon reflection, speakers of English know such facts about the *range* of possible meanings and implications. This suggests a severe constraint on semantic theories: they should explain why a given sound has the meanings it does have *and no others*.

Satisfying this constraint requires the postulation of structure that goes well beyond audible word order. And since this is important at several junctures below, it is worth being clear about it now. Consider Chomsky's (1965) famous examples (27–8).

(27)    John is easy to please

(28)    John is eager to please

In (27), 'John' is construed as the *object* of 'please', while 'John' is construed as the *subject* of 'please' in (28). In this respect, (27–8) are like (29–30),

(29)    It is easy for us to please John

(30)    John is eager that he please us

where the pronoun in (30) is understood as referentially dependent on 'John'. Other things being equal, one would assume that the transitive verb 'please' is always associated with two argument positions, whether or not those positions are occupied by overt (pronounced) argument expressions. And this suggests that in (27), 'John' is associated with the grammatical position occupied by 'John' in (29); while in (28), 'John' is associated with the grammatical position occupied by 'he' in (30). So Chomsky proposed that (27–8) have the grammatical structures indicated in (27G) and (28G),

(27G)   [John is easy [*e* to please___]]

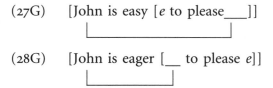

(28G)   [John is eager [__ to please *e*]]

and not those indicated in (27G*) and (28G*);

(27G*)   [John is easy [__ to please *e*]]

(28G*)   [John is eager [*e* to please___]]

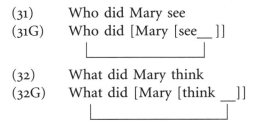

where the "links" indicate relations between 'John' and an argument position associated with the embedded transitive verb, with '*e*' indicating the other argument position (also unpronounced but *not* referentially dependent on another expression in the sentence).[13]

If this suggestion seems recherché, note that audible word-position is often a poor guide to grammatical role. Questions provide obvious examples, as in (31–3).

(31)    Who did Mary see
(31G)   Who did [Mary [see__ ]]

(32)    What did Mary think
(32G)   What did [Mary [think __]]

---

[13] The idea is that [*e* to please __ ] means, roughly, that some relevant entity or entities please__; [ __to please *e*] means, roughly, that __ please(s) some relevant entity or entities. One can also use coindexing to indicate the relevant facts, as in: [John₁ is easy [*e* to please *e*₁]]. This leaves various details open; see Chomsky (1981), Higginbotham (1985), Hornstein (2001) for discussion. Is (28) the result of a transformation in which 'John' *moved* to the matrix subject position? Or does (28) contain an unpronounced pronominal element referentially dependent on 'John'?

(33)    I wonder who Mary saw
(33G)    [I wonder who [Mary [saw __]]]
                    └_____┘

Linguists in the transformational-grammar tradition provide a wide array of evidence for such proposals, independent of purely semantic considerations; see Radford (1988), Haegeman (1994), and Jackendoff (1993) for introductions. For example, one can argue that there are *constraints* on displacement of wh-expressions—and hence, that wh-expressions can be displaced. Note that (34*) is somehow ill-formed,

(34*)    Who did I wonder Mary saw

while (31) and (33) are perfectly fine sentences. But there is nothing wrong with the following question: which individual is such that I wonder whether Mary saw that individual?

Autonomous constraints on grammatical structure can help explain facts about (non)ambiguity (see Higginbotham, 1985). Consider, for example, the unambiguous question (35),

(35)    Was the child who lost kept crying?

which has only the reading suggested by (35G), corresponding to 'The child who lost was kept crying'.

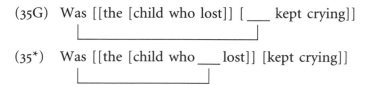

(35G)    Was [[the [child who lost]] [ ___ kept crying]]

(35*)    Was [[the [child who ___ lost]] [kept crying]]

The question suggested by (35*)—The *child who was lost* kept crying?—is not a possible meaning for (35), even though it is the question one might expect given the individual words. And while (36) is a fine sentence, (37*) is word salad.

(36)    The man who was yelling stole my wallet
(37*)    Was the man who yelling stole my wallet?

One can start to explain these facts by saying that natural language prohibits displacement of auxiliary verbs from relative clauses— and hence, that (35G) is the only available grammatical structure for (35).[14]

A similar point is illustrated by another pair of contrasts due to Chomsky.

(38)   John ate.
(39)   John ate a fish.
(40)   John is too clever to catch.
(41)   John is too clever to catch a fish.

Sentence (38) means, roughly, that John ate something (edible); and if (39) is true, so is (38). But (40) does not mean that John is too clever to catch something. Rather, (40–1) are paraphrased by (42–3).

(42)   John is too clever for us to catch him
(43)   John is too clever for him to catch a fish

Sentences (41) and (43) convey the idea, which would be expressed only in strange circumstances, that John will not catch a fish because he is too clever to do so. Extending this paradigm, (44)

(44)   The goose is too clever to eat

can mean that the goose is either too clever *(for us) to eat it,* or too clever *(for it) to dine.* This suggests a structural ambiguity, as indicated by (44G) and (44G′).

(44G)   [[The goose] is [too clever [*e* to eat ___]]]

(44G′)   [[The goose] is [too clever [___ to eat *e*]]]

Likewise, 'The goose is ready to eat' can mean that the goose is *pret-à-manger,* or that it is ready to dine. So it seems that lexical and

---

[14] See Ross (1967). Then one can seek an explanation for this constraint; see Travis (1984), Baker (1988), Chomsky (1995).

structural facts interact: 'ready' creates an ambiguity that 'eager' and 'easy' do not. Correlatively, it is a substantive fact that (27–8) are *un*ambiguous, and that speakers know this.

(27)  John is easy to please
(28)  John is eager to please

All of which suggests that (23) has only the grammatical structures (23G) and (23G′).

(23G)   [[The prince] [attacked the [duke from Gloucester]]]
(23G′)  [[The prince] [[attacked the duke] [from Gloucester]]]

But as (23*) reminds us, this is to assume—correctly, but substantively—that there are endlessly many grammatical structures that the string of words in (23) cannot instantiate.

(23*)   [[[The [prince ___]] [attacked the duke]] [from Gloucester]]

Moreover, if we want to *explain* why (23) can have only two meanings, we need a theory according to which neither (23G) nor (23G′) can support the meaning that (23) cannot have. In particular, we need a theory according to which (23G′) cannot mean that the prince satisfied the following complex condition: he attacked the duke, and he was from Gloucester. This is a nontrivial desideratum. According to Conjunctivism, and as desired, (23G′) means that something satisfied the following complex condition: its Agent was the prince; it was an attack; its Theme was the duke; and it was from Gloucester. But whatever we say about this particular case, our theories cannot be silent on the question of *how* form is related to meaning. For even *given* a grammatical structure, there are negative facts to explain.

It is hard to overstate the importance of this point. There are endlessly many facts about what strings of words cannot mean. These facts call for explanation, especially when the "nonmeanings" are perfectly coherent interpretations, given the relevant word meanings. Explaining such facts requires hypotheses about grammatical structure *and* how such structure is (and is not) related to the meaning of a complex expression. Correspondingly, I assume that sound–meaning associations are *constrained* by grammatical structure in ways that a semantic theory should reveal. And absent argument to the contrary, I assume that ambiguity should be diagnosed as homophony: just as semantically distinct words may sound alike ('beat'/'beet', 'patience'/'patients'), semantically distinct ways of arranging the same lexical items may sound alike, as in many of the examples above. If we don't describe ambiguity this way, it is hard to see how we can explain the *nonambiguity* of complex expressions in terms of grammatical structure and its relation to meanings (see Higginbotham, 1985).[15]

Recasting a point stressed in §1.3 above, each linguistic sound confronts us with three questions: what can it mean; what grammatical forms can it have; and how are these forms related to the possible meanings? It is a wonderful fact, worthy of reflection in its own right, that linguists have been able to pose such questions and begin to answer some of them. There was no guarantee that such investigation would be productive. But it isn't surprising that investigation has led to descriptions of linguistic facts that were previously unimagined. Successful inquiry has *always* led us beyond surface appearances.

## 2.5. *Facts Discovered along the way*

The brief sketch in this section hardly constitutes a survey of all the semantic facts. Moreover, investigation often *reveals* explananda, while casting doubt on old beliefs. (Anyone who insisted that celestial mechanics was concerned only with planetary motions, and that facts about tides or falling bodies were irrelevant, got the

---

[15] One can use 'ambiguity' more broadly. But then I am using the term in a restricted and technical sense: since expressions are *structured* things, not mere word-strings, no *expression* is structurally ambiguous; although distinct expressions can be homophonous.

theory he deserved.) So one shouldn't try to define the scope of semantic theorizing in advance of investigation. It turns out, for example, that quantificational words like 'every' and 'most' have some nonobvious properties (discussed in Chapter 2) that are intimately connected with the meanings of such expressions. It would be crazy to stipulate that a property cannot be semantic if we didn't recognize it as such prior to theorizing. As we just saw, constraints on displacement are arguably crucial to semantics; yet this was hardly a pre-theoretic thought.

The last fifty years of linguistics should also leave us receptive to the idea that facts about language *acquisition* are germane to theories of meaning. Within a few years, any normal child will come to associate sounds with meanings in (more or less) the same way that local adults do. So experience and human biology must somehow conspire to this end. Various "poverty of stimulus" arguments, based on facts illustrated with examples like (23–44) above, suggest that human biology somehow imposes substantive and theoretically interesting limits on how children *can* associate sounds with meaning. So facts about what children can(not) learn bear on questions about what sounds can(not) mean. And in any case, a normal speaker's capacity to associate sounds with meanings is a capacity that developed under conditions of normal human experience. So the principles governing sound–meaning associations must be such that a normal speaker can (under conditions of normal human experience) come to associate sounds with meanings in that way.[16]

---

[16] See e.g. Chomsky (1957, 1965, 1986), Hornstein and Lightfoot (1981), Jackendoff (1993). For discussion of relevant psycholinguistic studies, and replies to recent critics of poverty of stimulus arguments, see Crain and Pietroski (2001, 2002), Laurence and Margolis (2001). Some readers will be waiting to hear about what they take to be the central semantic fact—namely, that words bear certain relations to the things speakers talk about. But while it is a truism that speakers can use 'dog' to talk about dogs, it is less clear that a theory of meaning needs to characterize some relation R (other than *can be used by speakers to talk about*) such that the word 'dog' bears R to dogs. Is there something speakers talk about by using 'every'? If our best theory of meaning associates words with things speakers refer to (and not just in the sense that meaning *constrains* reference), so be it.

One cannot determine a priori which facts a semantic theory should explain. In any domain, what a theory *should* explain depends on what gets discovered. And we can discover semantic facts, just as we can discover biological facts. In my view, insensitivity to this point still pervades philosophy of language, despite Chomsky (1955, 1957, 1965, 1966, 1970, 1977, 1981, 1986, 1995, 2000*b*) and the remarkably successful research program he initiated. Of course, one can define 'semantics' as one likes; and there is a tradition of using the term to talk about the enterprise of defining models for expressions of an invented language. But following Chomsky, we can study human language as a natural phenomenon, which is whatever it is. Members of a certain species have a rather striking trait. As theorists, our job is to describe and explain as best we can. In studying natural language, tools used to invent formal languages have often proved useful. But these tools do not determine the facts of interest, much less the form of correct explanations, with regard to natural phenomena that are independent of our theorizing.

The questions addressed here concern whatever portion of the world—presumably something about human psychology—is responsible for the facts, whatever they turn out to be, concerning what complex expressions mean and how speakers understand such expressions. No stipulation can ensure that a particular body of facts constitutes the explananda we must explain in order to have an adequate theory of the relevant portion of the world. Explaining some facts may well require description and explanation of facts not yet imagined. That said, we need to start somewhere. And we have enough to begin.

But that is something to be argued for, not a manifest fact to be explained. That said, the hypothesis I will adopt associates at least many expressions with "Semantic Values"; see Ch. 1. And one is free to say, if one wants to, that speakers can use 'dog' to talk about dogs because the dogs are the Semantic Values of 'dog'. The question will be whether this 'because'-claim is true.

# 1

# Elementary Cases

As discussed in the Introduction, Conjunctivism is a thesis about semantic composition in natural language: when expressions are concatenated, they are interpreted as (conjoinable) monadic predicates; and the resulting phrase is interpreted as a predicate satisfied by whatever satisfies both constituents. Functionism is the more common thesis that a complex expression is composed of (i) an expresssion that stands for some function and (ii) an expression that stands for some entity in the domain of that function, with the whole standing for the value of the function given the relevant argument. In this chapter, I argue that Conjunctivism is theoretically viable and attractive. By the end of Chapter 2, I will have shown how Conjunctivists can handle the usual range of textbook constructions—at least as well, and often better, than Functionists. Chapter 3 extends the case that Conjunctivism is preferable, on empirical grounds, across a range of specific constructions in which verbs combine with grammatical arguments.

I begin by showing that Conjunctivism is fully compatible with some plausible assumptions about the general shape of a semantic theory for *any* language with endlessly many sentences that exhibit relations of implication. This helps distinguish these assumptions from the more substantive hypothesis of Functionism. Next, I argue that Conjunctivism is not *ad hoc* compared with Functionism. Each view requires an auxiliary hypothesis, since predicates can combine with arguments (as in 'hugged Chris') or adjuncts (as in 'red ball' or 'sang loudly'); and arguments differ, grammatically and semantically, from adjuncts. One can adopt the view that Functionism is correct for predicate–argument concatenation, while Conjunctivism is correct for predicate–adjunct concatenation. But none of these proposals is intrinsically simpler than the others. Conjunctivism predicts that grammatical relations between predicates and their arguments are semantically significant, and that sentences involve covert quantification over things like events, in which other things "participate". But this is a good thing.

Perhaps surprisingly, Conjunctivists can easily accommodate transitive verbs, sentential connectives, and quantifiers. This last topic, connected with issues about plural noun-phrases, merits its own chapter; providing the semantics for quantificational constructions is an illuminating exercise. But as we shall see, Conjunctivists can handle simple examples like (1).

(1)   Pat did not sing or Chris hugged every linguist

Given *two* ways of handling such cases, it becomes clear that Functionism can and should be construed as an empirical hypothesis about natural language—not a mere convention, with roots in the study of formal languages, for how to encode facts about what expressions mean.

Absent an alternative, it is hard to assess Functionism for plausibility given its familiarity. But if we could start over, and ask what concatenation signifies in natural language, we would presumably consider the idea that forming a phrase corresponds to conjoining the semantic properties of the constituents. When sentences are combined in discourse without connectives, we hear the combination conjunctively. And if children *could* interpret speech by treating subsentential concatenation as a sign of predicate-conjunction, one might expect children to do so, at least if the alternative is to treat subsentential concatenation as a sign of function-application. So if Conjunctivism is compatible with known facts, that is worth knowing. For then we can start comparing alternative hypotheses.

## 1. A Fregean Framework

Building on two millenia of prior work, Frege (1879, 1892*a*, *b*) bequeathed to us some tools—originally designed for the study of logic and arithmetic—that can be used in constructing theories of meaning for natural languages. Given the minimal assumption that (declarative) sentences can be evaluated in a binary fashion, we can treat meanings as compositionally determined constraints on how expressions can be evaluated; where such constraints can be represented by associating expressions with *Semantic Values* (or simply *Values*) of various kinds.[1] Adopting this framework does not commit us to any particular view about the semantic role of natural language syntax. But we must distinguish (i) plausible Fregean claims about the abstract semantic architecture of any language that allows for endlessly many evaluable expressions, from (ii) tendentious claims about how this architecture is realized in human languages. The debate between Functionists and Conjunctivists concerns (ii), not (i).

## 1.1. *Values and Explanations*

The unboundedness of natural language suggests that a semantic theory will take the following form: a list of "lexical" axioms that associate each meaningful primitive expression with something—an entity, property, constraint, or whatever—that we  can call a lexical meaning; some "compositional" axiom(s), corresponding to the semantically significant way(s) of combining expressions; and rules of inference that license the derivation of theorems that associate complex expressions with their meanings.[2] What remains,

---

[1]  I use capital letters as a reminder that '(Semantic) Value' is a technical notion. In the end, terminology doesn't matter. But I prefer 'Value' to 'referent' as an analog of Frege's term of art *Bedeutung*. Many expressions, like 'every linguist' and 'loudly', are not used as devices for referring to (or even talking *about*) particular things. I also want to leave open the possibility that predicates have *many* Values. And it seems odd to say that a predicate has many referents. But I do not claim that expressions somehow "have" Values independently of speakers who evaluate expressions. In my view, to say that expression $\Sigma$ has the Value(s) it has is just to say that $\Sigma$ has certain semantic properties, and is thus evaluated in a certain way by competent speakers.

[2]  Reference to meanings, as opposed to quantification over Values, plays no role in the *theories* on offer. But one can talk about meanings, without illicit reification, since one can talk about the semantic properties of expressions. If 'ball' is subject

one might think, is just the task of specifying plausible axioms and rules. But if we want *explanations*, and not just plausibility, we also need the right *kinds* of axioms.

For example, merely assigning compositionally determined meanings to (2) and (3)

    (2)  Pat sang
    (3)  I sang

will not explain why these sentences differ semantically. Let '♯' and '♭' and '♪' stand, respectively, for the meanings of 'Pat' and 'I' and 'sang'. Assume that ♯ and ♪, together with the relevant grammatical structure, determine the meaning of (2); while ♭ and ♪ likewise determine the meaning of (3). Indeed, let ♯^♪ and ♭^♪ *be* the meanings of (2) and (3). It doesn't follow that these sentences differ semantically, unless one assumes that ♯ differs from ♭, *and* that this difference is not effaced by combining these lexical meanings with ♪. Nor does it follow that (3) is context-sensitive in a way that (2) is not. To capture these facts, we need further claims about the relevant meanings and how they combine.

Similarly, merely assigning compositionally determined meanings to (2–3) and (4–5)

    (4)  Someone sang
    (5)  Pat sang loudly

provides no explanation for why these sentences exhibit a certain pattern of implication. Let '𝄞' and '𝄞^♪' stand for the meanings of 'someone' and (4). This doesn't yet distinguish 𝄞 from ♯, ♭, or the meaning of 'everyone'. So if one wants a theory that specifies the meanings of 'someone' and 'Pat' in ways that reveal why (2) implies (4), but not conversely, one needs more than just *correct* specifications of meanings. One needs theoretically *perspicuous* specifications. Analogous remarks apply to (2) and (5). One can say, correctly

to the constraint that x is a Value of that word iff x is a ball, we can talk about this constraint (which bears on how speakers use 'ball' to talk about the world).

but uninformatively, that 'loudly' has a meaning such that 'sang loudly' has the compositional meaning it does. But this leaves many (nonactual) possibilities open—e.g., that 'sang loudly' means what 'sang or was loud' actually means—and thus fails to explain various facts that more substantive semantic theories can and do explain.[3]

Moreover, the meaning of a sentence seems to be importantly different than the meaning of a single word, and the meaning of 'every' seems to differ *in kind* from the meanings of 'Pat' and 'sang'. Speakers can, quite naturally, use declarative sentences to make statements that can be true or false; they can use names to refer to things; they can use 'I' as a device of self-reference; etc. But such facts are not even encoded, much less explained, if we merely introduce a scheme for saying that (i) each word means what it does, and (ii) any semantic contribution of syntax preserves the compositionality of meanings. This suggests that semantic theorizing should begin with some assumptions about the semantic *categories* to which various expressions belong; though of course, one wants to start with the sparest assumptions required to explain the facts. It is not obvious what the best starting point is. But Frege provided a suggestion that has proven fruitful.

Suppose that (declarative) sentences are associated with a distinctive range of (Semantic) Values, which reflect the ways that sentences can be evaluated. Then one can hypothesize that sentences are associated with Values in a way that ensures the following: relative to any context, each sentence is associated with exactly one Value from the range of potential Values for sentences; synonymous sentences are always associated with the same Value; one of the potential Values for sentences—call it 't' to suggest truth—is such that every tautology (like 'Pat sang if Pat sang') has this Value; and a sentence S1 semantically implies another sentence S2 iff relative to

---

[3] Compare §2 of the Introduction. I stress this point because some authors seem to think that providing an adequate theory of meaning is simply a matter of specifying an algorithm (which can be largely disquotational) for associating expressions with compositionally determined meanings. See Horwich (1997, 1998); see Pietroski (2000*a*) for discussion.

every context, S1 has the Value **t** *only if* S2 has the Value **t**. This requires at least two potential Values for sentences, to avoid the absurd consequence that each sentence implies every sentence. So, following Frege, let's make the minimal assumption that there are exactly two—calling the second sentential Value '**f**' to suggest falsity.[4]

A further hypothesis is that a sentence has the Value **t** relative to a context iff the sentence is *true* relative to that context. This may be plausible for the arithmetic sentences that most interested Frege. It is certainly a convenient idealization. And on any view, the meaning of a sentence S is a major factor in determining whether or not an *utterance* of S is true in a given conversational situation. But one might suspect, as I do, that the truth or falsity of a sentential utterance often depends on conversational factors beyond those that determine a Value for the *sentence* in question; see Pietroski (2003, forthcoming, in progress). For now, though, we needn't worry about this.

The important point is that the Fregean strategy for explaining implication limits what one can say about *how* the meanings of sentences are compositionally determined. Consider (6–8).

(6)  Pat sang
(7)  Pat sang or Chris danced
(8)  Pat sang and Chris danced

If we want to explain why (6) is implied by (8), we need a theory which ensures that (6) gets the Value **t** if (8) does; and similarly with respect to the other implications exhibited by these sentences. This constrains hypotheses about the semantic contributions of

---

[4] For purposes of explaining "semantic links" between sentences, it doesn't matter what **t** and **f** *are*. They could be the numbers 1 and 0, Noam Chomsky and Donald Davidson, or any two objects. The important point is that we want a theory according to which: S1 implies S2 iff *it follows from the theory* that (relative to any context) S1 has a designated Value only if S2 also has that Value (which will be the value associated with tautologies). Implications are thus characterized as by-products of constraints, characterized by the theory, on Values.

sentential connectives and syntax. We want a theory from which it follows that any sentence of the form 'P and Q' gets the Value **t** iff both 'P' and 'Q' get the Value **t**. And similarly, *mutatis mutandis*, for other "logical" expressions. As we'll see, there is more than one way to achieve this result. But there are also many ways to fail. In general, facts about implications constrain hypotheses about lexical meanings and how they compose.[5]

A special case of implication concerns inferences like 'Bruce is Batman and Bruce sang, so Batman sang'—or in conditional form, 'Batman sang if Bruce is Batman and Bruce sang'. Speakers recognize the "risk-free" character of many conditionals with the "substituting" form indicated below;

(SUB)   ⟨...N1...⟩ if⟨N1 is N2 and ⟨...N2...⟩⟩

where 'N1' and 'N2' are names, and angled brackets indicate sentences. One can explain such facts by adopting a theory according to which: each name is associated with at most one entity (from a range of potential Values for names); in a sentence like 'Bruce sang', the effect of the name on the Value of the sentence is exhausted by the Value of the name; and if N1 is N2, then 'N1' and 'N2' have the *same* Value. On such a theory, 'Bruce' and 'Batman' have the same Value if Bruce is Batman; so given that 'Bruce sang' differs from 'Batman sang' only by substitution of one name for the other, and given that Bruce is Batman, 'Bruce sang' has the Value **t** (if and) only if 'Batman sang' has the Value **t**.[6]

Of course, there are also conditionals like (9),

(9)   The mayor knows that Batman sang if
Bruce is Batman and the mayor knows that Bruce sang

---

[5] One can hold that sentences exhibit relations of semantic implication, much as they exhibit relations of rhyme, even if one suspects that sentential Values should not be identified with truth-values; see Chomsky (2000a). For semantic implication may be insensitive to the gap between **t** and truth.

[6] This must all be relativized to contexts, given that more than one individual is called 'Bruce'. And we must allow for names (like 'Vulcan') that name nothing. Following Burge (1973), I suspect that proper names in English have covert structure, as in 'the Bruce' (or drawing on Kaplan (1989), 'dthat Bruce'); where x is a

which speakers do *not* regard as truisms. Since the mayor might not *know* that Bruce is Batman, it seems clear that 'Bruce is Batman and the mayor knows that Bruce sang' does not imply 'The mayor knows that Batman sang'. So not every instance of (SUB) is even true, much less risk-free. An even more obvious counterexample to (SUB) is (10).

(10)   The mayor said 'Batman sang' if Bruce is Batman and the mayor said 'Bruce sang'.

If a speaker assertively utters (the sentence) 'Bruce sang', it does not follow that he assertively uttered 'Batman sang', no matter who Batman is. But let's assume—deferring further discussion until Chapter 3—that sentences like 'The mayor knows that Bruce sang' and 'The mayor said "Bruce sang" ' are special cases, in which the effect of 'Bruce' on the Value of the whole sentence is not exhausted by the Value of 'Bruce'.[7] If this assumption is defensible, we can adopt a semantic theory according to which 'N1' and 'N2' have the same Value if N1 is N2. Such a theory would let us account for the truistic character of endlessly many conditionals like 'Cicero spoke if Cicero was Tully and Tully spoke'. So let's suppose, tentatively, that the (widely endorsed) Fregean framework is on the right track.

## 1.2.   *Values, Functions, and Syntax*

This is to accept constraints "from above" and "from below" on how compositionality is to be explained: each sentence must be (conditionally) associated with **t** or **f**; if one sentence implies another, the former is associated with **t** only if the latter is; and each name is to

Value of the proper *noun* 'Bruce' relative to a context iff x is a contextually relevant thing that is (properly) called 'Bruce', leaving open the possibility that the world contains nothing called 'Bruce'. But for present purposes, we can adopt the idealizing assumption that each name has exactly one bearer.

  [7]  See Pietroski (1996) for discussion, references, and a specific implementation— drawing on Davidson (1968) and others—of Frege's (1892*b*) own response to "Frege's Puzzle".

be associated with some entity, subject to the condition just discussed on when names are associated with the same entity. This limits what we can say about the semantic contributions of verbs and natural language syntax. But this is a constraint on the *joint* contribution of verbs, which can take names as grammatical arguments, and the syntax of combining verbs with their arguments. This constraint may initially suggest Functionism. But in fact, it leaves ample room for Conjunctivism, as well as other hypotheses about how verbs and syntax conspire to produce their joint semantic effect. (Similar remarks apply, as we'll see in Chapter 2, to determiners like 'every' and their grammatical arguments.)

Let's pretend, for now, that the grammatical structure of 'Pat sang' is as simple as it appears to be: $\langle \text{Pat}_\alpha \text{ sang}_\Pi \rangle$. And let's say that the Value of $\text{Pat}_\alpha$ is **Pat**. In this notation, $\text{Pat}_\alpha$ and $\text{sang}_\Pi$ are lexical items—an argument and a predicate—while **Pat** is a Value of the sort a name can have. If only for simplicity, suppose that **Pat** is a certain person in a domain of things that some speakers are talking about. Given the Fregean assumptions, there has to be some compositionally determined condition, such that the sentence $\langle \text{Pat}_\alpha$ $\text{sang}_\Pi \rangle$ has the Value **t** iff that condition obtains. In which case, there is a smallest function F from things in the relevant domain (of potential Values for names) to **t** or **f**, such that: $\langle \text{Pat}_\alpha \text{ sang}_\Pi \rangle$ has the Value **t** iff $F(\textbf{Pat}) = \textbf{t}$, and $\langle \text{Pat}_\alpha \text{ sang}_\Pi \rangle$ has the Value **f** iff $F(\textbf{Pat}) = \textbf{f}$. Given that $\langle \text{Pat}_\alpha \text{ sang}_\Pi \rangle$ has exactly one of the two sentential Values, we can abbreviate: $\langle \text{Pat}_\alpha \text{ sang}_\Pi \rangle$ has the Value **t** iff $F(\textbf{Pat}) = \textbf{t}$. Correspondingly, a way of specifying F quickly springs to mind: $F(x) = \textbf{t}$ iff x sang, and $F(x) = \textbf{f}$ iff x did not sing; or abbreviating, $F(x) = \textbf{t}$ iff x sang.[8]

That is, we can think about the sentence $\langle \text{Pat}_\alpha \text{ sang}_\Pi \rangle$ *minus the name Pat$_\alpha$* as having a semantic correlate that maps potential Values of names onto **t** or **f**. This mapping will be determined by the semantic contributions of $\text{sang}_\Pi$ *and* the syntax of combining such

---

[8] If this seems utterly trivial, imagine confronting the expression 'Gnas tap'. One could learn something by learning that it has the Value **t** iff $F(\textbf{Pat}) = \textbf{t}$. Likewise, from the perspective of someone acquiring English, it is far from trivial that 'Pat sang' has the Value **t** iff $F(\textbf{Pat}) = \textbf{t}$.

a predicate with a name like Pat$_\alpha$. This makes it tempting to say that function F *is* the semantic contribution of sang$_\Pi$, and that concatenation signifies function-application, with the result that the Value of $\langle$Pat$_\alpha$ sang$_\Pi\rangle$ is indeed F(**Pat**). But this temptation can be resisted. I'll spend the rest of the book arguing that it should be resisted. It is worth getting clear, though, about why and how it *can* be resisted. For I suspect that failure to be clear about this accounts for at least some of Functionism's initial appeal.

Let's say that $\langle\ldots$ sang$_\Pi\rangle$ is the sentence $\langle$Pat$_\alpha$ sang$_\Pi\rangle$ minus the name Pat$_\alpha$, assuming that this "sentence-frame" is also the sentence $\langle$Chris$_\alpha$ sang$_\Pi\rangle$ minus the name Chris$_\alpha$. Given our basic assumptions, $\langle\ldots$ sang$_\Pi\rangle$ is importantly like the arithmetic function-expression 'S(x) = x + 1'. As Frege (1892*a*) noted, one can make the "unsaturated" aspect of this function-expression more vivid as in 'S( ) = ( ) + 1', where the "gap" can be filled by (two occurrences of) any numeral. Of course, the successor function maps numbers onto numbers—S(1) = 2, S(2) = 3, and so on—while the function corresponding to $\langle\ldots$ sang$_\Pi\rangle$ maps things like **Pat** onto **t** or **f**. But the analogy can be improved, following Frege, by considering a "t-variant" of the successor function: S*(x, y) = [**t** if y = x + 1, and **f** otherwise]; or abbreviating, S*(x, y) = [**t** iff y = x + 1]. Similarly, we can consider a t-variant of the two-place addition function, as indicated below.

$$A(x, y) = x + y \qquad A^*(x, y, z) = [\mathbf{t} \text{ iff } x + y = z]$$

In general, every n-place function has an (n + 1)-place **t**-variant; and while 'sang' does not suggest relationality, we can still associate $\langle\ldots$ sang$_\Pi\rangle$ with a function from individuals to **t** or **f**. But nothing follows about how this function should be specified for purposes of semantic theorizing, or how the verb sang$_\Pi$ is related to this function. *Perhaps* the Value of sang$_\Pi$ just *is* the smallest function F such that F(x) = **t** iff x sang. This effectively treats the verb as a predicate satisfied by individual singers. But another possibility is that sang$_\Pi$ is satisfied by past events of singing, and that semanticists should specify the relevant function accordingly: F(x) = **t** iff ∃e

[Agent(e, x) & Past-Singing(e)]; or rewriting variables, $F(x') = t$ iff $\exists x[\text{Agent } (x, x') \ \& \ \text{Past-Singing}(x)]$, where 'Agent' expresses a relation that holds between events (whatever *they* turn out to be) and things like **Pat**.

On this view, something over and above the verb itself corresponds to '$\exists x[\text{Agent}(x, x') \ \& \ldots]$'; see Parsons (1990) on "subatomic" semantics. As we shall see, this is independently plausible. But in any case, the initial Fregean assumptions do not determine the Values of verbs. Nor do they determine the semantic character of syntax, even if every *declarative sentence minus an argument-term* maps Values of argument-terms onto **t** or **f**. In this context, it is especially important not to confuse the natural languages our theories are about with the formal metalanguage we use to state the theories. In familiar formal languages, combining a one-place predicate with an argument-term (surrounded by brackets) creates a device for referring to the *value* of the function associated with the predicate given the relevant argument. If 'S' indicates the successor function, 'S(3)' is a way of describing the number four; if 'P' indicates the predecessor function, 'P(3)' is a way of describing the number two; and 'S(P(3))' is a way of describing the number three. One could also adopt a formal metalanguage in which '^' signifies function-application, with the result that: 'S^3' is a way of describing the number four; 'P^3' is a way of describing the number two; and 'S^[P^3]', with brackets reflecting the order function-application, is a way of describing the number three. But this interpretation of concatenation is not mandatory.

One could invent a perverse language in which the Value of '___ (...)' is the result of doubling the Value of '...', then applying the function associated with '___', and then doubling again. In such a language, 'S(3)' would be a way of describing the number fourteen, and 'P(3)' would be a way of describing the number ten. So the existence of a function F, such that $\langle \text{Pat}_\alpha \ \text{sang}_\Pi \rangle$ has the Value **t** iff F(**Pat**), shows only that the semantic contribution of the *verb and syntax* can be specified in terms of *F and function-application*. This doesn't tell us what the verb and syntax each contribute, or how they conspire to produce their joint effect. *If* the semantic contribution of natural language syntax is function-application, then the semantic contribution of a verb like sang$_\Pi$ should be represented as a function from things like **Pat** to **t** or **f**. But the antecedent of this conditional may not be true. This rather abstract point is absolutely crucial to what follows. So I propose to make it again, in a slightly different way, drawing on Frege (1892*a*).

## 1.3. *Concepts versus Sets*

Let's focus on arithmetic sentences, which are especially friendly to Functionism, and adopt the following (simplifying) assumptions: each numeral is a name whose Value is the number we typically refer to by using the numeral; 'is prime' is a simple predicate, with the copula playing no semantic role of its own; and a sentence of the form ⟨N$_\alpha$ is prime$_\Pi$⟩ has the Value **t** iff the Value of N$_\alpha$ is prime. Then ⟨3$_\alpha$ is prime$_\Pi$⟩ has the Value **t** iff 3 is prime. So given the arithmetic facts, ⟨3$_\alpha$ is prime$_\Pi$⟩ has the Value **t**. But there are still *two* semantic roles associated with ⟨... is prime$_\Pi$⟩: *selection* of a certain function from potential Values of names to **t** or **f**, and *application* of that function to the Value of the relevant name N$_\alpha$.

We can highlight the first role by contrasting two sets of ordered pairs, one corresponding to ⟨... is prime$_\Pi$⟩, and the other corresponding to ⟨... is even$_\Pi$⟩:

{ <x, y>: y = **t** iff x is prime, and y = **f** iff x is not prime}

{ <x, y>: y = **t** iff x is even, and y = **f** iff x is not even}.

These sets have different members. The former contains <3, **t**>, while the latter contains <3, **f**>. So we can say that ⟨... is prime$_\Pi$⟩ and ⟨... is even$_\Pi$⟩ select different functions. We can highlight the second role by contrasting the Value of ⟨3$_\alpha$ is prime$_\Pi$⟩—namely, **t**—with the following short list of abstract objects: 3, {<x, y>: y = **t** iff x is prime, and y = **f** iff x is not prime}. There may be a sense in which this list is more "naturally" associated with **t** than with **f**. But the list is not identical with **t**. Likewise, the semantic contribution of ⟨ . . . is prime$_\Pi$⟩ is not exhausted by the selected set.

Frege (1892*a*) thus distinguished *Value-Ranges*—i.e. sets of ordered pairs <x, y>, such that x is the Value of an argument-term (or an n-tuple of such Values) and y is either **t** or **f**—from *Concepts*; where talk of Concepts was supposed to help mark the difference between a sentence and a mere list. (Compare Kant's distinction between truth-evaluable judgments and mere combinations of ideas.) While each Concept was said to be associated with a certain Value-Range, Frege stipulated that Concepts are *not* sets; so Concepts are not functions in the modern sense.[9] One can think of {x: x is prime}, or {<x, y>: y = **t** iff x is prime, and y = **f** iff x is not prime}, as the "extent" of the Concept associated with ⟨ . . . is prime$_\Pi$⟩. But the Concept, unlike the associated set, was supposed to incorporate the further role of associating each Concept-entity combination with the *value of* the associated function given the entity as argument. This led Frege to say, while asking his readers for a "pinch of salt", that Concepts cannot *be* Values—not even Values of the word 'Concept'. But one need not endorse this (arguably paradoxical) way of talking to admit the distinction Frege wanted to stress, between a function and applying it.

To repeat, our framework assumptions guarantee that ⟨ . . . is prime$_\Pi$⟩—the predicate *plus* the surrounding sentential syntax—is associated with a function F such that for any numeral 'N', the result of saturating the sentence-frame with 'N' is a sentence whose Semantic Value is **t** iff **t** is the value of F given the Semantic Value of 'N' as argument. But this doesn't tell us *how* to divide the semantic work done jointly by the lexical predicate prime$_\Pi$ and the surrounding syntax. The usual terminology, now entrenched, can lull one into thinking otherwise. We say that predicates (like functions) take arguments, and that predicate–argument combinations have (Semantic) Values, while functions map their arguments onto values. But terminological homophony cannot guarantee that

---

[9] A function is a set **s** of ordered pairs, such that if <x, y> ∈ **s**, there is no z (z ≠ y) such that <x, z> ∈ **s**.

functions are the Values of predicates like prime$_\Pi$ and sang$_\Pi$. This is an empirical claim about the semantics of natural language.

It will be useful, here and below, to employ some standard notation for talking about functions. Let '$\lambda x . \Phi x$' stand for the smallest function that maps each entity in the domain over which the variable '$x$' ranges onto a value as specified by '$\Phi x$'. If '$x$' ranges over integers, then '$\lambda x . x + 1$' describes the successor function, which maps each integer x onto $x + 1$. Hence, $[\lambda x . x + 1](3) = 4$, and $[\lambda x . x + 1](27) = 28$. Similarly, $[\lambda x . \mathbf{t}$ iff x is prime$](3) = \mathbf{t}$ iff 3 is prime; and $[\lambda x . \mathbf{t}$ iff x is prime$](28) = \mathbf{t}$ iff 28 is prime. Since 3 is prime, $[\lambda x . \mathbf{t}$ iff x is prime$](3) = \mathbf{t}$; and since 28 is not prime, $[\lambda x . \mathbf{t}$ iff x is prime$](28) = \mathbf{f}$. Now let '$\|...\|$' stand for *the Semantic Value of* the enclosed expresssion. (Cf. Montague (1970); see Heim and Kratzer (1998) for discussion in the context of transformational grammar.) This notation makes it easy to state the main issue concisely.

By hypothesis: $\|3_\alpha\| = 3$; for any sentence $\langle ...\rangle$, $\|\langle ...\rangle\|$ is either $\mathbf{t}$ or $\mathbf{f}$; and $\langle ...$ is prime$_\Pi\rangle$ is associated with the function $[\lambda x . \mathbf{t}$ iff x is prime$]$.[10] But this does not determine the Values of lexical predicates. One can *hypothesize* that $\|$is prime$_\Pi\| = \|$prime$_\Pi\| = [\lambda x . \mathbf{t}$ iff x is prime$]$. And this invites a corresponding thought about the semantic role of concatenation: the Semantic Value of any expression composed of a predicate $\Pi$ and a syntactic argument $\alpha$ is the *value of the function* associated with $\Pi$ given the Semantic Value of $\alpha$ as *argument to that function*; that is, $\|\Pi^\wedge \alpha\| = \|\Pi\|(\|\alpha\|)$. Given this Functionist hypothesis about semantic composition, and the convention that bracketing (like '$^\wedge$') indicates concatenation,

---

[10] If we *assume* that the Value of 'N is prime' is $\mathbf{t}$ or $\mathbf{f}$, we could simply write '$\lambda x . x$ is prime', understanding this as a description of a function from things to sentential Values. And if we stipulate that 'F' expresses the relevant function of this sort, '$\lambda x . Fx$' and '$\lambda x . \mathbf{t}$ iff Fx' are equivalent. But I will be explicit that the functions in question map things onto $\mathbf{t}$ or $\mathbf{f}$. If the need arises, we can make the notation more explicit. Let '$[\lambda x . \Phi_{<\alpha,\beta>}x]$' stand for the smallest function $\Phi$, from entities of type $\alpha$ to entities of type $\beta$, that maps each entity in the domain over which the variable '$x$' ranges onto the value of $\Phi$ given x as argument. We can also specify the relevant variable domains explicitly, instead of relying on variable types, as in '$[\lambda x{:}x{\in}D_\alpha . \mathbf{t}$ iff $\Phi_{<\alpha,\beta>}x]$'; see Heim and Kratzer (1998) for discussion.

$\|\langle 3_\alpha \text{ is prime}_\Pi \rangle\| = \|\text{is prime}_\Pi\|(\|3_\alpha\|) = [\lambda x . \mathbf{t} \text{ iff } x \text{ is prime}](3) = \mathbf{t}$ iff 3 is prime.

There is, however, no a priori guarantee that concatenating an expression whose Semantic Value is some entity x with an expression whose Semantic Value is some function F (with x in its domain) results in a complex expression whose Semantic Value is F(x). This is the obvious conjecture *if* the Semantic Values of (one-place) predicates are functions from the Semantic Values of syntactic arguments to **t** or **f**. But there is nothing incoherent in the supposition that concatenation has a different semantic role, not even if the Semantic Values of predicates are functions of the relevant sort.

One can imagine a perverse language in which $\|\Pi^\wedge \alpha\| = \|\Pi\|(\|\alpha\|)$ *unless* $\|\alpha\|$ *is an odd number*, in which case $\|\Pi^\wedge \alpha\| = \|\Pi\|(\|\alpha\| + 1)$. Suppose that in such a language: $\langle 3_\alpha{}^\wedge \P_\Pi \rangle$ is a sentence, $\|3_\alpha\| = 3$, and $\|\P_\Pi\| = [\lambda x . \mathbf{t} \text{ iff } x \text{ is prime}]$. Given that $\|3_\alpha\|$ is an odd number, and that $3 + 1 = 4$, it follows that

$$\|3_\alpha{}^\wedge \P_\Pi\| = \|\P_\Pi\|(\|3_\alpha\| + 1) = [\lambda x . \mathbf{t} \text{ iff } x \text{ is prime}](3 + 1)$$
$$= \mathbf{t} \text{ iff 4 is prime}$$

In such a language, $\langle \ldots \P_\Pi \rangle$ differs semantically from $\langle \ldots \text{ is prime}_\Pi \rangle$, even though $\|\P_\Pi\| = \|\text{is prime}_\Pi\|$. Alternatively, suppose that in the imagined language, $\|\P_\alpha\| = [\lambda x . \mathbf{t} \text{ iff } x - 1 \text{ is prime}]$. Given that $\|3_\alpha\|$ is an odd number, and that $(3 + 1) - 1 = 3$, it follows that

$$\|3_\alpha{}^\wedge \P_\Pi\| = \|\P_\Pi\|(\|3_\alpha\| + 1) = [\lambda x . \mathbf{t} \text{ iff } x - 1 \text{ is prime}](3 + 1)$$
$$= \mathbf{t} \text{ iff 3 is prime.}$$

In such a language, combining a name for an odd prime number with $\P_\Pi$ has the same (**t**-conditional) effect as combining a name for that number with our predicate prime$_\Pi$, even though $\|\P_\Pi\| \neq \|\text{prime}_\Pi\|$.

In short, the result of applying $[\lambda x . \mathbf{t} \text{ iff } x \text{ is prime}]$ to the number 3 can be obtained by applying $[\lambda x . \mathbf{t} \text{ iff } x - 1 \text{ is prime}]$ to the number 4. And the result of applying $[\lambda x . \mathbf{t} \text{ iff } x \text{ is prime}]$ to 4 can be obtained by applying [λx . **t** iff x + 1 is prime] to 3. So one cannot *stipulate* that in any language with predicates and arguments, $\|\Pi^\wedge \alpha\| = \|\Pi\|(\|\alpha\|)$. Nor can one stipulate that $\|\text{prime}_\Pi\| = [\lambda x . \mathbf{t}$ iff x is prime]. These are substantive proposals that go beyond the initial Fregean assumptions.

## 2. A Conjunctivist Strategy

Other, less contrived alternatives to Functionism illustrate the same point.

### 2.1. *One Value or Many Values*

If $\|\text{is prime}_\Pi\| = \|\text{prime}_\Pi\| = [\lambda x . \mathbf{t}$ iff x is prime], then $\text{prime}_\Pi$ has a *single* Semantic Value. It is also true, on this view, that $\|\text{prime}_\Pi\|$ is a *set* with elements like <3, **t**> and <4, **f**>. But a set is still a thing, and predicates differ semantically from names for sets. One can stipulate that $\text{Euclid}_\alpha$ is a name for the set {<x, y>: y = **t** iff x is prime, and y = **f** iff x is not prime}; in which case, $\|\text{Euclid}_\alpha\| = \|\text{prime}_\Pi\|$. Yet $\text{prime}_\Pi$ and $\text{Euclid}_\alpha$ have different semantic roles, as manifested in how they (can and cannot) combine semantically with other expressions. Functionists can mark this distinction in terms of a semantic typology that parallels the grammatical distinction between expressions that take arguments and the arguments taken. One can say that names like $3_\alpha$ and $\text{Euclid}_\alpha$ are of type <x>. And one can hypothesize that predicates like $\text{prime}_\Pi$ are of type <x, **t**>, linguistic devices that express functions from entities to sentential Values. This encodes the idea that $\text{prime}_\Pi$ can combine with an expression of type <x> to form a sentence whose Value is **t** iff $\|\text{prime}_\Pi\|$ maps the relevant entity to **t**; see Chierchia and Turner (1988) for discussion. But there are other ways of capturing the difference between predicates and names.

In particular, one can describe predicates as expressions that can have *many* Semantic Values, encoding this as follows: Val(x, $\text{prime}_\Pi$) iff x is prime; where 'Val(x, ... )' means that x is a Value of '...';

see Larson and Segal (1995), Higginbotham (1986). I discuss some theoretical virtues of this notation, due essentially to Tarski (1933, 1984), in §2.4 and Chapter 2. For now, just note that it lets us say that words like 'red' and 'ball' are predicative in the following sense: such expressions can (and often do) apply to more than one thing; to know what such an expression means is to know that the expression applies to anything that satisfies a certain condition, which can be satisfied by more than one thing without violating any categorical constraint. We can capture the contrasting idea that proper names have *unique* Values with axioms like the following: Val(x, $3_\alpha$) iff x = 3; that is, x is a Value of $3_\alpha$ iff x *is identical with* the number 3. And it is easy to formulate the Conjunctivist thesis in these terms: Val(x, $\Phi^\wedge\Psi$) iff Val(x, $\Phi$) & Val(x, $\Psi$), where $\Phi$ and $\Psi$ range over expressions of any kind. On this view, x is a Value of the complex expression $3_\alpha^\wedge$[is prime$_\Pi$] iff x is a Value of $3_\alpha$ *and* x is a Value of prime$_\Pi$.[11]

At first glance, this appears to violate the requirement that the Value of a sentence be **t** or **f**. But the Fregean apparatus does not tell us what *sentences* are. Maybe a sentence is something more than the mere concatenation of a grammatical predicate with an argument, much as a judgment is something more than a mere concatenation of ideas. There is a long tradition of treating the category of sentence as somehow special, in a way that grammatical categories like noun-phrase and verb-phrase are not. This is unsurprising if we focus on truth-evaluability and semantic implication. So perhaps we should think of a sentence as a complex expression that has been "capped off" in a way that makes it binarily evaluable, and thus an expression of a type such that expressions of that type can exhibit relations of implication.

There are various ways of implementing this suggestion. But suppose we distinguish the predicative *phrase* [$3_\alpha$ is prime$_\Pi$]$_{\Pi P}$,

---

[11]  This presupposes universal closure of the axioms, which will officially include generalizations like '∀x[Val(x, $\Phi^\wedge\Psi$) iff Val(x, $\Phi$) & Val(x, $\Psi$)]'. Eventually, we must also mark the *differences* between nouns and adjectives; see Baker (2003). But for simplicity, I am abstracting away from such differences.

where 'ΠP' indicates that a predicate has combined with an argument to form a "grammatically saturated" expression, from the *sentence* $\langle [3_\alpha \text{ is prime}_\Pi]_{\Pi P} \rangle$. This leaves it open whether the angled brackets, which reflect sentencehood, correspond to (i) some aspect of grammatical structure, not yet indicated with notation like '$[3_\alpha \text{ is prime}_\Pi]_{\Pi P}$', or (ii) something else involved in the interpretation of sentences as such. Setting this issue aside for now, consider the following hypothesis: Val($t$, $\langle [\ldots]_{\Pi P} \rangle$) iff for some x, Val(x, $[\ldots]_{\Pi P}$). This is, in effect, to say that labelling a phrase *as* a sentence has the semantic effect of existential closure.

On this view, a sentence of the form $\langle [\ldots]_{\Pi P} \rangle$ has the Value $t$ iff at least one thing is a Value of the predicative phrase $[\ldots]_{\Pi P}$. Concatenating a predicate with an argument corresponds to conjunction, and labelling the resulting complex expression *as* a sentence corresponds to existential closure. This proposal may be wrong; though as we'll see, Functionists also need to posit covert existential closure. And in any case, there is more than one way to map the Value of a name onto a sentential Value.

$$S \Rightarrow [\lambda x \,.\, t \text{ iff } x \text{ is prime}](3)$$
$$/ \quad \backslash$$
$$3 \Leftarrow \alpha \quad \Pi \Rightarrow [\lambda x \,.\, t \text{ iff } x \text{ is prime}]$$

$$S \Rightarrow t \text{ iff } \exists x \,(x = 3 \,\&\, x \text{ is prime})$$
$$\Pi P \Rightarrow x \text{ iff } (x = 3 \,\&\, x \text{ is prime})$$
$$/ \quad \backslash$$
$$x \text{ iff } x = 3 \Leftarrow \alpha \quad \Pi \Rightarrow x \text{ iff } x \text{ is prime}$$

Similarly, one could say that $t$ is a Value of $\langle [\text{Pat}_\alpha \text{ sang}_\Pi]_{\Pi P} \rangle$ iff something is a Value of $\text{Pat}_\alpha$ and $\text{sang}_\Pi$.

This implies that $\langle [\text{Pat}_\alpha \text{ sang}_\Pi]_{\Pi P} \rangle$ gets the Value $t$ only if **Pat** is a Value of $\text{sang}_\Pi$. But again, there are alternatives. Just as there may be more to the interpretation of a sentence than one might initially suspect, there may be more to the interpretation of a syntactic *argument* than one might initially suspect. Suppose the grammatical form of 'Pat sang' is correctly represented as follows: $\langle [\Theta\text{-Pat}_\alpha \text{ sang}_\Pi]_{\Pi P} \rangle$; where '$\Theta$' indicates that $\text{Pat}_\alpha$ is the *subject of* a certain kind of verb—intuitively, a verb that associates its subjects with the thematic role of Agency. One can hypothesize that any such verb is grammatically related to its subject in a semantically significant way. This makes room for the idea that certain verbs have events as their Values, where events are things in which potential Values of names *participate*.

For example, one could adopt the following view, according to which sang$_\Pi$ and its subject are both interpreted as monadic predicates: Val(x, sang$_\Pi$) iff Past-Singing(x); and Val(x, $\Theta$-...) iff $\exists x'[\text{Agent}(x, x') \,\&\, \text{Val}(x', ...)]$, where '...' can be replaced by any name like Pat$_\alpha$. Or rewriting for notational convenience, with 'o' as a variable associated with predicates,

$$\text{Val}(o, \text{sang}_\Pi) \text{ iff Past-Singing}(o)$$
$$\text{Val}(o, \Theta\text{-}...)\text{iff } \exists x[\text{Agent}(o, x) \,\&\, \text{Val}(x, ...)].^{[12]}$$

This requires a distinction between the name Pat$_\alpha$, as a lexical item independent of any grammatical relations, and Pat$_\alpha$ as it appears in the configuration indicated by '$\Theta$'. But we can draw such a distinction.

The semantic axiom for Pat$_\alpha$, 'Val(x, Pat$_\alpha$) iff x = **Pat**', reflects a claim about the semantic contribution of Pat$_\alpha$ to complex expressions in which the name appears. But one can *add* the hypothesis that certain grammatical relations are semantically significant, with the result that the semantic axiom for a name does not by itself capture

---

[12] I use 'o' to avoid any suggestion that all predicates have events as their Values. But the notation is otherwise in concious imitation of Higginbotham's (1985) discussion of theta-marking. Perhaps '$\Theta$' corresponds to a real *feature* assigned to Pat$_\alpha$ in the course of constructing the sentence, and not just a *structural relation*; see Hornstein (2001, 2002). But I do not assume this. And nothing hangs on the distinction between 'o' and 'x'. Formally, there is nothing wrong with 'Val(o, sang$_\Pi$) iff o sang', which says that something is a Value of sang$_\Pi$ iff it sang, and likewise for 'Val(x, The Renaissance$_\alpha$) iff x was The Renaissance'. In general, one should not be misled by the typographic conventions of using letters to indicate variable positions. If not for type-setting difficulties, I would use notation like the following.

$$\text{Val(\_\_, } \Theta\text{-Pat}_\alpha) \text{ iff } \exists[\text{Agent(\_\_, \_\_)} \,\&\, \text{\_\_} = \textbf{Pat}$$

Of course, one can hypothesize that natural language distinguishes event-variables from individual-variables. But whatever notation one uses, one must allow for sentences like 'That was a loud explosion'.

the semantic contribution of the name *as occupier of a certain grammatical role*, like being the subject of a verb like sang$_\Pi$. Given that

$$\text{Val}(o, \Theta\text{-}\ldots) \text{ iff } \exists x[\text{Agent}(o,x) \ \& \ \text{Val}(x,\ldots)],$$

it follows that Val(o, $\Theta$-Pat$_\alpha$) iff $\exists x[\text{Agent}(o, x) \ \& \ x = \textbf{Pat}]$. Or simplifying,

$$\text{Val}(o, \Theta\text{-Pat}_\alpha) \text{ iff Agent}(o, \textbf{Pat}).$$

One can view '$\Theta$' as the mark of a certain grammatical relation, and read 'Val(o, $\Theta$-Pat$_\alpha$)' as follows: o is a Value of *Pat$_\alpha$ as marked* in the way that subjects of verbs like sang$_\Pi$ get marked.

Conjunctivists can go on to say that something is a Value of the predicative phrase [$\Theta$-Pat$_\alpha$ sang$_\Pi$]$_{\Pi P}$ iff it is a Value of both constituents, treating $\Theta$-Pat$_\alpha$ (i.e., the name as marked, not the bare lexical item) as the compositionally relevant constituent. More formally,

$$\text{Val}(o, [\Theta\text{-Pat}_\alpha \ \text{sang}_\Pi]_{\Pi P}) \text{ iff Val}(o, \Theta\text{-Pat}_\alpha) \ \&$$
$$\text{Val}(o, \text{sang}_\Pi); \text{ hence,}$$
$$\text{Val}(o, [\Theta\text{-Pat}_\alpha \ \text{sang}_\Pi]_{\Pi P}) \text{ iff Agent}(o, \textbf{Pat}) \ \& \ \text{Past-Singing}(o).$$

So if we add the assumption that sentencehood involves existential closure of the variable,

$$\text{Val}(\textbf{t}, \langle[\ldots]_{\Pi P}\rangle) \text{ iff } \exists o[\text{Val}(o, [\ldots]_{\Pi P})]$$

we get the desired result:

$$\text{Val}(\textbf{t}, \langle[\Theta\text{-Pat}_\alpha \ \text{sang}_\Pi]_{\Pi P}\rangle) \text{ iff } \exists o[\text{Agent}(o, \textbf{Pat}) \ \& \ \text{Past-Singing}(o)].$$

That is, the sentence 'Pat sang' gets the Value **t** iff **Pat** was the Agent of some event of singing.[13]

---

[13] Or put another way, Val(t, $\langle[\Theta\text{-Pat}_\alpha \ \text{sang}_\Pi]_{\Pi P}\rangle$) iff

$$\exists[\exists[\text{Agent}(\underline{\quad}, \underline{\quad}) \ \& \ \underline{\quad} = \textbf{Pat}] \ \& \ \text{Past-Singing}(\underline{\quad})]$$

Let me repeat this important point. Initially, one might think that Conjunctivism is incompatible with the claim that action verbs are predicates of events. After all, 'Pat sang' can be true; yet *nothing* is both **Pat** and a past event of singing. But the apparent "mismatch" vanishes if the relevant grammatical relation signifies a thematic relation that **Pat** can bear to an event (by "participating" in the event in a certain way). I'll return to this point, because I think it suggests an *explanation* for the fact that certain grammatical relations are indeed semantically (and thematically) significant: given a fundamentally Conjunctivist language, this is a simple way of allowing for predicates of *events* that can combine with names of *individuals*, while avoiding rampant mismatches. A language-learner who treats concatenation as a sign of predicate-conjunction, and thus deals easily with phrases like 'red ball', can accommodate grammatical arguments by assigning thematic significance to grammatical relations. But for now, let me just note that this is a coherent way of describing the relation between the Value of a name and the Values of sentences in which the name appears.

Functionism is *one* way of implementing a Fregean framework in which each sentence is conditionally associated with one of exactly two sentential Values, and each grammatical argument has a Value that—together with the rest of the sentence—determines this conditional association. This is not to deny that natural language semantics has nonconjunctive aspects that can be characterized in functional terms. Even if Conjunctivism is correct, one can describe the significance of being an argument of sang$_\Pi$ in terms of the function $[\lambda x . [\lambda o . t \text{ iff } x \text{ is the Agent of } o]]$, which maps things like **Pat** to functions (from *events* to **t** or **f**). And one can describe existential closure in terms of a function, $\lambda F . t \text{ iff } \exists o[F(o) = t]$, which maps functions (from *events* to **t** or **f**) to **t** or **f**. I don't think this is an illuminating description. But the issue is not whether there are non-conjunctive aspects of meaning.

The issue concerns the semantic contributions of predicates, concatenation, and grammatical relations. We should all agree with Frege that a sentence is not a list, since (utterances of) sentences can be evaluated for truth or falsity; sentences, unlike lists, exhibit implications. Conjunctivists should also grant—indeed, they should argue—that grammatical relations between predicates and arguments are semantically significant in ways that go beyond conjunction (and ordering arguments). For if this is correct, it is an explanandum that Conjunctivism might help us explain.[14]

## 2.2. *Transitive Constructions and Thematic Roles*

The main point of this section is to show that Conjunctivists can deal with a range of basic constructions. So without suggesting that we're done with intransitive verbs, let's turn to examples like (11).

(11)   Pat hugged Chris

For purposes of illustrating the usual Functionist account, suppose that (11) has the following structure: $\langle \text{Pat}_\alpha \, [\text{hugged}_{\Pi^*} \, \text{Chris}_\alpha]_\Pi \, \rangle$; where $\text{Chris}_\alpha$ is the *internal* argument of $\text{hugged}_{\Pi^*}$, and $\text{Pat}_\alpha$ is the *external* argument. I'll have more to say about internal and external arguments below. But 'hugged Chris' is a predicative constituent of (11), while 'Pat hugged' is not. In this sense, 'Chris' is more closely related to 'hugged' than 'Pat' is; see Williams (1980), Marantz (1984). Indeed, one can view 'Pat' as *the* argument of the complex monadic predicate 'hugged Chris'. And presumably, '5 precedes 6' exhibits the same grammatical structure: $\langle 5_\alpha \, [\text{precedes}_{\Pi^*} \, 6_\alpha]_\Pi \rangle$. Given Functionism, the Value of $[\text{precedes}_{\Pi^*} \, 6_\alpha]_\Pi$ has to be a function from entities to sentential Values. That is, $\|\text{precedes}_{\Pi^*} \, 6_\alpha\|$ has to be of type $\langle \mathbf{x}, \mathbf{t} \rangle$. So $\|\text{precedes}_{\Pi^*}\|$ has to be of type $\langle \mathbf{x}, \langle \mathbf{x}, \mathbf{t} \rangle \rangle$,

---

[14] Conjunctivists do not deny that concatenation corresponds to a function, since predicate-conjunction can obviously be so described: $\|^\wedge\| = \lambda \mathbf{o} \, . \, \mathbf{v}$ iff $\exists F \exists G[\mathbf{o} = \langle F, G \rangle \, \& \, \mathbf{v} = \lambda \mathbf{o}' \, . \, \mathbf{t} \text{ iff } F(\mathbf{o}') = \mathbf{t} \, \& \, G(\mathbf{o}') = \mathbf{t}]$. One can also encode Functionism in terms of assigning a semantic value to concatenation: $\|\Pi^\wedge \alpha\| = \|^\wedge\|(\langle \|\Pi\|, \|\alpha\| \rangle)$; where $\|^\wedge\| = \lambda \mathbf{o} \, . \, \mathbf{v}$ iff $\exists F \exists x[\mathbf{o} = \langle F, x \rangle \, \& \, F(x) = \mathbf{v}]$, and 'F' ranges over functions from individuals to truth-values (and '**o**' ranges over ordered pairs of functions and elements of the relevant domains). The empirical question is whether concatenation in natural language signifies the specific semantic content of conjunction, as well as signifying that the phrase is not just a list of two predicates, or whether concatenation makes a "minimal" contribution in that it *just* signifies function-application.

a function from entities to *functions* of type $<x, t>$. On this view, $\|\text{precedes}_{\Pi*}\| = [\lambda y \,.\, [\lambda x \,.\, \mathbf{t} \text{ iff } x \text{ precedes } y]].$[15]

If this is correct, and $\|\Pi^\wedge \alpha\| = \|\Pi\|(\|\alpha\|)$, then

$$\|\text{precedes}_{\Pi*} 6_\alpha\| = \|\text{precedes}_{\Pi*}\|(\|6_\alpha\|)$$
$$= [\lambda y \,.\, [\lambda x \,.\, \mathbf{t} \text{ iff } x \text{ precedes } y]](6)$$
$$= [\lambda x \,.\, \mathbf{t} \text{ iff } x \text{ precedes } 6].$$

The phrase $[\text{precedes}_{\Pi*} \, 6_\alpha]_\Pi$ is of the form '$\Pi^\wedge \alpha$'; although in this case, the Value of the complex expression is said to be a function (as opposed to $\mathbf{t}$ or $\mathbf{f}$). And given that $\|5_\alpha \, [\text{precedes}_{\Pi*} \, 6_\alpha]_\Pi\| = \|\text{precedes}_{\Pi*} \, 6_\alpha\|(5)$, it follows that

$$\|5_\alpha [\text{precedes}_{\Pi*} 6_\alpha]_\Pi\| = [\lambda x \,.\, \mathbf{t} \text{ iff } x \text{ precedes } 6](5)$$
$$= \mathbf{t} \text{ iff } 5 \text{ precedes } 6.$$

Likewise, if $\|\text{hugged}_{\Pi*}\| = [\lambda y \,.\, [\lambda x \,.\, \mathbf{t} \text{ iff } x \text{ hugged } y]]$, then

$$\|[\text{hugged}_{\Pi*}\text{Chris}_\alpha]_\Pi = [\lambda y \,.\, [\lambda x \,.\, \mathbf{t} \text{ iff } x \text{ hugged } y]](\mathbf{Chris})$$
$$= [\lambda x \,.\, \mathbf{t} \text{ iff } x \text{ hugged } \mathbf{Chris}]; \text{ and}$$

$$\|\text{Pat}_\alpha[\text{hugged}_{\Pi*}\text{Chris}_\alpha]_\Pi\| = [\lambda x \,.\, \mathbf{t} \text{ iff } x \text{ hugged } \mathbf{Chris}](\mathbf{Pat})$$
$$= \mathbf{t} \text{ iff } \mathbf{Pat} \text{ hugged } \mathbf{Chris}.$$

For purposes of illustrating a Conjunctivist alternative, let's make the grammatical relations between the verb and its arguments explicit as in (11G),

$$(11G) \quad \langle [\text{ext-Pat}_\alpha \; [\text{hugged}_{\Pi*} \; \text{int-Chris}_\alpha]] \rangle$$

with 'ext' and 'int' highlighting external and internal arguments, respectively. Recall that Conjunctivists distinguish the sentence, indicated with angled brackets, from the syntactically saturated phrase. And $\langle [\text{ext-Pat}_\alpha \; [\text{hugged}_{\Pi*} \; \text{int-Chris}_\alpha]] \rangle$ is just $\langle [\text{Pat}_\alpha \; [\text{hugged}_{\Pi*} \text{Chris}_\alpha]_\Pi]_{\Pi P} \rangle$ by another name. The bracketing and phrasal subscripts determine what is an argument of what. One can hypothesize that, because the grammatical relations are significant, $\text{Pat}_\alpha$ is interpreted

---

[15] This is the (smallest) function—call it $\mathscr{F}$—that maps y onto the (smallest) function F such that $F(x) = \mathbf{t}$ iff x precedes y. Thus, $\mathscr{F}(1) = [\lambda x \,.\, \mathbf{t} \text{ iff } x \text{ precedes } 1]$; $\mathscr{F}(2) = [\lambda x \,.\, \mathbf{t} \text{ iff } x \text{ precedes } 2]$; etc.

as an Agent-specifier, while Chris$_\alpha$ is interpreted as a Theme-specifier; where the Theme of a hugging is the individual hugged, as opposed to Agent who does the hugging.[16] Given Conjunctivism, (11) has the Value **t** iff something is a Value of ext-Pat$_\alpha$, hugged$_{\Pi^*}$, and int-Chris$_\alpha$. The further claim is that o is a Value of all three conjuncts iff the Value of Pat$_\alpha$ was the *Agent* of o, o was an *event* of hugging, and the Value of Chris$_\alpha$ was the *Theme* of o.

One might implement this proposal with the axioms below.

$$\text{Val}(o, \text{ext-} \dots) \text{ iff } \exists x[\text{Agent}(o, x) \ \& \ \text{Val}(x), \dots]$$

$$\text{Val}(o, \text{int-} \dots) \text{ iff } \exists x[\text{Theme}(o, x) \ \& \ \text{Val}(x), \dots]$$

It follows from these axioms that Val(o, ext-Pat$_\alpha$) iff $\exists x$[Agent (o, x) & Val(x, Pat$_\alpha$)]; and since Val(x, Pat$_\alpha$) iff x = **Pat**, Val(o, ext-Pat$_\alpha$) iff Agent(o, **Pat**). Similarly, it follows that Val(o, int-Chris$_\alpha$) iff Theme(o, **Chris**). On this theory, every external argument is an Agent-specifier, and every internal argument is a Theme-specifier. But prima facie, 'Pat resembles Chris' does not imply that **Pat** was an Agent, and '5 precedes 6' does not imply that anything happened. This suggests that the significance of being an argument can *vary*, presumably within constraints, across verbs. Conjunctivists can adopt a correspondingly more flexible view.

At least for now, let 'External(o, x)' mean that x is the external participant of o, and let 'Internal(o, x)' mean that x is the internal participant of o—leaving it open what it is for one thing to be the external or internal participant of something else. And consider the following axioms:

$$\text{Val}(o, \text{ext-} \dots) \text{ iff } \exists x[\text{External}(o, x) \ \& \ \text{Val}(x, \dots))]$$

$$\text{Val}(o, \text{int-} \dots) \text{ iff } \exists x[\text{Internal}(o, x) \ \& \ \text{Val}(x, \dots))].$$

---

[16] For reasons noted in Ch. 3, it has become standard to use 'Theme' instead of 'Patient' to talk about the thematic relation associated with direct-objects of action verbs. This lets us say that "things" like songs can be Themes—if I played a song, the song is what I played, and it "measures" (in Tenny's (1994) sense) the duration of the playing—even if such things are not *affected* by Agents. But intuitively, the Theme of a hugging is the individual affected by the Agent's action.

This is still to say that grammatical relations are significant. For example, o is a Value of Pat$_\alpha$ *marked as an external argument* iff **Pat** is the external participant of o; and o is a Value of Chris$_\alpha$ *marked as an internal argument* iff **Chris** is the internal participant of o. Or abbreviating, Val(o, ext-Pat$_\alpha$) iff External(o, **Pat**); and Val(o, int-Chris$_\alpha$) iff Internal(o, **Chris**).[17] So given Conjunctivism,

Val(o, [ext-Pat$_\alpha$[hugged$_{\Pi*}$ int-Chris$_\alpha$]$_\Pi$]$_{\Pi P}$) iff

External(o, **Pat** & Val(o, hugged$_{\Pi*}$) & Internal(o, **Chris**).

But it doesn't yet follow that the Values of hugged$_{\Pi*}$ are events with Agents and Themes.

The biconditional above is compatible with the Values of hugged$_{\Pi*}$ being *ordered pairs* of individuals, where the ordered pair <**Pat, Chris**> has **Pat** as its external participant and **Chris** as its internal participant. One can stipulate that, for any ordered pair, its first element is the external participant, and its second element is the internal participant. So one could adopt the following notational variant of a Functionist axiom for hugged$_{\Pi*}$: Val(o, hugged$_{\Pi*}$) iff $\exists x \exists y[o = <x, y> \& x$ hugged $y]$. I'll soon discuss some reasons for rejecting such axioms for action verbs. But the proposed construal of grammatical relations leaves the issue open.

The more interesting Conjunctivist proposal is that the Values of hugged$_{\Pi*}$ are *events*, where for any event o and individual x: x is the external participant of o iff x is the Agent of o; and x is the internal participant of o iff x is the Theme of x. That is,

Val(o, hugged$_{\Pi*}$) iff Event(o) & Past-Hugging(o); and

Event(o) $\rightarrow$ {$\forall$x[External(o, x) iff Agent(o, x)]

& $\forall$x[Internal(o, x) iff Theme(o, x)]}.

On this view, Pat$_\alpha$ is an Agent-specifier in (11) because Pat$_\alpha$ is the external argument of an event-predicate, and Chris$_\alpha$ is a

---

[17] In Ch 2, I defend second-order versions of these hypotheses concerning the significance of being an internal or external argument. This allows for events with *many* internal and/or external participants. But for now, we can ignore this possibility and restrict attention to the first-order proposal.

Theme-specifier because Chris$_\alpha$ is the internal argument of an event-predicate. But 'ext' and 'int' do not themselves signify the relations "Agent-of" and "Theme-of". The grammatical relations signify generic participation relations, "External-of" and "Internal-of"; and certain lexical predicates demand that their Values be of a certain sort, such that Values of that sort have certain kinds of participants. In particular, a transitive action verb like hugged$_{\Pi^*}$ has Values whose external/internal participants of are Agents/Themes. Metaphorically, such verbs "infuse" grammatical relations (which by themselves have purely formal significance) with specific thematic significance.[18]

It follows that

$$\text{Val}(o, [\text{ext-5}_\alpha[\text{precedes}_{\Pi^*}\text{int-6}_\alpha]_\Pi]_{\Pi P}) \text{ iff}$$

$$\text{External}(o, 5) \;\&\; \text{Val}(o, \text{precedes}_{\Pi^*}) \;\&\; \text{Internal}(o, 6).$$

But so long as precedes$_{\Pi^*}$ is not an event-predicate, it does not follow that the number 5 is an Agent if it precedes anything. In this (very special) case, it may be plausible to treat the (mathematical) verb as a predicate satisfied by certain ordered pairs:

$$\text{Val}(o, \text{precedes}_{\Pi^*}) \text{ iff } \exists x \exists y[o = <x, y> \;\&\; \text{Predecessor-of}(x, y)];$$

where 'Predecessor-of' is defined in mathematical terms. Or perhaps the Values of 'precedes' are *states*, as Parsons (1990) suggests; where the participants of states are Subjects and Objects, as opposed to Agents and Themes. This is not implausible for verbs like 'hates' and 'resembles'. But let me set these issues aside for now.[19] The more immediately important point is that on a Conjunctivist view, each

---

[18] On this view, an event of kissing with Romeo as its external participant and Juliet as its internal participant is presumably distinct from any event with Juliet as its external participant and Romeo as its internal participant. See Schein (2002) for arguments that we want to individuate the Values of action verbs (at least) this finely. Those who want to reserve 'event' for spatiotemporal particulars individuated less finely should mentally replace 'event' in the text with the technical term 'event*'; cf. n. 34 below.

[19] Some authors hold that perceptual verbs—like 'saw' or 'heard'—take subjects that represent "Experiencers" (as opposed to Agents) of events. Following Baker (1997), who draws on Dowty (1979, 1991), I adopt a more inclusive notion of 'Agent' according to which being a perceiver counts (for purposes of semantic theory) as a

argument of a transitive verb gets interpreted in terms of some "participation relation" that can hold between a Value of the verb and the Value of a name.

Let me stress that Conjunctivism *requires* this kind of approach to transitive constructions. As we saw in §2.1, one could (though I don't) say that sang$_\Pi$ is a predicate satisfied by individuals like **Pat**. In this sense, something could be a Value of both Pat$_\alpha$ and sang$_\Pi$, just as something can be a Value of both Pat$_\alpha$ and linguist$_\Pi$. But nothing could be a Value of Pat$_\alpha$ and hugged$_{\Pi^*}$ and Chris$_\alpha$, unless **Pat** is identical with **Chris**, and **Pat/Chris** is a Value of hugged$_{\Pi^*}$; and then 'Pat hugged Chris' would mean something like *Pat hugged, and Pat is Chris*. In this sense, Conjunctivists are forced to say that certain grammatical relations are associated with participation relations. Initially, one might think this tells against Conjunctivism. Shouldn't a semantic theory be able to accommodate elementary facts about verbs without appeal to "things" in which other things participate? But one can invert this thought. Conjunctivism *predicts* that transitive verbs have Values to which the Values of internal and external arguments can be related—and hence, that grammatical arguments can be semantically associated with thematic roles. This prediction is evidently correct; see Gruber (1965, 1976), Jackendoff (1972, 1987), Chomsky (1981, 1995), Baker (1988, 1997), Dowty (1991), Grimshaw (1990), Pesetsky (1995), etc.

I review some relevant data in later chapters. But consider a striking negative generalization about natural language: there are no transitive action verbs with meanings such that (in active voice) the grammatical subject is represented as the thing affected, while the direct-object is represented as the actor. Principles of natural language evidently preclude the possibility of a verb 'V' such that a sentence of the form 'x (V y)', with 'y' as the internal argument, means that there was a hugging of x by y; see Baker (1988, 1997). If we

way of being an Agent. But one could also draw further distinctions among events: events$_{action}$ whose external participants are Agents, and events$_{perception}$ whose external participants are Experiencers. Examples like 'Chicago is west of Boston' merit further discussion. But if Functionists say that $\|west\| = \lambda y . [\lambda x . \mathbf{t}$ iff x is west of y], Conjunctivists can treat '(is) west (of)' like 'precedes'.

want to say that Chris was hugged by Pat, with 'Chris' as the subject, we use passive voice. In Functionist terms, there is no verb whose Value is [λy . [λx . **t** iff y hugged x]]. The same holds for other action verbs, even on an inclusive conception of action. There is no verb 'glubbed' such that 'x glubbed y' means that y pushed/ate/stole/loved/saw/built x. One wants to know why.

Perhaps some "filter" rules out Values like [λy . [λx . **t** iff y hugged x]]; see Chapter 3 for discussion. But another possibility is that transitive verbs are semantically monadic, with lexical meanings that do *not* preclude the unobserved thematic order of arguments, and that the constraint reflects the thematic significance of verb–argument *relations*. (If external arguments of event-predicates must be interpreted as Agent-representers, there cannot be event-predicates with external arguments that are interpreted as Theme-representers.) Appeal to thematic differences between intransitive verbs—compare the intuitively agentive 'sang' with the intuitively nonagentive 'fell'—also correlate with differences in how such verbs are grammatically related to their arguments. For example, it is independently plausible that 'Pat' is an external argument in 'Pat sang', but a (displaced) internal argument in 'Pat fell'.[20] So in the end, it may be a virtue of Conjunctivism that it cannot accommodate 'Pat hugged Chris' without appeal to things in which the Values of names can participate, and hypotheses about *how* participation relations and grammatical relations are connected.

## 2.3. *Extending the Strategy*

With this in mind, let me offer the obvious hypotheses about prepositions and sentential connectives.

---

[20] See Ch.3 n. 12. There is, of course, an inverse of 'precedes': x precedes y iff y succeeds x. Though in my view, this is further reason for treating the mathematical notion as a (very) special case, in which the "verb" is so thematically bleached that one can treat it as a predicate of ordered pairs (and in that sense equivalent to 'is a predecessor of'). Being the subject of a "natural" verb carries semantic significance beyond that of merely indicating the first relatum of an asymmetric relation. Even verbs like 'married', which describe "symmetric" transactions, carry the implication that the (Value of) grammatical subject is represented *as* the Agent.

One might have wondered how 'hugged Chris in Paris on Monday' could be a conjunctive predicate. Even if 'Chris' is (by virtue of its grammatical role) interpreted as a predicate of events, 'in' and 'on' are not. But one can hypothesize that 'on Monday' is interpreted as a monadic predicate because 'on' marks 'Monday' in a thematically significant way. I take up the details in §3. But one can say that o is a Value of 'hugged Chris in Paris on Monday' iff: o is a Value of 'hugged'; *and* for some x, x is both a Value of 'Chris' and the internal participant of o; *and* for some x, x is both a Value of 'Paris' and a place in which o occurred; *and* for some x, x is both a Value of 'Monday' and a time (interval) at which o occurred. Associating adverbial prepositional phrases with thematic roles is natural enough with respect to phrases like 'was a hugging *of* Chris *by* Pat'. The broader idea is that natural language includes a finite number of elements (like prepositions) and grammatical relations (like subject and object) that make it possible to interpret a name as a constituent of a logically complex monadic predicate satisfied by things to which the name's Value is suitably related.[21]

The connective 'or' and the sentential constituents of (12)

(12)    Pat sang or Chris danced

can also be interpreted as conjoinable monadic predicates. Suppose the grammatical form of (12) is as shown in (12G), suppressing subsentential structure for simplicity.

(12G)    $\langle[\text{ext-}\langle\text{Pat sang}\rangle_{\underline{\alpha}}\ [\text{or}_{\underline{\Pi}^*}\ \text{int-}\langle\text{Chris danced}\rangle_{\underline{\alpha}}\ ]_{\underline{\Pi}}]_{\underline{\Pi P}}\rangle$

Here, underlining indicates *sentential* predicates and arguments, with the latter marked as either external or internal arguments of 'or'. The idea is that sentential connectives, like transitive verbs, combine with arguments (of the right sort) to form a sentence; see

---

[21] If prepositions were productive, or even if there were lots of them, I would worry that this is cheating. Conjunctivism would be trivialized if phrases could always be interpreted as predicates by treating one constituent as a device for turning the other into a predicate. But if Conjunctivism is on the right track, and the number of psychologically important participation relations exceeds the number of grammatical relations that can carry thematic significance, prepositions are not surprising.

Larson and Segal (1995) for discussion. This makes it possible to say that (12) has the Value **t** iff for some o,

$\exists x[\text{External}(o, x)\ \&\ \text{Val}(x, \langle \text{Pat sang} \rangle_\alpha)]\ \&\ \text{Val}(o, \text{or}_{\Pi^*})\ \&$

$\exists x[\text{Internal}(o, x)\ \&\ \text{Val}(x, \langle \text{Chris danced} \rangle_\alpha)].$

On this view, o is a Value of $\text{or}_{\Pi^*}$ only if o has sentential Values as its external and internal participants. But there are at least four such things—namely, the ordered pairs $\langle \mathbf{t}, \mathbf{t} \rangle$, $\langle \mathbf{t}, \mathbf{f} \rangle$, $\langle \mathbf{f}, \mathbf{t} \rangle$, and $\langle \mathbf{f}, \mathbf{f} \rangle$.[22] And one can say that $\text{or}_{\Pi^*}$ is satisfied by the first three of these, writing the axiom as follows:

$\text{Val}(o, \text{or}_{\Pi^*})$ iff $\exists x \exists y[\text{External}(o, x)\ \&\ \text{Internal}(o, y)\ \&$

$(x = \mathbf{t} \text{ or } y = \mathbf{t})].$

In which case, (12) has the Value **t** iff there is something such that:

its external participant = **t** iff Val(**t**, ⟨Pat sang⟩);

its internal participant = **t** iff Val(**t**, ⟨Chris danced⟩); and

its external participant = **t** or its internal participant = **t**.

Something satisfies all three conditions iff Val(**t**, ⟨Pat sang⟩) or Val(**t**, ⟨Chris danced⟩). So as desired, (12) has the Value **t** iff Val(**t**, ⟨Pat sang⟩) or Val(**t**, ⟨Chris danced⟩). In general, 'S1 or S2' has the Value **t** iff Val(**t**, S1) or Val(**t**, S2). Similar remarks apply to sentential conjunction and material conditionals.

$\text{Val}(o, \text{and}_{\Pi^*})$ iff $\exists x \exists y[\text{External}(o, x)\ \&\ \text{Internal}(o, y)$

$\&\ (x = \mathbf{t} \text{ and } y = \mathbf{t})];$

$\text{Val}(o, \text{if}_{\Pi^*})$ iff $\exists x \exists y[\text{External}(o, x)\ \&\ \text{Internal}(o, y)$

$\&\ \text{Internal}(o, y)\ \&\ (x = \mathbf{t} \text{ if } y = \mathbf{t})].$

---

[22] The remarks in n. 12 apply here. One could say that (12) has the Value **t** iff

$\exists[\exists[\text{Ext}(\_\_, \_\_)\ \&\ \text{Val}(\_\_, \langle \text{Pat sang} \rangle_\alpha)]\ \&\ \text{Or}(\_\_)\ \&\ \exists[\text{Int}(\_\_, \_\_)\ \&\ \text{Val}(\_\_, \langle \text{Chris danced} \rangle_\alpha)]]$

Initially, one might balk at specifying the meanings of sentences like (12) in terms of purely formal "participation" relations that elements of an ordered pair x bear to x itself. But this is just the Conjunctivist version of the common claim that sentential connectives are relevantly like transitive verbs. Functionists will say that $\|\text{or}_{\underline{\Pi}*}\|$ is a function of type $\langle t \langle t, t \rangle\rangle$, $\lambda y . [\lambda \underline{x} . t \text{ iff } \underline{x} = t \text{ or } \underline{y} = t]$, with '$\underline{x}$' and '$\underline{y}$' ranging over sentential Values. Conjunctivists replace function-application with participation relations, conjunction, and existential closure. In cases like (12) and '5 precedes 6', this may be a distinction without a difference. But recall that, at this stage, the goal is to show that Conjunctivists *can* handle the usual range of elementary examples.

Sentential negation is another example of this sort. Suppose that $\text{Val}(o, \text{not}_{\underline{\Pi}})$ iff $o = f$, and that (13) has the underlying grammatical form shown in (13G)—with $\text{not}_{\underline{\Pi}}$ taking one sentential argument, and pronunciation reflecting displacement.

(13)    Chris is not a linguist
(13G)    $\langle [\text{not}_{\underline{\Pi}} \langle \text{Chris is a linguist}\rangle]_{\underline{\Pi}P}\rangle$

Then on a Conjunctivist view, (13) has the Value **t** iff for some o, $o = f$ *and* $\text{Val}(o, \langle \text{Chris is a linguist}\rangle)$. That is, (13) has the Value **t** iff $\text{Val}(\mathbf{f}, \langle \text{Chris is a linguist}\rangle)$. Functionists can get the same result, saying that $\|\text{not}_{\underline{\Pi}}\| = [\lambda \underline{x} . t \text{ iff } (\underline{x} = \mathbf{f})]$. For then, $\|\langle \text{not}_{\underline{\Pi}} \langle \text{Chris is a } \text{linguist}\rangle_{\underline{\alpha}}\rangle\| = \|\text{not}_{\underline{\Pi}}\|(\|\text{Chris is a linguist}\|) = [\lambda \underline{x} . t \text{ iff } (\underline{x} = \mathbf{f})]$ $(\|\text{Chris is a linguist}\|) = \mathbf{t}$ iff $(\|\text{Chris is a linguist}\| = \mathbf{f})$. So there is no support here for either view. But perhaps surprisingly, (13) does not pose a serious difficulty for Conjunctivism.[23]

## 2.4. *One or Many (again): Vagueness*

I conclude this section with a digression from the tour of textbook cases. Recall an earlier question: does a predicate have a set as its sole Value, or can a predicate have many Values? One might think

---

[23] At least not unless the need for covert existential closure tells against Conjunctivism. My thanks to Kent Johnson, who saw before I did that Conjunctivists could say that **f** is the sole Value of 'not'.

this is a matter for terminological decision: say that the Value of 'linguist' is $\{<x, y>: y = t$ iff x is a linguist & $y = f$ iff x is not a linguist$\}$; or say that x is a Value of 'linguist' iff x is a linguist, with the linguists as the Values of the predicate. But the first way of talking creates a difficulty at the outset. As Sainsbury (1990) stresses, metalanguage expressions like '$\{x: x$ is a linguist$\}$' and '$\{x: x$ is bald$\}$' do not specify *sets* if natural language predicates like 'linguist' and 'bald' do not have precise extensions. And, prima facie, such predicates are *vague*; since they admit of borderline cases, they do not have precise extensions.

The meaning of 'bald' seems to allow for individuals who are neither (determinately) bald nor (determinately) not bald. And given such individuals, it seems that *no* set is the set of bald individuals. In which case, neither '$\{x: x$ is bald$\}$' nor '$\{<x, y>: y = t$ iff x is bald & $y = f$ iff x is not bald$\}$' specifies a set; hence, '$\lambda x . t$ iff x is bald' does not specify a function. So if natural language predicates are vague, Functionist axioms like '$\|bald\| = \lambda x . t$ iff x is bald' do not assign Values to such predicates after all. By contrast, vagueness does not preclude us from saying that 'bald' has many Values. This is one reason for not insisting on Functionist specifications of Values.

Let me concede at once that everyone has to face the (ancient and much discussed) paradoxes of vagueness eventually.[24] But my worry is not that Functionism somehow makes the paradoxes worse. It is

---

[24] If one denies that 'bald' has an extension, one need not grant that each individual is either in the extension of 'bald' or not. But I have nothing new to say about *what* is wrong with arguments like the following: someone with no hair is bald; and if someone is bald, then anyone with just one more hair is also bald; so everyone is bald. For useful discussion, see Williamson (1994), Keefe and Smith (1996), Graff (2000). For present purposes, we don't need an analysis of what it is for a predicate to be vague. The intuitive notion will suffice: 'V' is a vague predicate if it seems to allow for indeterminate cases—things that are neither clearly V nor clearly not V; the paradoxes of vagueness arise with respect to such predicates; 'bald' and 'red' are paradigm examples. Upon reflection, most predicates of natural language are vague. Singing shades off into talking and screeching. For any individual who is clearly a linguist, there was a time at which she wasn't, and a time at which it was unclear whether she was a linguist; and other individuals, say a philosopher by training in a linguistics department, might remain vague cases.

rather that (i) the actual vagueness of predicates like 'bald' and 'linguist' has the consequence that metalanguage expressions like '$\|\text{bald}\| = \lambda x$ . **t** iff x is bald' and '$\|\text{linguist}\| = \lambda x$ . **t** iff x is a linguist' do not express hypotheses, and (ii) the hypotheses in the vicinity are implausible. If this is correct, it tells against the idea that each predicate has some *thing*, which may have elements, as its one Value. (Though I don't know how much weight this consideration carries: how likely is it that the best response to the paradoxes will, in retrospect, make the worry seem misguided?) But in any case, using the apparatus of set theory to formulate plausible semantic hypotheses is not as easy as initial appearances might suggest. So one cannot just assume that Functionism offers a perfectly fine way of talking about natural language semantics, and then adopt it on grounds of familiarity.

The crucial point, which also figures importantly in Chapter 2, is that an expression can look like a set-description even if there is no set that it describes. Consider Russell's famous example, which does not involve vague predicates. The expression '$\{x: x \text{ is a set } \& x \notin x\}$' does not describe a set, since there is no set whose members are all and only the nonselfelemental sets.[25] The prime numbers *do* form a set. So there is a set that '$\{x: x \text{ is a prime number}\}$' describes, and '$\lambda x$ . **t** iff x is a prime number' describes a function. But it is hardly obvious that '$\{x: x \text{ is bald}\}$' describes a set. While this might seem like a mere technical point, there is a serious question here. Can theorists correctly describe the semantic properties of natural language predicates in set-theoretic terms?

We would be suspicious of a theory according to which the Value of 'bald' was a certain rock, or an alleged largest prime number.

---

[25] Suppose there is such a set, **s**. Either (i) $\mathbf{s} \in \mathbf{s}$, or (ii) $\mathbf{s} \notin \mathbf{s}$. If (i), then $\mathbf{s} \in \{x: x \text{ is a set } \& x \notin x\}$, and so $\mathbf{s} \notin \mathbf{s}$; in which case, $\mathbf{s} \in \mathbf{s}$, and $\mathbf{s} \notin \mathbf{s}$. So not (i). If (ii), then since **s** is a set, $\mathbf{s} \in \{x: x \text{ is a set } \& x \notin x\}$, and so $\mathbf{s} \in \mathbf{s}$; in which case, $\mathbf{s} \notin \mathbf{s}$ and $\mathbf{s} \in \mathbf{s}$. So not (ii). So neither (i) nor (ii). So there is no such set. Likewise, on standard (Zermelo-Frankl) conceptions of sets, there is no set of all sets; so no set **s** is such that '$\{x: x \text{ is a set}\}$' describes **s**. Indeed, there are endlessly many "paradoxical" set-descriptions that cannot (on pain of contradiction) describe any set, given the usual interpretation of the formalism; and as we'll see in Ch 2, nonstandard interpretations are unlikely to help semanticists.

Perhaps we should also be suspicious of theories that associate 'bald' with an alleged set of bald things. By definition, there are no vague cases of set membership. Given any set **s**, if something is a member of **s**, it is determinately a member of **s**; and if something is not a member of **s**, it is determinately not a member of **s**. So if some man is such that '{x: x is bald}' fails to specify an entity such that the man is neither determinately a member of the entity nor determinately not a member of the entity, then '{x: x is bald}' does not specify a set. (And even the possibility of a vague case raises concerns about the hypothesis that predicates have sets as Values. One doesn't want to say that 'linguist' fails to have a Value *if* there is a vague case.)

Consider a closely related argument; cf. Benacerraff (1965). If '{x: x is bald}' specifies a set, there is a set that it specifies. So given this set and some others that '{x: x is bald}' *might* specify, for all we know, there is a fact of the matter as to *which set* it does specify. But given some individuals who are (intuitively) neither clearly bald nor clearly not bald, many sets are equally good—and equally bad—candidates for being the alleged set of bald things. There seems to be no fact of the matter as to which of these is the alleged set. So perhaps we should conclude that '{x: x is bald}' does not specify any set.

Say that **b** is a *candidate* for being the set of bald things iff for every individual x: x is a member of **b** if x is clearly bald; x is not a member of **b** if x is clearly not bald; if x is a member of **b**, then so is any individual at least as bald as x; and if x is not a member of **b**, neither is any individual at least as hirsute as x (see Fine (1975), Kamp (1975) ). Since there are vague cases, there is more than one candidate for being the alleged set of bald things. There are sets that include all the clearly bald individuals and just a few vague cases; sets that include a few more vague cases; and so on. (It is also vague just *which* sets are the candidates; with regard to some individuals, it won't be clear whether they are clearly bald or vague cases; and for other individuals, it won't be clear whether they are vague cases or clearly not bald.) In my view, there is no fact of the matter about which of the candidates is specified by '{x: x is bald}'. But I'm not sure how to *argue* for this, except by repeating what is standardly said. It is hard to see how there could be a fact of the matter, given that otherwise competent speakers are both unable to discern it and unable to say what would settle the question.

One can bite the bullet and insist that 'bald' does have a precise extension: it's just that speakers *can't tell* whether or not certain individuals are in the extension of the predicate; and so far as we know, third-person descriptions of speakers' (perhaps unconscious) psychology won't settle the question either. Perhaps it is a brute fact that one person is bald, while another person with one more hair is not bald. With respect to the study of logic—the most general principles governing truth and falsity—this may even be the right way to think about predication; see Williamson (1994). We do sometimes think about predicates as devices that let us make distinctions that we ourselves cannot make; and we may have a "regulative ideal" according to which predicates in a "logically proper" language make sharp distinctions, even if no one can say how. But if the goal is to study how speakers understand natural language, this conception of predication seems to be inappropriately detached from human psychology.[26]

Put another way, even if one insists on logical grounds that every predicate has an extension whose boundaries may elude us, one still has to *argue* that 'bald' is a predicate whose extension is also its Semantic Value. Prima facie, taking Values to be sets mischaracterizes the facts about how speakers understand natural language. And as Wright (1975) discusses, vagueness need not reflect *inadequacies* of natural language. There are domains of human interest, like morality and law, in which we may well *want* predicates that are "tolerant" in the following sense: very small differences—say, smaller than those noticeable by any normal human—cannot mark the distinction between being or not being a Value of the predicate. If natural

---

[26] Were I committed to the idea that sentences really have *truth*-values relative to contexts, I would be more inclined to adopt Williamson's view that 'bald' really does have a classical extension, given his trenchant criticisms of alternatives. But it seems to me that Williamson has offered excellent reasons for *not* insisting that sentences of natural language have (context-sensitive) *truth*-conditions; see Pietroski (forthcoming) for related discussion.

language includes tolerant predicates, semantic theories must accommodate them. And if this tells against the idea that each predicate has a set as its Value, so be it.

Before considering a common Functionist reply, and ending this digression, let's be clear that a reply is needed. If '$\lambda$x . t iff x is bald' fails to specify a function, this hybrid English-Formalese expression is relevantly like 'Vulcan' and 'Phlogiston', which allegedly denoted something but didn't. One can, by adopting a suitable logic, allow for the use of such expressions in one's metalanguage. But when speakers learn that a name has no bearer, their reaction is unlike their reaction at being reminded of vagueness. And if the axiom '$\|$bald$\| = \lambda$x . t iff x is bald' associates *no* function with the predicate 'bald', then the axiom either says that 'bald' has no Value, or it says nothing about the semantic properties of 'bald'. In which case, claims like '$\|\langle$Pat$_\alpha$ is bald$_\Pi\rangle\| = $ t iff $\|$bald$_\Pi\|($**Pat**$) = $ t' are false or undefined, even if **Pat** is clearly bald. Applying *no* function to **Pat** does not yield a Value. Likewise for 'linguist', 'sang', 'hugged', and just about all English predicates.

By contrast, admitting vague cases does not preclude using 'Val(x, bald$_\Pi$) iff x is bald' to offer a revisable hypothesis about the semantic properties of the predicate. One can just admit that a vague case is neither determinately a Value of 'bald' nor determinately not a Value of 'bald', and that 'Val' does not express a *function* from expressions to Values. (If one says that predicates have potentially many Values, one is not obliged to find a set-like thing to be *the* Value of the predicate.) In some domains, like mathematics, we rightly want theories not expressed with vague terms. But I see nothing wrong with using vague terms to specify the Values of natural language predicates, especially given the alternatives.

Of course, if 'bald' does not have some set as its extension, there is no *set* of those things that are the Values of 'bald'. In this respect, '{x: Val(x, bald$_\Pi$)}' is no better than '{x: x is bald}'. So I eschew notation like '{x: Val(x, bald$_\Pi$)}', even with respect to the semantics of quantification and plurality; see Chapter 2. And if **Pat** is neither clearly bald nor clearly not bald, then without additional devices, a compositional semantic theory will have the consequence that t is neither determinately a Value of the sentence 'Pat is bald' nor determinately not a Value of the sentence; likewise for **f**. But the biconditional 'Val(**t**, ⟨Pat is bald⟩) iff ∃x[x = **Pat** & x is bald]' can still be a theorem of such a theory. The explanations that a semantic theory provides do not rely on the assumption that each declarative sentence has a determinate Value. The assumption is that there are exactly two sentential Values, with no sentence having both, and that each sentence Σ is associated with a condition C such that: if C obtains, Σ has the Value **t**; otherwise, Σ has the Value **f**. This does not yet require that condition C be determinate.

Put another way, one can adopt a Fregean framework without making an assumption of determinacy part of one's *hypothesis* about the semantics of *natural* language. But to repeat, I am not saying that one can avoid the paradoxes of vagueness simply by denying that predicates of natural language have extensions. My point is that the apparent fact of vagueness creates a difficulty for even *stating* Functionist axioms that actually assign Values to predicates of natural language. In this sense, Functionism does not (as it first appears) provide an especially simple and innocuous way of assigning Values to expressions. Perhaps this just shows that semanticists should replace talk of sets and function-application with talk of sets* and function*-application, where there are cases of vague set* membership. But this isn't obviously simpler than saying that predicates can have many Values, and that some things are neither clearly Values nor clearly not Values of vague predicates.

One might reply that $\|bald_{\Pi}\|$ is a function *from contexts to* extensions, and that this matters. There are, no doubt, senses in which 'bald' is context-sensitive. In some conversational situations, the standard for baldness is very high, so that (in those situations) only individuals with *no* visible hair count as bald. This rules out many individuals who would count as vague cases in many other situations. And many expressions of natural language have meanings that are usefully characterized as mappings from contexts to Values. For example, with regard to the pronoun 'I', one wants to say something like the following: x is the Value of 'I' *relative to* context **c** iff x is the speaker in **c**. But it doesn't follow that every kind of context-sensitivity should be characterized by relativizing Values to contexts. It is important to distinguish 'contexts' used as a term of art for whatever Values of expressions like 'I' get relativized to, from 'contexts' used as a term for the conversational situations in which expressions get used; see Pietroski (2003*b*, forthcoming). But one can advance the following hypothesis: function F is the Value of 'bald' relative to context **c** iff F is the "precisified" candidate (for being [λx . **t** iff x is bald]) associated with **c**; where, by stipulation, each context is associated with exactly one precisification of each vague term. (Compare supervaluationist approaches to the logic of vagueness, e.g. Fine (1975).)

Perhaps the claim that 'bald' has an extension *relative to each context* is more plausible than the claim that 'bald' has a single (context-invariant) extension. But is either claim plausible? Prima facie, there will be vague cases in any conversational situation. Even if it is stipulated that someone counts as bald iff he has less than 1,000 hairs on his head, it can be unclear whether or not someone has less than 1000 hairs on his head. (Where does the head stop and the back start? What about loose hairs? And of course, such stipulation is rare.) So appeal to contexts will help, in this regard, only if the contexts to which Values are relativized are *absolutely* precisifying in a way that actual conversational situations are not. Each conversational situation **c** will have to be associated with potentially many contexts—each of which is, in effect, an arbitrary precisification (compatible with the standards operative in **c**) of each relevant predicate; see, for example, Lewis (1972, 1979).[27]

---

[27] Drawing on Stalnaker (1974, 1978), as Lewis (1979) does, one might identify contexts with functions that determine a "presupposed" set of possible worlds—and then say that while each proposition (i.e. each potential assertion/presupposition) is determinately true or determinately false at each world, a typical conversational situation leaves it indeterminate exactly which possible worlds are presupposed. But one cannot also assume (without begging the question at hand) that speakers *understand* sentences in terms of relativization to contexts so construed. Prima facie, our understanding of vague predicates leaves room for vague cases even relative to a determination of both the nonlinguistic facts and the linguistic context.

This is a coherent view, and it may be the best Functionist option. As a psychological hypothesis, the idea would be that speakers evaluate vague expressions relative to precisifications; though in any communicative situation, speakers are indifferent as to which of the associated precisifications they relativize to. But one might wonder if there is any real motivation for this conception of context and understanding—especially given that natural languages appear to have tolerant predicates—apart from the desire to maintain that predicates have Functions as Values. And even if that is sufficient motivation, the resulting version of Functionism comes with substantive implications that are by no means obviously correct. So if we understand '$\lambda x$ . t iff x is bald' as shorthand for the more sophisticated view, we must not forget that the shorthand masks a very substantive hypothesis.

I have belabored this apparently technical point because at least since Frege, who was mainly interested in logic and the foundations of arithmetic, there has been a tradition of taking sentences like 'Five precedes six' as semantic paradigms that should be analyzed in the simplest possible way. This can make it seem that appeal to events and thematic roles, like considerations having to do with vagueness, concern aspects of natural language that are "secondary" from a semantic perspective: features of natural language that we should view as somehow "added onto" or "departures from" the simple Functionist ideal manifested by formal languages of the sort Frege invented. The use of formal apparatus, along with talk of functions and precision, can also encourage the thought that Functionist hypotheses are sure to be clear and appropriately "theoretical"—the only question being which such hypotheses are correct. But this may be all wrong. We don't know in advance which theoretical tools are appropriate for purposes of describing and explaining natural phenomena, or which cases should be our theoretical paradigms. Mathematical examples were important to Frege. But they may be *very* special cases in which the *absence* of thematic roles and vagueness fosters the illusion that the Value of a predicate is a function.

# 3. Grammatical Relations and Existential Closure for All

Let's return, now, to the tour of textbook cases. From a Conjunctivist perspective, phrases like 'red ball' and 'even prime' reveal semantic composition in its pure form: something is a Value of the phrase iff it is a Value of both constituents. Examples of predicate–argument concatenation, like 'Pat sang' and 'hugged Chris', illustrate a semantic interaction effect: concatenation still signifies conjunction, but the grammatical relations are also significant. Correlatively, auxiliary hypotheses are required to handle phrases formed by combining a predicate with an argument. From a Functionist perspective, these phrases reveal semantic composition in its pure form: concatenation signifies function-application, and predicates signify functions. But if this is correct, auxiliary hypotheses are required to handle cases of predicate–adjunct concatenation, like 'red ball' and 'even prime'. (Readers who know about type-shifting will know where this is heading: while Conjunctivism requires a limited kind of type-adjustment for arguments, Functionism requires at least as much type-adjustment overall.) It turns out that Functionists also need to posit covert quantification over events. So even in this respect, Conjunctivism is no more complicated. Indeed, it is arguably part of the simplest account of both arguments and adjuncts.

## 3.1. *Adjuncts and Functionism*

Suppose that '2 is a prime number' and '2 is an even prime number' have the grammatical structures indicated below, where 'is a(n)' plays no semantic role.

$$\langle 2_\alpha (\text{is a})[\text{prime}_\Pi \ \text{number}_\Pi]_\Pi\rangle$$
$$\langle 2_\alpha (\text{is an})[\text{even}_\Pi \ [\text{prime}_\Pi \ \text{number}_\Pi]_\Pi]_\Pi\rangle$$

As indicated, some complex predicates are concatenations of simpler predicates. (And in some cases, such combination is extendable *ad nauseam*, as in 'Pat is a rich tall attractive . . . intelligent doctor'.)

But the Functionist principle, $\|\Pi^\wedge\alpha\| = \|\Pi\|(\|\alpha\|)$, does not apply to concatenations of predicates. And it won't help to say that $\|\Pi_1{}^\wedge\Pi_2\| = \|\Pi_1\|(\|\Pi_2\|)$. For if $\|\text{prime}_\Pi\| = [\lambda x \ . \ \mathbf{t} \text{ iff x is prime}]$, and $\|\text{number}_\Pi\| = [\lambda x \ . \ \mathbf{t} \text{ iff x is a number}]$, neither $\|\text{prime}_\Pi\|$ nor $\|\text{number}_\Pi\|$ maps the other function to $\mathbf{t}$. So regardless of order, $\|\Pi_1\|(\|\Pi_2\|)$ will be either $\mathbf{f}$ or undefined, depending on whether or not functions are entities in the relevant domain. But unless $\|[\text{prime}_\Pi \ \text{number}_\Pi]_\Pi\| = [\lambda x \ . \ \mathbf{t} \text{ iff x is a prime number}]$, Functionists cannot say that $\|[\text{prime}_\Pi \ \text{number}_\Pi]_\Pi\|(\|2_\alpha\|) = [\lambda x \ . \ \mathbf{t} \text{ iff x is a prime number}](2) = \mathbf{t}$ iff 2 is a prime number. So suppose that $\|\text{prime}_\Pi \ \text{number}_\Pi\|$—outer brackets omitted for simplicity—is a function of type $\langle \mathbf{x}, \mathbf{t} \rangle$. The first difficulty remains. If $\|\text{even}_\Pi\| = [\lambda x \ . \ \mathbf{t} \text{ iff x is even}]$, neither $\|\text{even}_\Pi\|$ nor $\|\text{prime}_\Pi \ \text{number}_\Pi\|$ maps the other to $[\lambda x \ . \ \mathbf{t} \text{ iff x is an even prime number}]$. But if this isn't the Value of $[\text{even}_\Pi \ [\text{prime}_\Pi \ \text{number}_\Pi]_\Pi]_\Pi$, Functionists cannot handle the sentence $\langle 2_\alpha \text{ is an } [\text{even}_\Pi \ [\text{prime}_\Pi \ \text{number}_\Pi]_\Pi]_\Pi \rangle$. And so on.

A well-known response, which can be encoded in various ways, is that the grammatical *relation* between concatenated predicates is relevant to the interpretation of the phrase. Suppose we represent the grammatical structure of 'prime number' as follows: $[ad\text{-prime}_\Pi \ \text{number}_\Pi]_\Pi$; where '*ad-*' indicates that prime$_\Pi$ has been *adjoined to* (and is a modifier of) number$_\Pi$. Then a Functionist can maintain that $\|\text{prime}_\Pi\| = [\lambda x \ . \ \mathbf{t} \text{ iff x is prime}]$, while advancing the following auxiliary hypothesis, where 'X' ranges over functions of type $\langle \mathbf{x}, \mathbf{t} \rangle$:

(AH)    $\|ad\text{-}\ldots_\Pi\| = \lambda X \ . \ [\lambda x \ . \ \mathbf{t} \text{ iff } X(x) = \mathbf{t} \ \& \ \|\ldots_\Pi\|(x) = \mathbf{t}]$; and

$\|ad\text{-}\ldots_\Pi{}^\wedge\Pi\| = \|ad\text{-}\ldots_\Pi\|(\|\Pi\|)$

On this view, $\|ad\text{-prime}_\Pi\|$ is a function from functions to functions, and modified predicates are treated as semantic arguments of adjuncts. So

$\|ad\text{-prime}_\Pi\| = [\lambda X \ . \ [\lambda x \ . \ \mathbf{t} \text{ iff } X(x) = \mathbf{t} \ \& \ \|\text{prime}_\Pi\|(x)]]$; and

$\|ad\text{-prime}_\Pi \ \text{number}_\Pi\| = \|ad\text{-prime}_\Pi\|(\|\text{number}\|)$; hence,

$$\|ad\text{-prime}_\Pi \text{ number}_\Pi\| = [\lambda X \ . \ [\lambda x \ . \ \textbf{t} \text{ iff } X(x) = \textbf{t}$$
$$\& \ \|\text{prime}_\Pi\|(x) = \textbf{t}]](\|\text{number}\Pi\|)$$
$$= \lambda x \ . \ \textbf{t} \text{ iff } \|\text{number}_\Pi\|(x) = \textbf{t}$$
$$\& \ \|\text{prime}_\Pi\|(x) = \textbf{t}$$
$$= \lambda x \ . \ \textbf{t} \text{ iff } x \text{ is a number } \& \ x \text{ is prime.}[28]$$

Likewise, $\|ad\text{-even}_\Pi\| = \lambda X \ . \ [\lambda x \ . \ \textbf{t} \text{ iff } X(x) = \textbf{t} \ \& \ \|\text{even}_\Pi\|(x) = \textbf{t}]$. And

$$\|ad\text{-even}_\Pi[ad\text{-prime}_\Pi \text{ number}_\Pi]\|$$
$$= \|ad\text{-even}_\Pi\|(\|ad\text{-prime}_\Pi\text{number}_\Pi\|)$$
$$= \lambda x \ . \ \textbf{t} \text{ iff } x \text{ is even } \& \ (x \text{ is a number } \& \ x \text{ is prime}).$$

This proposal can be extended to other kinds of adjuncts. Suppose that the preposition 'from' is a two-place predicate that combines with an argument like 'Boston' to form a one-place predicate whose Value is a function of type $<\textbf{x, t}>$: $\|\text{from}_{\Pi*} \text{ Boston}_\alpha\| = [\lambda x \ . \ \textbf{t} \text{ iff } x \text{ is from Boston}]$. Then, given (AH), the Value of a prepositional phrase *adjoined to* a common noun is a function from functions of type $<\textbf{x, t}>$ to such functions. For example, in the complex noun-phrase $[\text{linguist}_\Pi \ ad\text{-}[\text{from}_{\Pi*} \text{ Boston}_\alpha]_\Pi]_\Pi$,

$$\|ad\text{-}[\text{from}_{\Pi*}\text{Boston}_\alpha]_\Pi\| = \lambda X \ . \ [\lambda x \ . \ \textbf{t} \text{ iff } X(x) = \textbf{t}$$
$$\& \ \|\text{from}_{\Pi*}\text{Boston}_\alpha\|(x) = \textbf{t}].$$

So if $\|\text{linguist}_\Pi\| = [\lambda x \ . \ \textbf{t} \text{ iff } x \text{ is a linguist}]$, then

$$\|\text{linguist}_\Pi \ ad\text{-}[\text{from}_{\Pi*}\text{Boston}_\alpha]_\Pi\|$$
$$= [\lambda x \ . \ \textbf{t} \text{ iff } x \text{ is a linguist } \& \ x \text{ is from Boston}].$$

Similarly, suppose that 'who Pat hugged' is a complex predicate formed by displacing 'who' from the object-position of 'hugged', and that $\|[\text{who}_i \ [\text{Pat hugged } t_i]]_\Pi\| = [\lambda x \ . \ \textbf{t} \text{ iff Pat hugged } x]$. Then

---

[28] Converting a Value-specification in accordance with the relevant principle— x is $\Phi$ iff $[\lambda x \ . \ \textbf{t} \text{ iff } x \text{ is } \Phi](x) = \textbf{t}$—is innocuous, in that it adds nothing new to a Functionist semantic theory. I return to issues surrounding quantification over functions in chapter two.

$\|\text{linguist}_\Pi$ $ad\text{-}[\text{who}_i$ $[\text{Pat hugged } t_i]]_\Pi\| = \|ad\text{-}[\text{who}_i$ $[\text{Pat hugged } t_i]]_\Pi\|(\|\text{linguist}_\Pi\|) = [\lambda x \ . \ t \text{ iff } x \text{ is a linguist \& Pat hugged } x]$. As we'll see, adverbs introduce a further twist. But a Functionist can account for at least many cases of adjunction with (AH).

Correlatively, the auxiliary hypothesis will end up doing a lot of work. And as the notation indicates, (AH) effectively introduces an axiom of function-*conjunction*. For there are two aspects to the hypothesis. First, a certain grammatical relation—adjunction of one predicate to another—is associated with a *type-shift*: the adjoined predicate is interpreted as a function of type $\ll x, t>, <x, t\gg$, from functions to functions, as opposed to a function of type $<x, t>$. Second, the "shifted Value" of the adjoined predicate $\Pi_1$ is conjunctive in the following sense: if function F is the "unshifted" Value of $\Pi_1$ (i.e. the value of $\Pi_1$ without regard to its being grammatically marked as an adjunct), and $\Pi_1$ is adjoined to $\Pi_2$, then the Value of the resulting phrase $ad\text{-}\Pi_1{}^\wedge\Pi_2$ is the function $[\lambda x \ . \ t \text{ iff } F(x) = t \ \& \ \|\Pi_2\|(x) = t]$.

Indeed, instead of appealing to such shifting (associated with '*ad*', which indicates adjunction), one might adopt *two* compositional axioms. In particular, following Heim and Kratzer (1998), one might just add a second axiom for cases of adjunction.

$$\|\Pi^\wedge\alpha\| = \|\Pi\|(\|\alpha\|)$$
$$\|\Pi_1{}^\wedge\Pi_2\| = \lambda x \ . \ t \text{ iff } \|\Pi_1\|(x) = t \ \& \ \|\Pi_2\|(x) = t$$

A committed Functionist will view the "second" axiom as notational abbreviation for (AH) and appeal to type-shifting. (I return to this view.) But one can offer the two axioms as the hypothesis that the semantic contribution of concatenation is not uniform: when predicates combine with arguments, concatenation signifies function-application; when predicates combine with predicates, concatenation signifies function-conjunction.[29] I think we should take this mixed view very seriously. For perhaps, all things considered, (i) appeal to

---

[29] Compare Higginbotham's (1985) distinction between theta-marking and theta-linking. Yet another interpretation of the "mixed" view is that the second axiom is a Functionist rewrite of Conjunctivism, while the "first" axiom is a Functionist rewrite of appeal to participation relations along with the significance of 'ext' and 'int'.

type-shifting is implausible, at least for relatively simple cases of adjunction, but (ii) Conjunctivism is less plausible than theories that assign functions to at least some expressions that combine with arguments (whose Values are in the relevant domains).

Unsurprisingly, I endorse (i) but not (ii). Though my reasons will not fully emerge until later chapters: many cases of *predicate–argument* combination are best described in Conjunctivist terms, since Functionist descriptions require appeal to type-shifting and conjunction. For now, just note that the mixed view is no *simpler* than Conjunctivism supplemented with the hypothesis that predicate–argument relations are semantically significant. (This is especially clear if it is independently plausible that those relations are often thematically significant.)

Likewise, supplemented Conjunctivism is no more *ad hoc* than Functionism supplemented with its auxiliary claims about adjunction. On both of these views, concatenation makes a uniform semantic contribution across all constructions, despite the fact that adjoining to a predicate differs semantically from "saturating" a predicate with an argument. And the two responses to this fact are parallel: if one mode of combination reveals semantic composition in its pure form, the other mode reveals some kind of interaction effect. According to Functionists, predicate–adjunct combinations reveal the semantic contribution of concatenation *and* the significance of being an adjunct. According to Conjunctivists, predicate–argument combinations reveal the semantic contribution of concatenation *and* the significance of being an (internal or external) argument. The diagram below may help the formally-minded.

|  | Functionism | Conjunctivism |
|---|---|---|
| Arguments | $F(\alpha)$ | $\Theta(x, \alpha)\ \&\ F(x)$ |
|  | $/\quad\backslash$ | $/\quad\backslash$ |
|  | $\alpha\quad F(x)$ | $\Theta(x, \alpha)\quad F(x)$ |
|  |  | $\alpha$ |
| Adjuncts | $F(x)\ \&\ G(x)$ | $F(x)\ \&\ G(x)$ |
|  | $/\quad\backslash$ | $/\quad\backslash$ |
|  | $\lambda X\,.\,F(x)\ \&\ X(x)\quad G(x)$ | $F(x)\quad G(x)$ |
|  | $F(x)$ |  |

## 3.2. *Conjunction Reduction and Type Adjustment*

There are, however, at least two ways of thinking about type-shifting. And it is worth being clear about this, if only to be clear about the sense in which I do (and don't) appeal to type-shifting by saying that Val(o, ext-Pat$_\alpha$) iff ∃x[External(o, x) & Val(x, Pat$_\alpha$)]. Consider, once again, (AH).

(AH)   $\|ad\text{-}\ldots_\Pi\| = \lambda X$ . $[\lambda x$ . $\mathbf{t}$ iff $X(x) = \mathbf{t}$ & $\|\ldots_\Pi\|(x) = \mathbf{t}]$; and
       $\|ad\text{-}\ldots_\Pi{}^\wedge\Pi\| = \|ad\text{-}\ldots_\Pi\|(\|\Pi\|)$

Taken at face value, this is a hypothesis about the significance of a certain mode of grammatical composition. So construed, Functionism supplemented with (AH) can indeed look like a notational variant of the mixed view, absent independent reasons for thinking that adjuncts are somehow "marked" as type-shifters. But on another conception, type-shifting does *not* reflect the significance of any grammatical relation in natural language. One might think that type-shifting reflects a different kind of fact about natural language: it allows for the construction of phrases that would be uninterpretable if each predicate had a fixed semantic type, *given* that concatenation uniformly signifies function-application (as it does in a Fregean formal language); see Montague (1974), Partee and Rooth (1983), Partee (1987).

The thought here is that natural language allows for combinations that would be semantically incoherent *if* predicates like prime$_\Pi$ and number$_\Pi$ *always* had the Value-type $<\mathbf{x}, \mathbf{t}>$. So perhaps some expressions have "flexible" semantic types: while such an expression may have a "default" Value-type like $<\mathbf{x}, \mathbf{t}>$, it can also be interpreted as having a "higher" Value-type like $\ll\mathbf{x}, \mathbf{t}>,<\mathbf{x}, \mathbf{t}\gg$, if this would allow for a coherent interpretation of the phrase in which the expression appears. This raises questions about why such expressions are (allegedly) as flexible as they are, but not more or less so—and how children associate grammatical types with semantic types in the right way.[30] Correlatively, if one wants to *explain* why

---

[30] In my view, the prospects for answers to such questions are slim. But this is tendentious; cf. Partee (1987), Partee and Rooth (1983), who offer useful discussion and motivate the flexible approach.

something satisfies 'red ball' only if it satisfies 'ball', one cannot just say that the shifted Value-type of red$_\Pi$ is $\ll$**x**, **t**$>$,$<$**x**, **t**$\gg$. But neither can one stipulate that for all x, $\|$red$_\Pi$ ball$_\Pi\|$(x) $=$ **t** only if $\|$ball$_\Pi\|$(x) $=$ **t**; see Taylor (1985) for discussion. One has to explain why the shifted *Value* of red$_\Pi$ is a function F* such that F*$\|$ball$_\Pi\|$(x) $=$ **t** only if $\|$ball$_\Pi\|$(x) $=$ **t**.

Why, for example, isn't the shifted Value of red$_\Pi$ a function F* such that F*$\|$ball$_\Pi\|$(x) $=$ **t** iff x is red *or* x is a ball, or a function F* such that F*$\|$ball$_\Pi\|$(x) $=$ **t** iff x is red *if* x is a ball? In general, why *doesn't* 'red ball' have the meanings it doesn't have? Such questions take on renewed significance if the relation between grammar and meaning is said to be flexible. Recall from the Introduction that, in many respects, the relation *isn't* flexible; see Higginbotham (1985). Of course, examples like 'fake diamond' and 'alleged crook' must eventually be accommodated. But these apparently nonconjunctive phrases may not be mere two-word concatenations. Similarly, one wants an account that handles 'big ant' and 'small elephant'. Is x a Value of the former iff x is a Value of both 'big' and 'ant', while x is a Value of the latter iff x is a Value of both 'small' and 'elephant'? But such examples, discussed briefly in Chapter 2, present complications on any view; see Kamp (1975). And in any case, there seems to be an "adjunct-as-conjunct" generalization that one is getting at with (AH), the mixed view, or Conjunctivism.

Red balls are red, and big ants are ants. Other things being equal, one wants a semantic theory to account for these obvious implications. Otherwise, we need another account of why the implications are obvious. So there is pressure on Functionists to either (i) provide an independently plausible account of why Value-shifting has the semantic character it would need to have, in order to explain the relevant facts about natural language, or (ii) endorse something like (AH) as a hypothesis about the significance of adjunction, at least in "typical" cases—even if this latter strategy ultimately leads to the mixed view.

Given (AH), one can say that the Value of red$_\Pi$ is uniformly [$\lambda$x . **t** iff x is red], modulo vagueness. On this view, the "shift" is due to the hypothesized significance of a certain grammatical relation: two expressions of type $<x, t>$, like 'red' and 'ball', can combine to form a phrase of the same type; but since adjunction matters semantically, the adjoined predicate is interpreted *as though* it had a different type. Analogously, there is a limited sense in which my version of Conjunctivism appeals to a kind of type-adjustment with regard to arguments. One can maintain that the Value of $Pat_\alpha$ is always **Pat**. For the "shift", from a name for an individual to a predicate of things with participants, is due to the hypothesized significance of certain grammatical relations.[31] But in my view, this auxiliary hypothesis enjoys two prima-facie virtues that (AH) does not. First, as noted in §2, it is independently plausible that being the subject or object of a verb often has thematic significance. Second, as noted in the Introduction, adjunction is the more clearly *recursive* case.

To be sure, there are verbs that combine with sentential arguments, as in 'said that Pat hugged Chris'. And this introduces a kind of recursion: Pat said that Chris thinks that . . . Sam hugged Hilary. But in Chapter 3, I'll argue that Conjunctivism actually offers a better account of such cases.[32] If one sets these aside, and ignores the trivial kind of recursion associated with sentential connectives, it seems that natural language allows for arbitrarily complex expressions *because* it allows for the expansion of predicates by means of adjuncts (i.e. adjectives, adverbs, prepositional phrases, and relative clauses). Each natural language predicate takes a very finite number of arguments—one, two, or at most three for ditransitive verbs like 'give'. By contrast, Fregean formal languages allow for predicates with arbitrarily many arguments. One can define a 26-place predicate 'Q' satisfied by a 26-tuple $<a, b, . . . , x, y, z>$ iff $z$ is bigger than $y$, which is smaller than $x$, which . . . than $b$, which is to the left of $a$.

---

[31] One *could* say that expressions like $Pat_\alpha$ have "flexible" semantic types. But that would introduce an unneeded (and unwanted) degree of freedom between grammar and meaning. Just so, I suspect, for the traditional conception of type-shifting.

[32] Independently, many theorists have held that sentential arguments have adjunct-like grammatical properties; see Munro (1982). And from a semantic perspective, such arguments call for special treatment on any view; see Ch. 3.

Natural language is constrained with regard to the number of arguments, but not adjuncts, that can combine with a predicate to form a phrase. And if the open-endedness of natural language resides mainly with adjunction, it seems odd to treat adjunction as the semantically special case. If the significance of concatenation is uniform, why think that the uniformity is tailored to predicate–argument combinations, while all the other cases reflect a semantic interaction effect? Note that even the mixed view posits the *resources* for dealing with predicates that take arbitrarily many arguments. Why not say instead that natural language exploits just a few grammatical relations to signify participation relations? If there are just a few candidate grammatical relations, the limitation on adicity would be unmysterious. While these considerations don't show that Conjunctivism is true, they can help motivate it. In any case, there is nothing especially simple about a semantics that treats adjunction as the special case.

## 3.3. *Initial Evidence for Covert Quantification over Events*

Even if appeal to thematic roles and (limited) type-adjustment for arguments is not *ad hoc*, Conjunctivists also need to posit covert existential closure to account for the semantic character of sentences. So at least in this respect, one might think that Functionism is simpler. But there is ample independent motivation for positing covert quantification with regard to sentences like (14) and (15),

(14)   Caesar died
(15)   Brutus stabbed Caesar

as in the following paraphrases: *there was a* death of Caesar; and *there was a* stabbing of Caesar by Brutus. Existential closure may play a larger role for Conjunctivists. Though again, this may reflect a correct prediction, rather than a basis for objection.

It is an ancient idea that many verbs are used to describe events (changes, happenings). It is, however, a further step to say that a sentence like (15) *means that* there was an event of a certain sort. Ramsey (1927) took this step, in the context of distinguishing facts from events. He held that the event of Brutus stabbing Caesar, which occurred in a certain place at a certain time, was distinct from the fact that Brutus stabbed Caesar—the latter being the (abstract) fact that *there was a* stabbing of Caesar by Brutus. Davidson (1967b) went further, arguing that a compositional semantic theory for a natural language should specify the meanings of many sentences in terms of such quantification over events. His main reason was that a sentence like (15) is implied by endlessly many sentences that exhibit a network of implications, which can be explained in terms of covert quantification and conjunction-reduction.

Consider (15a-f), each of which semantically implies (15).

(15a)   Brutus stabbed Caesar angrily
(15b)   Brutus stabbed Caesar in Boston
(15c)   Brutus stabbed Caesar with a cucumber
(15d)   Brutus stabbed Caesar angrily in Boston
(15e)   Brutus stabbed Caesar in Boston with a cucumber
(15f)   Brutus stabbed Caesar with a cucumber angrily

Note also that (15d) implies (15a) and (15b); (15e) implies (15b) and (15c); (15f) implies (15c) and (15a). Moreover, (15f) implies and is implied by (15g), while (15h) implies each of the others.

(15g)   Brutus stabbed Caesar angrily with a cucumber
(15h)   Brutus stabbed Caesar angrily, in Boston, with a cucumber

These facts can be explained with a theory according to which: (15) has the Value **t** iff something was a stabbing of Caesar by Brutus; each (lexical or phrasal) adverbial modifier is interpreted as a monadic predicate of events; and each adverbially modified sentence has the Value **t** iff something was a stabbing of Caesar by Brutus *and also* a Value of each adverbial constituent.

Given such a theory, (15d) has the Value **t** iff something was a stabbing of Caesar by Brutus, a Value of 'angrily', and a Value of 'in Boston'. Likewise, (15a) has the Value **t** iff something was both a stabbing of Caesar by Brutus and a Value of 'angrily'. So given an elementary principle of reasoning—if something satisfies each of two conditions, then something satisfies the first condition—it follows that (15a) imples (15). Similarly, (15d) implies (15a). Let's say that something satisfies the predicate 'S', short for 'Stabcaebrutish', iff it was a stabbing of Caesar by Brutus. Then trivially,

$$\exists o[S(o) \& Angrily(o) \& In(o, Boston)] \rightarrow \exists o[S(o) \& Angrily(o)]; and$$
$$\exists o[S(o) \& Angrily(o)] \rightarrow \exists o[S(o)].$$

This reflects the correlation between adjunction-reduction and conjunction-reduction. While Davidson did not provide an explicit theory of the sort he envisioned, his insight can be encoded in various ways; see Pietroski (2003a) for a more extensive review. But before turning to a Conjunctivist proposal, it is worth noting (as Ramsey did) that while (15) implies only one stabbing, it is compatible with multiple stabbings of Caesar by Brutus. This helps account for some *non*implications, as illustrated with examples due to Gareth Evans and discussed in detail by Taylor (1985).

Suppose that Shem poked Shaun *twice* at the same time: once softly, with a red stick (held in Shem's left hand); and once sharply, with a blue stick (held in Shem's right hand). And suppose that these were the *only* pokings of Shaun by Shem. Then intuitively, (16) is true twice over,

   (16)   Shem poked Shaun

much as 'Someone sang' is true twice over if two boys sang. Again, there is a network of implications in which adjuncts seem to be conjuncts: since Shem poked Shaun softly with a red stick, Shem poked Shaun softly; etc. But note that while (17) and (18) are true, (19) and (20) are false.

   (17)   Shem poked Shaun softly, and Shem poked Shaun with a blue stick
   (18)   Shem poked Shaun sharply, and Shem poked Shaun with a red stick
   (19)   Shem poked Shaun softly with a blue stick
   (20)   Shem poked Shaun sharply with a red stick

Correlatively, (17) does not imply (19), and (18) does not imply (20).

This is expected if each sentence is associated with existential closure of an event-variable. Let's say that something satisfies 'P' iff it was a poking of Shaun by Shem. Then (17) has the Value **t** iff $\exists o[P(o) \, \& \, Softly(o)] \, \& \, \exists o[P(o) \, \& \, With(o, \text{ a blue stick})]$, while (19) has the Value **t** iff $\exists o[P(o) \, \& \, Softly(o) \, \& \, With(o, \text{ a blue stick})]$. So (17) does not imply (19); the existence of a soft poking and a blue-stick poking does not ensure the existence of a soft, blue-stick poking. Similarly, the existence of a sharp poking and a red-stick poking does not ensure the existence of a sharp, red-stick poking; so (18) does not imply (20). But if we think simply in terms of ordered pairs $<x, y>$ such that x poked y, it is hard to *distinguish* the pairs associated with 'poked softly with a blue stick' from the pairs associated with both 'poked softly' and 'poked with a blue stick', while still *capturing* the implications from 'poked softly with a blue stick' to 'poked softly' and 'poked with a blue stick'.[33]

By contrast, events with $n$ participants are individuated more finely than ordered $n$-tuples of those participants—or even $(n+1)$-tuples consisting of the participants and a moment in time. One can think of events as "things" that encode more than just temporal information. This raises questions about how events *are*

---

[33] One cannot think of predicate restriction as follows: 'poked' specifies a set, **s**, of ordered pairs; a complex predicate like 'poked forcefully' or 'poked with a blue stick' specifies a subset of **s**; and a doubly complex predicate like 'poked forcefully with a blue stick', or 'poked with a blue stick forcefully', specifies the *intersection* of the relevant subsets. This would ensure the "order invariance" of modifiers. But it incorrectly predicts that (17) and (19) are truth-conditionally equivalent; cf. Montague (1970). One could say that (19) is true iff Sharply-Poked-With$_3$(Shem, Shaun, a blue stick); see Kenny (1963). But as Davidson (1967*b*) noted, pursuing this strategy requires an open-ended number of complex predicates that take differing numbers of arguments: 'Shem poked Shaun with a blue stick at noon' is true iff Poked-With-At$_4$(Shem, Shaun, a blue stick, noon); etc. And without meaning postulates that effectively encode the relevant implications, the truth of 'Poked-With-At$_4$(Shem, Shaun, a blue stick, noon)' does not ensure the truth of 'Poked-With$_3$(Shem, Shaun, a blue stick)' or 'Poked$_2$(Shem, Shaun)'. See Taylor (1985), who also provides an argument for an eventish semantics based on the ambiguity of 'Henry gracefully ate all the crisps'—which could mean either that *each* eating of a crisp by Henry was graceful, or that the complex event of eating all the crisps was graceful.

individuated.[34] Though we can take up such questions after we have a better sense of which semantic facts are explained in terms of events; see Schein (2002). For now, events are the Values of event-variables in natural language.

## 3.4. *Functionist and Conjunctivist Implementations*

One does not need thematic roles, much less the idea that verbs are monadic predicates, to distinguish the Values of verbs that take $n$ arguments from $n$-tuples. Following Davidson (1967b), one might represent the meaning of (16) as in (16a), as opposed to (16b);

(16a)    $\exists e[\text{Poked}_3(\text{Shem, Shaun, e})]$
(16b)    $\exists o[\text{Agent}(o, \text{Shem}) \ \& \ \text{Past-Poking}(o) \ \& \ \text{Theme}(o, \text{Shaun})]$

where 'e' is explicitly introduced as a variable associated with the "extra" argument position of certain verbs, and 'Poked$_3$' is satisfied by an ordered triple $<x, y, e>$ iff e was a poking of y by x. This does not assume that Poked$_3$(Shem, Shaun, e) iff Agent(e, Shem) & Past-Poking(e) & Theme(e, Shaun); though this possibility is left open.[35] One can stipulate that Poked$_2$(Shem, Shaun) iff $\exists e[\text{Poked}_3(\text{Shem}, \text{Shaun, e})]$. So a Davidsonian Functionist might say that

$$\|\text{poked}_{\Pi^*}\| = [\lambda y \ . \ [\lambda x \ . \ \mathbf{t} \text{ iff Poked}_2(x, y)]]$$
$$= [\lambda y \ . \ [\lambda x \ . \ \mathbf{t} \text{ iff for some event e, e was a poking}$$
$$\text{of y by x}]].$$

---

[34] Is event x identical with event y if x and y have all the same *spatio*temporal properties? What if x and y satisfy the same event sortal, and have the same participants in the same roles? But criteria of individuation, as in Kim (1993), may be premature—especially if the relation between meaning and truth is not simple—given how hard it is to distinguish semantic from metaphysical questions in this area.

[35] Say that 'R' corresponds to the red-stick-poking and 'B' corresponds to the blue-stick-poking. Then one can represent the two events as follows: (Shem, Shaun, R), (Shem, Shaun, B). One might think of R and B as event-*features* that distinguish two simultaneous pokings with the same Agent and Theme. But one can also think of R and B as the distinct *events* of poking, with each ordered triple explicitly reflecting two ("external" and "internal") participants of the third element.

This effectively treats the covert event-variable as the verb's most *internal* argument, with this argument bound before the verb combines with any arguments, so that $\|poked_{\Pi*}\|$ is still a function that maps things like $\|Shaun_\alpha\|$ to functions from things like $\|Shem_\alpha\|$ to **t** or **f**.

Initially, this might look like a good hypothesis. But suppose that $\|[poked_{\Pi*} \ Shaun_\alpha]_\Pi\| = [\lambda x \ . \ \mathbf{t}$ iff for some event e, e was a poking of Shaun by x], and that $\|softly_\Pi\| = [\lambda e \ . \ \mathbf{t}$ iff e was soft]. We still need a compositional axiom that determines the Value of the modified verb phrase. And (AH)

(AH)    $\|ad\text{-}_{...\Pi}\| = \lambda X \ . \ [\lambda x \ . \ \mathbf{t}$ iff $X\,(x) = \mathbf{t} \ \& \ \|_{...\Pi}\|(x) = \mathbf{t}]$; and

       $\|ad\text{-}_{...\Pi}{}^\wedge\Pi\| = \|ad\text{-}_{...\Pi}\|(\|\Pi\|)$

won't help. If 'e' and 'x' are variables of the same type, then '$\lambda e \ . \ \mathbf{t}$ iff e was soft' is equivalent to '$\lambda x \ . \ \mathbf{t}$ iff x was soft', and (AH) applies and delivers a wrong result: $\|[poked_{\Pi*} \ Shaun_\alpha]_\Pi \ ad\text{-}softly_\Pi\| = [\lambda x \ . \ \mathbf{t}$ iff x was soft & for some event e, e was a poking of Shaun by x]; hence, Shem poked Shaun softly iff there was a poking of Shaun by Shem, *and Shem* was soft. This mischaracterizes the adjunct, which purports to describe an event, not an Agent. Yet if 'e' and 'x' are variables of different types—capturing the idea that 'softly' applies to things *done* softly—then (AH) does not apply, since it deals with phrases formed by combining expressions whose Values are functions of the same type. Functionists might *want* to say that $\|[poked_{\Pi*} \ Shaun_\alpha]_\Pi \ softly_\Pi\| = [\lambda x \ . \ \mathbf{t}$ iff for some event e, e was a poking of Shaun by x & e was done softly]. But once the event-variable is closed, additional predicates cannot be linked to it.[36]

---

[36] Similar remarks apply to the mixed view if $\|poked_{\Pi*}\| = \lambda y \ . \ [\lambda x. \ \mathbf{t}$ iff some event e was a poking of Shaun by x]. And given this hypothesis about the verb, it won't help to say that the grammatical structure of 'poked Shaun softly' is really $[[poked_{\Pi*} \ ad\text{-}softly]_{\Pi*} \ Shaun_\alpha]_\Pi]$. One can invent an auxiliary hypothesis according to which: $\|ad\text{-}red_\Pi \ ball_\Pi\| = \lambda x \ . \ \mathbf{t}$ iff $\|red_\Pi\|(x) = \mathbf{t} \ \& \ \|ball_\Pi\|(x) = \mathbf{t}$; and adjoining an adverb to $[poked_{\Pi*} \ Shaun_\alpha]_\Pi$ effectively "reopens" the event variable so that $\|[poked_{\Pi*} \ Shaun_\alpha]_\Pi] \ softly_\Pi\| = \lambda x \ . \ \mathbf{t}$ iff for some event e, e was a poking of Shaun by x & was soft. But this version of Functionism is hardly simple. And it explains nothing about adjunction, since it stipulates everything.

Alternatively, a Functionist could say that

$$\|\text{poked}_{\Pi*}\| = \lambda y \, . \, [\lambda x \, . \, [\lambda e \, . \, \textbf{t} \text{ iff } e \text{ was a poking of } y \text{ by } x]].$$

This effectively treats the event-variable as the verb's most *external* argument. On this view,

$$\|\text{Shem}_\alpha[\text{poked}_{\Pi*}\text{Shaun}_\alpha]_\Pi\|$$
$$= [\lambda e \, . \, \textbf{t} \text{ iff } e \text{ was a poking of Shaun by Shem}].$$

This requires a distinction between a predicative *phrase*, saturated by the right number of (overt) syntactic arguments, and a *sentence* (indicated by angled brackets); where $\|\langle [\ldots]_{\Pi P}\rangle\| = \textbf{t}$ iff $\exists e\{\|[\ldots]_{\Pi P}\|(e)\} = \textbf{t}$. But perhaps Functionists should, like Conjunctivists, draw such a distinction.[37] Given (AH), and abstracting away from tense, one could say that $\|\text{softly}_\Pi\| = \|ad\text{-soft}_\Pi\| = \lambda X \, . \, [\lambda e \, . \, \textbf{t} \text{ iff } X(e) = \textbf{t} \, \& \, e \text{ was done softly}]$, and hence that

$$\|\text{Shem}_\alpha[\text{poked}_{\Pi*} \, \text{Shaun}_\alpha]_\Pi]_{\Pi P} \, ad\text{- soft}_\Pi\|$$
$$= [\lambda e \, . \, \textbf{t} \text{ iff } e \text{ was a poking of Shaun by Shem } \& \, e \text{ was done softly}]$$

Likewise, a Functionist could say that

$$\|\text{sang}_\Pi\| = [\lambda x \, . \, [\lambda e \, . \, \textbf{t} \text{ iff } e \text{ was a singing by } x]]$$
$$\|\text{Pat}_\alpha \, \text{sang}_\Pi\| = [\lambda e \, . \, \textbf{t} \text{ iff } e \text{ was a singing by Pat}]]$$
$$\|\langle[\text{Pat}_\alpha \, \text{sang}_\Pi]_{\Pi P}\rangle\| = \textbf{t} \text{ iff for some } e, \, e \text{ was a singing by Pat}$$
$$\|[\text{Pat}_\alpha \, \text{sang}_\Pi]_{\Pi P} ad\text{-loud}_\Pi\| = [\lambda e \, . \, \textbf{t} \text{ iff } e \text{ was a singing by Pat}$$
$$\& \, e \text{ was loud}]$$
$$\|[[\text{Pat}_\alpha \, \text{sang}_\Pi]_{\Pi P} ad\text{-loud}_\Pi]_{\Pi P}\rangle\| = \textbf{t} \text{ iff } \exists e[e \text{ was a singing by Pat}$$
$$\& \, e \text{ was loud}].$$

This preserves a unified account of adjunction. But it gives up the idea that 'sang loudly' and 'poked Shaun softly' are grammatical

---

[37] As discussed in §2.1, this leaves it open whether the angled brackets correspond to grammatical structure not yet indicated or some extragrammatical system that marks sentences as such.

constituents, in favor of the idea that $[\text{Pat}_\alpha \ \text{sang}_\Pi]_{\Pi P}$ and $[\text{Shem}_\alpha [\text{poked}_{\Pi*} \ \text{Shaun}_\alpha]_\Pi]_{\Pi P}$ are monadic predicates that can combine with adverbial modifiers. Of course, one can introduce a different compositional axiom for adjunction, according to which $\| [\text{poked}_{\Pi*} \ \text{Shaun}_\alpha]_\Pi \ \text{softly}_\Pi \| = [\lambda x \ . \ \mathbf{t}$ iff for some event e, e was a poking of Shaun by x & e was soft]; the idea would be that if an adverbial adjunct modifies a predicate with two variables, it attaches to the appropriate variable. But this still introduces a kind of complexity that a Conjunctivist does not need.

Conjunctivists can be agnostic about *where* adjuncts combine, letting the grammatical details fall as they may; see Cinque (1999) for discussion of these details. Given that $\text{Val}(\text{o}, \text{poked}_{\Pi*})$ iff x was an event of poking, and that $\text{Val}(\text{o}, \text{softly}_\Pi)$ iff x was done softly— adding the hypothesis that arguments are marked as such—a Conjunctivist semantics can accommodate any of the structures below.

$$[\text{ext-Shem}_\alpha [[\text{poked}_{\Pi*} \text{int-Shaun}_\alpha]_\Pi \text{softly}_\Pi]_\Pi]_{\Pi P}$$
$$[[\text{ext-Shem}_\alpha [\text{poked}_{\Pi*} \text{int-Shaun}_\alpha]_\Pi]_{\Pi P} \text{softly}_\Pi]_{\Pi P}$$
$$[\text{ext-Shem}_\alpha [[\text{poked}_{\Pi*} \text{softly}_\Pi]_{\Pi*} \text{int-Shaun}_\alpha]_\Pi]_{\Pi P}$$

In each case, x is a Value of the complex phrase iff: Shem was the Agent of x; and x was an event of poking; and Shaun was the Theme of x; and x was done softly. The order of conjuncts doesn't matter.

There is another sense in which Functionists must add an auxiliary hypothesis that Conjunctivists do not need. Recall from the Introduction that 'The prince attacked the duke from Gloucester' has no prince-from-Gloucester reading. So it is not enough to say just that $\| [\text{attacked the duke}]_\Pi \| = \lambda x \ . \ [\lambda e \ . \ \mathbf{t}$ iff e was an attack of the duke by x]. One wants to know why the adjunct 'from Gloucester' cannot be linked to the 'x'-variable, so that $\| [\text{attacked the duke}]_\Pi$ $[\text{from Gloucester}]_\Pi \| = \lambda x \ . \ [\lambda e \ . \ \mathbf{t}$ iff e was an attack of the duke by x & x is from Gloucester]. Conjunctivists can simply say that something is a Value of the complex verb-phrase iff it is a Value of both 'attacked the duke' and 'from Gloucester'; where something is a Value of 'attacked the duke' iff it was an attack whose Theme was the duke.

Of course, this doesn't show that a Conjunctivist implementation of Davidson's proposal is preferable all things considered. There may be alternative explanations of the relevant facts. My main point here is just that a Functionist implementation is no simpler.

I will be arguing for axioms like 'Val(o, poked$_\Pi$) iff x was a poking', as opposed to '$\|$poked$\| = \lambda y$ . [$\lambda x$ . [$\lambda e$ . t iff e was a poking by x of y]]'. But event-friendly Functionists can certainly account for many facts. In particular, one cannot establish Conjunctivism just by noting implications like the following: if Shem poked Shaun, then Shem did something, there was a poking, and something happened to Shaun (see Castañeda (1967)). Functionists can introduce thematic roles by elaborating Davidsonian claims about *lexical* meanings: $\|$poked$\| = \lambda y$ . [$\lambda x$ . [$\lambda e$ . t iff Agent(e, x) & Poking(e) & Theme(e, y)]]. Meanings are specified conjunctively on this view, discussed in Chapter 3. But the significance of predicate–argument combination is still function-application; see Levin and Rappaport Hovav (1995).

On the other hand, if this approach to action verbs is embedded in a mixed view according to which adjunction signifies predicate-conjunction, the net result looks a lot like Conjunctivism. And one still wants to know why there is no verb 'glubbed' such that $\|$glubbed$\| = \lambda y$ . [$\lambda x$ . [$\lambda e$ . t iff Theme(e, x) & Poking(e) & Agent(e, y)]]. But the best cases for Functionism, quantificational constructions, have not yet been considered. So for now, let me just repeat that we have two hypotheses about how predicates are semantically linked to their arguments: via lexical specification and function-application; or via grammatical relations and predicate-conjunction. After showing that the latter hypothesis can accommodate quantificational constructions at least as well as the former, I will argue that the more Functionism is elaborated in response to apparent difficulties, the more it looks like Conjunctivism.

## 3.5. *Other Evidence*

If action sentences involve covert quantification over events, there should be symptoms of this beyond semantic implications. And indeed there are. I will not try to review the large literature on this topic; see Parsons (1990), Larson and Segal (1995), Higginbotham, Pianesi and Varzi (2000). But a few examples will illustrate the kinds of considerations that are relevant. And since I want to review this evidence without presupposing Conjunctivism, or anything about thematic roles, I will use representations like '∃e[Poked$_3$ (Shem, Shaun, e)]' in these last pages of this chapter. Subsequently, I presuppose covert quantification over events in arguing for Conjunctivism.

First, there is the mundane but still germane fact that (15) and (21) are paraphrases.

> (15)    Brutus stabbed Caesar
> (21)    There was a stabbing of Caesar by Brutus

By itself, this doesn't show that (15) involves covert quantification. One might argue that the meaning of (21) should be represented with 'Stabbed$_2$(Brutus, Caesar)'. But prima facie, (21) involves quantification over events; a speaker can continue with 'It was done quickly', with 'It' used to talk about an event, thereby implying that Brutus stabbed Caesar quickly. And an event analysis predicts that (21) can be paraphrased with (15). Moreover, one can plausibly specify the meaning of (22) with (22a).

> (22)    Brutus fled after he stabbed Caesar
> (22a)   ∃e{Fled$_2$(Brutus, e) & ∃f[After$_2$(e, f) & Stabbed$_3$ (he, Caesar, f)]}

For (22) seems to be true iff an event of Brutus's fleeing occurred after an event of his stabbing Caesar.

So given an event analysis of (22), we can treat 'after' simply as a binary predicate satisfied by ordered pairs of events. And one can plausibly specify the meaning of (23) with (23a).

> (23)    Brutus dropped the knife before Caesar died
> (23a)   ∃e{Dropped$_3$(Brutus, the knife, e) & ∃f[Before$_2$(e, f) & Died$_2$(Caesar, f)]}

One can paraphrase (23) by using overt event nominals, as in (24).

(24)  A *dropping of the knife by Brutus* occurred before Caesar's death

And this bolsters the idea that 'Brutus dropped the knife' and 'Caesar died' covertly involve the kind of quantification over events that is overt in (23*a*). For the italicized expressions in (24) seem to be event descriptions, especially given the presence of words like 'before' and 'occurred'

Another source of evidence stems from sentences used to make perceptual reports. Notice that (25) differs in various ways from (26).

(25)  Cassius saw Brutus flee
(26)  Cassius saw that Brutus fled

In (25), 'flee' is untensed. And if Brutus was the noblest Roman, the truth of (25) ensures that Cassius saw the noblest Roman flee, but the truth of (26) does not ensure that Cassius saw *that* the noblest Roman fled. In (25) but not (26), 'Brutus' occupies a position in which its semantic contribution is exhausted by its Value; cf. 'The mayor thinks that Batman fled'. So following Higginbotham (1983) and Vlach (1983), one might well report the meaning of (25) with (25*a*):

(25*a*)  $\exists e\{Saw_3(Cassius, f, e) \ \& \ \exists f[Flee_2(Brutus, f)]\}$

there was a seeing by Cassius of a fleeing by Brutus. Similar remarks apply to (27) and (28).

(27)  Nora heard Nick shout
(28)  Nora heard Nick shout in the hallway

This helps explain the ambiguity of (28), which can mean either that Nora was in the hallway when she heard Nick's shouting, or that she heard Nick's shouting which was coming from the hallway. The idea is that 'in the hallway' can be predicated of the hearing *or* the shouting, as in (28*a*) and (28*b*).

(28*a*)  $\exists e\{Heard_3(Nora, f, e) \ \& \ \exists f[Shout_2(Nick, f) \ \& \ In_2$
(the hallway, e)]$\}$

(28*b*)    $\exists e\{Heard_3(Nora, f, e) \ \& \ \exists f[Shout_2(Nick, f) \ \& \ In_2(the$
hallway, f)]\}

A wealth of data concerning various "aspectual" properties of
verbs points in the same direction; see Tenny (1994), Levin and
Rappaport Hovav (1995), Pylkannen (1999), Tenny and Pustajevsky
(1999), Higginbotham, Pianesi, and Varzi (2000). To take just one
much discussed example, which also bears on the relation between
thematic roles and grammatical relations, consider (29–32).

(29)    Pat cleaned the room for an hour
(30)    Pat cleaned the room in an hour
(31)    Pat cleaned rooms for an hour
(32)    *Pat cleaned rooms in an hour

As the unacceptability of (32) reveals, the adverbial modifier 'in an
hour' cannot be used to extend an event description in which the
"Theme-representer" is indefinite. Intuitively, 'in an hour' cannot
be used to extend an event description that does not include a
description of when the event would be "finished". Thus, one can
run *to the store* in an hour, but one cannot run *to stores* in an hour;
see Vendler (1967), Tenny (1994), and the discussion in Chapter 3. It
is hard to see how one can even describe the relevant generalization,
much less explain it, without assuming that (29–31) involve quantification over events. For there seems to be a restriction on the
kinds of event descriptions that can be extended by using certain
prepositional phrases.

Arguments in later chapters for thematically elaborated event
analyses are also arguments for event analyses. (See also Taylor
(1985).) Let me end this section, however, by noting that the considerations already mentioned interact, as suggested by (33).

(33)    Nora heard Nick shout loudly in the hallway before
seeing him leave quickly.

Those who wish to avoid appeal to events need to provide theoretically perspicuous semantic representations that help explain the
relevant implications (and paraphrases) for each reading of (33).

## 4. Summary

The moral of §1 one was that we can (coherently) adopt a Fregean framework for semantics without adopting specifically Functionist hypotheses about the Values of predicates. In §2, I outlined a simple Conjunctivist semantics for sentences formed by combining a predicate with one or two names. Here, the main issues concerned the connections between grammatical relations and thematic relations, which can be viewed as special cases of "participation" relations. The simple account can be extended to accommodate sentential connectives. Along the way, I noted some potential sources of motivation for Conjunctivism and its implication that a predicate can have many Values (as opposed to having a function as its one Value).

A recurring theme, stressed in §3, was that Functionism is no simpler than Conjunctivism. Everyone needs to accommodate both cases of adjunction and cases of predicates combining with arguments. So one way or another, everyone needs to assign some kind of semantic significance to some grammatical relations. And I mentioned some motivations for assigning special significance to predicate–argument relations: there are independent reasons for thinking that such relations are thematically significant (in linguistically constrained ways); and there are severe limitations on the number of arguments that natural language predicates can have. It turns out that Functionists must also appeal to covert quantification over events. So while Conjunctivism requires appeal to covert quantification over things in which other things participate, this is not an objection.

It still needs showing that a Conjunctivist semantics can be extended to quantificational constructions, which may well provide the best case for Functionism. But given such an extension, we would have a serious alternative to the hypothesis that concatenation signifies function-application.

# 2

---

# Quantification and Plurality

At this point, we have a rudimentary Conjunctivist semantics—a "toy" theory—according to which grammatical subjects and objects are interpreted as monadic predicates. Recall (1) and the grammatical structure indicated in (1G), where 'ext' and 'int' make the relevant grammatical relations explicit.

(1)  Brutus stabbed Caesar
(1G)  $\langle$[ext-Brutus$_\alpha$ [stabbed$_{\Pi*}$ int-Caesar$_\alpha$]]$\rangle$

The idea was that something is a Value of *Brutus$_\alpha$ as an external argument* iff its external participant is the Value of Brutus$_\alpha$; Val(o, ext-Brutus$_\alpha$) iff External(o, **Brutus**). Likewise, Val(o, int-Caesar$_\alpha$) iff Internal(o, **Caesar**). So given that the Values of stabbed$_{\Pi*}$ are past events of stabbing, and that events have Agents/Themes as their internal/external participants,

Val(o, [ext-Brutus$_\alpha$[stabbed$_{\Pi*}$int-Caesar$_\alpha$]]) iff

Agent(o, **Brutus**) & Past-Stabbing(o) & Theme(o, **Caesar**).

So if a sentence involves existential closure of a variable—Val(**t**, $\langle\ldots\rangle$) iff $\exists$o[Val(o,$\ldots$)]—then (1) has the Value **t** iff $\exists$o[Agent(o, **Brutus**) & Past-Stabbing(o) & Theme(o, **Caesar**)].

This toy theory does not, however, accommodate sentences like (2–5).

(2)  Every bottle fell
(3)  Most bottles fell

(4)   He broke every bottle
(5)   They broke seven bottles

Initially, it is hard to see how the constituents of such sentences even could be interpreted as monadic predicates conjoined with others. But in fact, there are at least two ways of providing a Conjunctivist semantics for quantificational and plural constructions. One of them mimics a standard Functionist account. The other draws on less familiar resources; though it is better, on both conceptual and empirical grounds. The leading thought, due essentially to Frege, is that (2) can be evaluated as follows: pair the bottles with sentential Values, so that each bottle is associated with **t** if it fell and **f** otherwise; then ask whether every one of the resulting pairs associates something with **t**. The trick is to transform this thought into a plausible and suitably general theory, without lapsing (as Frege did) into paradox.

# 1.  Two Fregean Roads

I begin by sketching the two Conjunctivist strategies for dealing with (2), contrasting my own with a notational variant of a more familiar Functionist approach. These strategies are in turn associated with different theories of plural noun-phrases and different construals of *second*-order quantification (i.e. quantification into positions associated with predicates, as opposed to names). It will help to have a sense of how the various pieces fit together before turning to details. So this "introductory" section is really a short version of the whole chapter. It can be viewed initially as a roadmap, and later as a summary.

## 1.1. *Quantification Over Ordered Pairs of Sets*

As discussed in Chapter 1, Conjunctivists treat transitive action verbs as special cases of semantically monadic predicates that combine with two grammatical arguments. Sentential connectives like 'or' are treated the same way, even though the Values of 'or' are not events. The hypothesis is that each Value of 'or'—$<t, t>$, $<t, f>$, and $<f, t>$—has a sentential Value as its internal element and a sentential Value as its external element. Correlatively, 'or' is treated as a predicate that combines with an internal (sentential) argument and an external (sentential) argument. On this view, predicates that take two grammatical arguments can be satisfied by various "things": events with Agents and Themes, ordered pairs, or perhaps still other entities that can be said to have both internal and external "participants".

This kind of proposal is applicable to quantificational words like 'every', given the increasingly common assumption that such words also take internal and external (predicative) arguments. For simplicity of initial exposition, pretend that the grammatical structure of (2) is as follows: $\langle[[\text{every}_{\Delta^*} \text{ int-bottle}_\Pi]_\Delta \text{ ext-fell}_\Pi]\rangle$, with '$\Delta^*$' indicating a *determiner*.[1] For the moment, let's also ignore event analyses, and say that x is a Value of fell$_\Pi$ iff x is an individual that fell. Later, I abandon these simplifications in favor of a more plausible view: the external argument of a determiner is an *open sentence* like $\langle[\underline{\quad} \text{ fell}_\Pi]\rangle$; the Values of this open sentence can only be specified *relative* to an entity; and for each entity x, **t** is the Value of $\langle[\underline{\quad} \text{ fell}_\Pi]\rangle$ relative to x iff x was the Theme of a falling. But until §3, we can ignore the distinction between the verb fell$_\Pi$ and the homophonous open sentence, pretending that the Values of the verb are things that fell (as opposed to events of falling).

If determiners take internal and external arguments, Conjunctivists can say that determiners have ordered pairs as Values. Indeed, this leaves room for at least two specific proposals. One is that the Values of determiners are ordered pairs of sets. The other, which I favor, is that the Values of determiners are of the form $<t, x>$ or $<f, x>$; where x is an entity in the relevant domain. The second suggestion, which may initially seem obscure, will seem more natural after a brief discussion of the first.

---

[1] Angled brackets still indicate a sentence, which signifies existential closure for Conjunctivists. I return to questions about the distinction between $\langle[\ldots]_{\Delta P}\rangle$ and $[\ldots]_{\Delta P}$.

One could hypothesize that o is a Value of every$_{\Delta*}$ iff for some set $\alpha$ and some set $\beta$, o $= <\alpha, \beta>$, and $\alpha$ includes $\beta$. Abbreviating, Val(o, every$_{\Delta*}$) iff $\exists\alpha\exists\beta$(o $= <\alpha, \beta>$ & $\alpha \supseteq \beta$). Conjunctivists could then say that: (2) has the Value **t** iff $\exists$o[Val(o, every$_{\Delta*}$) & Val(o, int-bottle$_\Pi$) & Val(o, ext-fell$_\Pi$)]; where Val(o, int-bottle$_\Pi$) iff the internal element of o is the set of bottles, and Val(o, ext-fell$_\Pi$) iff the external element of o is the set of things that fell. The idea would be that o is both a Value of *bottle$_\Pi$ as the internal argument of a determiner* and a Value of *fell$_\Pi$ as the external argument of a determiner* iff o is the ordered pair $<\{$x: x fell$\}, \{$x: x is a bottle$\}>$. More generally, one could adopt the axioms below:

$$\text{Val(o, int-} \ldots {}_\Pi) \text{ iff Internal(o, } \{\text{x: Val(x,} \ldots {}_\Pi)\})$$

$$\text{Val(o, ext-} \ldots {}_\Pi) \text{ iff External(o, } \{\text{x: Val(x,} \ldots {}_\Pi)\})$$

cf. Larson and Segal (1995: ch. 8). On this view, (2) has the Value **t** iff $\{$x: x fell$\} \supseteq \{$x: x is a bottle$\}$.

This is a Conjunctivist implementation of Frege's (1879, 1884, 1892*a*) idea that quantificational words express relations between extensions—on analogy with transitive verbs, viewed as devices for expressing relations between more ordinary things. With 'o' ranging over ordered pairs, Frege could have agreed that (1) has the Value **t** iff $\exists$o[External(o, **Brutus**) & Stabbed(o) & Internal(o, **Caesar**)], and that (2) has the Value **t** iff $\exists$o[Every(o) & Internal(o, $\{$x: x is a bottle$\}$) & External(o, $\{$x: x fell$\}$)].[2] Correspondingly, a Conjunctivist can say that the Values of determiners are ordered pairs of extensions. But this is, unsurprisingly, a notational variant of a Functionist implementation of Frege's idea.

On a Functionist view, $\|$bottle$_\Pi\|$ and $\|$fell$_\Pi\|$ are functions from entities to sentential Values. So if every$_{\Delta*}$ takes bottle$_\Pi$ and fell$_\Pi$ as arguments, then $\|$every$_{\Delta*}\|$ presumably maps such functions—call

---

[2] Davidsonians can replace the axiom 'Val(o, stabbed$_{\Pi*}$) iff $\exists$x$\exists$y[o $= <$x, y$>$ & x stabbed y]' with: 'Val(o, stabbed$_{\Pi*}$) iff Past-Stabbing(o)', where 'o' ranges over both ordered pairs and events with external and internal participants; or 'Val(o, stabbed$_{\Pi*}$) iff $\exists$x$\exists$y[o $= <$e, (x, y)$>$ & e was a stabbing by x of y]', where by stipulation, x is the external participant and y is the internal participant of $<$e, (x, y)$>$.

them Preds—to *functions* that map Preds to sentential Values. Ignoring covert quantification over events, $\|\text{stabbed}_{\Pi*}\|$ maps entities to *functions* that map entities to sentential Values. So $\|\text{every}_{\Delta*}\|$ and $\|\text{stabbed}_{\Pi*}\|$ are both functions that map things of a certain type onto functions that map things of that type to **t** or **f**; see Montague (1974). If 'X' and 'Y' range over Preds, the hypothesis about every$_{\Delta*}$ is that

$\|\text{every}_{\Delta*}\| = \lambda Y$ . $[\lambda X$ . **t** iff every individual x such that
$Y(x) = \mathbf{t}$ is such that $X(x) = \mathbf{t}]$.

One can specify this second-order function in many ways: $\lambda Y$ . $[\lambda X$ . **t** iff $\forall x\{Y(x) = \mathbf{t} \rightarrow X(x) = \mathbf{t}\}]$; $\lambda Y$ . $[\lambda X$ . **t** iff $\{x: X(x) = \mathbf{t}\} \supseteq \{x: Y(x) = \mathbf{t}\}]$; etc. But whatever the details, the idea is that every$_{\Delta*}$ is associated with a relation between functions—or more simply, between sets of entities—much as stabbed$_{\Pi*}$ is associated with a relation between more basic entities.

This fits nicely with the thought that (2) has the following simple grammatical structure: $[[\text{every}_{\Delta*} \text{ bottle}_{\Pi}]_{\Delta} \text{ fell}_{\Pi}]$. If there is no independent reason for positing existential closure of a variable associated with every$_{\Delta*}$, Functionists need not say that the sentence is associated with such closure. They can just say that

$\|[\text{every}_{\Delta*}\text{bottle}_{\Pi}]_{\Delta}\text{fell}_{\Pi}\| = [\|\text{every}_{\Delta*}\|(\|\text{bottle}_{\Pi}\|)](\|\text{fell}_{\Pi}\|) = \mathbf{t}$
iff every individual x such that $\|\text{bottle}_{\Pi}\|(x) = \mathbf{t}$
is such that $\|\text{fell}_{\Pi}\|(x) = \mathbf{t}$.

But as we have seen, one can recode this account in Conjunctivist terms, by assuming that predicates like bottle$_{\Pi}$ and fell$_{\Pi}$ have extensions. The claim that determiners express relations between extensions does not itself presuppose any specific view about how syntax contributes to meaning. The hypothesis that concatenation signifies conjunction is logically compatible with the hypothesis that determiners are satisfied by ordered pairs of sets. But consistency is one thing, plausibility another.

## 1.2. *Concerns about Quantifying over Extensions*

Conjunctivists say that a predicate can have many Values. But why deny that bottle$_\Pi$ has a function as its sole Value if one is going to say that *from the perspective of a determiner*, bottle$_\Pi$ stands for a set? It seems like cheating to reproduce a Functionist account of quantification in Conjunctivist terms, just as it seems like cheating to reproduce a Conjunctivist account of adjunction in Functionist terms. I think it also violates the spirit of Conjunctivism to say that determiners express relations between sets of Values. The leading idea is supposed to be that predicates and their grammatical arguments are interpreted, like Davidsonian adjuncts, as conjoinable *monadic* predicates. And the empirical content of this idea is diluted, in so far as it is defended by appealing to lexical meanings that reproduce the kinds of relationality permitted by Functionism. Part of what makes Conjunctivism theoretically interesting, with potentially interesting implications for language acquisition, is the suggestion that interpretation is constrained in ways that Functionism does not predict. I don't want to give up this suggestion with regard to determiners, at least not without exploring the options.[3]

These are reasons Conjunctivists have for not recoding Functionist theories of quantification. But there are also reasons for being suspicious of such theories, quite apart from particular theoretical commitments. While talk of sets is often convenient, it turns out that appeal to extensions is unneeded—and in many cases unwanted—in

---

[3] Recall the discussion, in Ch. 1, of thematic roles and their relation to grammatical relations. This is not to say that Conjunctivists cannot assign ordered pairs as Values. (My own proposal does just this.) But without constraints on what the elements of such ordered pairs can be—so that certain relations *cannot* be encoded this way—the theory becomes less interesting. As we shall see, one imposes a severe constraint by saying that determiners have Values of the form <v, x>. And in Ch. 3, I argue that (once a Conjunctivist account of quantification is in place), Functionists concede most of what matters in the debate if they appeal to (conjunctive and thematic) lexical meanings like $\lambda y . [\lambda x . [\lambda e . \mathbf{t}$ iff Agent(e, x) & Stabbing(e) & Theme(e, y)]]$, along with constraints on how thematic relations can be associated with grammatical relations.

theories of meaning for natural languages. This is so, even setting aside considerations of vagueness. As Russell's paradox shows, logic imposes limits on which sets there are. Functionist accounts are in constant danger of running afoul of such limitations, with the consequent need for *ad hoc* remedies. For example, such accounts can handle the truistic (6), but they have trouble with the equally truistic (7).

(6)   Every pet that does not own itself is a pet
(7)   Every set that does not contain itself is a set

While there may be a set of all the nonselfowning pets, there is no set of all the nonselfelemental sets.

Following Boolos (1984, 1998) and Schein (1993), I think this illustrates a general problem for any compositional semantics that relies on the following assumption: for each predicate Π, there is a set whose elements are all and only the things that satisfy Π. A better view is that a predicate can have many Values, which need not form a set. From this perspective, 'nonselfowning pet' and 'nonselfelemental set' are semantically on a par. Moreover, if we say that determiners express relations between extensions, we face a hard question: why are there certain relations that no determiner expresses?

This point is closely related to a medieval observation, discussed by Barwise and Cooper (1981) among others. When evaluating 'Every bottle fell', one need not—and intuitively, one does not—consider any nonbottles. One can focus solely on the bottles, and ask whether every one of them fell. Correspondingly, it is a truism that every bottle fell iff every bottle is a bottle that fell. Likewise, some/no/most/seven bottles fell iff some/no/most/seven bottles are bottles that fell. Using Barwise and Cooper's terminology, say that relation **R** is *conservative* iff for any sets $\alpha$ and $\beta$, $\alpha$ bears **R** to $\beta$ iff $(\alpha \cap \beta)$ bears **R** to $\beta$. Inclusion is a conservative relation; $\alpha \supseteq \beta$ iff $(\alpha \cap \beta) \supseteq \beta$. So is intersection; $\alpha \cap \beta$ iff $(\alpha \cap \beta) \cap \beta$. But equinumerosity, corresponding one-to-one, is not conservative. Suppose that three things fell, and there are three bottles, but no bottle fell. Then {x: x fell} is equinumerous with {x: x is a bottle}, while the intersection of these sets is not equinumerous with {x: x is a bottle}.

As we shall see, the pattern seems to be that no determiner expresses a nonconservative relation. There is, for example, no determiner 'Equi' such that 'Equi bottles fell' means that the fallen are equinumerous with the bottles. This negative generalization calls for explanation. If determiners express relations, the explanation will presumably take the form of a constraint on *which* relations determiners can express. But in my view, the prospects for finding an independently plausible constraint are dim, given relations like *corresponds one-to-one with*. I will suggest instead that the relevant negative generalization follows from a Conjunctivist analysis of words like 'every' as monadic predicates.

## 1.3. *Plural Quantification Over Basic Things*

To formulate my proposal, I need to introduce a little terminology. Let's say that Π is a *potentially plural predicate* if some things can (together) be Values of Π, even if each of those things fails to be a Value of Π. Suppose that some bottles are arranged so that they form a triangle. If no one of the bottles forms a triangle, 'form a triangle' seems to be a potentially plural predicate. But one might hold that, strictly speaking, there are no such predicates in natural language. Perhaps the bottles in question are not Values of 'form a triangle'. Maybe *the collection of* those bottles is a Value of the predicate, which is essentially singular: some things are Values of it only if each of them is a Value of it.[4]

---

[4] Or more permissively, one might say that the bottles are (many) Values of 'form a triangle', but only in an indirect and attenuated sense—namely, they are elements of some collection that is a Value of the predicate. Of course, a Functionist might object to the very idea of a predicate having Values. But let a *functional-satisfier* of a predicate Π, whose Value is function F, be any individual x such that $F(x) = \mathbf{t}$. Then each bottle is a functional-satisfier of 'bottle'. But if no bottle is a functional-satisfier of 'formed a triangle', then presumably, some bottles are (together) functional-satisfiers of the predicate iff the collection of those bottles is a functional-satisfier of the predicate. In which case, the (real) Value of 'formed a triangle' would have to be a function from collections to sentential Values, and the predicate would not be potentially plural.

Following Boolos (1998) and others, I think this common view is mistaken. As we shall see, natural language apparently includes many potentially plural predicates, and at least some predicates that are essentially plural; where no single thing, not even a collection, can be a Value of an essentially plural predicate, even though some things can (together) be Values of the predicate. Boolos illustrates the general point by noting that utterances of 'The rocks rained down' can be true, even though no one thing can rain down. I want to press this point, drawing on Schein's (1993) account of plural noun-phrases, for two reasons. First, given a line of thought developed below, Conjunctivism predicts that predication in natural language is regularly plural predication; whereas Functionism leads to the contrary prediction that natural language predication is essentially singular. Second, once we allow for the possibility of plural predication (and not just singular predication in disguise), we can provide an attractive Conjunctivist semantics for quantificational constructions like (2).

(2)   Every bottle fell.

The idea is that determiners and their arguments are interpreted as monadic plural predicates, whose Values are ordered pairs consisting of an entity and a sentential Value. More specifically, the Values of determiners (every$_{\Delta^*}$, most$_{\Delta^*}$, *etc.*) are of the form $<\mathbf{t}, x>$ or $<\mathbf{f}, x>$, with x as the internal element. Call such pairs "Frege-Pairs", since they reflect Frege's insight that a predicate like fell$_\Pi$— or more precisely, an open sentence like $\langle[\_\_\text{fell}_\Pi]\rangle$—can be viewed as an expression (of a Concept) that associates each relevant entity with a sentential Value.

One can hypothesize that, given some Frege-Pairs, they are Values of every$_{\Delta^*}$ iff every one of them associates its internal element with $\mathbf{t}$; they are Values of no$_{\Delta^*}$ iff no one of them associates its internal element with $\mathbf{t}$; and so on. Correlatively, one can say that some Frege-Pairs are Values of int-bottle$_\Pi$ iff they associate (all and only) the Values of bottle$_\Pi$ with sentential Values, and that some Frege-Pairs are Values of ext-fell$_\Pi$ iff each of them associates its internal element x with **t** iff x is a Value of fell$_\Pi$. Given Conjunctivism, the net result is that some things are Values of [[every$_{\Delta^*}$ int-bottle$_\Pi$] ext-fell$_\Pi$] iff: *every* one of them is of the form $<\mathbf{t}, x>$; their internal elements are the *bottles*; and each of them has **t** as its external element iff its internal element *fell*. In which case,

Val(**t**, $\langle$[[every$_{\Delta^*}$int-bottle$_\Pi$] ext-fell$_\Pi$]$\rangle$) iff

$\exists$O[Val(O, every$_{\Delta^*}$) & Val(O, int-bottle$_\Pi$) & Val(O, ext-fell$_\Pi$)];

where '$\exists$O . . .' means that *there are some things, the Os, such that* . . . , and 'Val(O, . . . )' means that the Os are Values of the expression in question.[5] I'll have much more to say about this notation below. But as we'll see, this helps explain the "conservativity generalization". And the proposal accommodates sentences with quantificational direct objects, as in (4).

(4)   He broke every bottle

My conclusion will be that Conjunctivists should not mimic a Functionist account of quantificational constructions. The more honestly Conjunctivist treatment is better, even though determiners and their arguments initially seem to provide support for Functionism. But the connections between quantification and plurality run deep, making it necessary to discuss both topics when defending an account of either. It needs showing that Conjunctivists can employ quantifiers like 'There are some things' without thereby quantifying over plural entities. And various facts do invite the hypothesis that plural nouns are associated with functions from collections to sentential Values. So let me end this overview by indicating the planned reply.

---

[5] The official gloss of '$\exists$X' will be 'There are *one or more* things, the Xs'. We can use '$\exists$X:Plural(X)' to say that that Xs are plural—i.e. more than one. It will still follow that 'Every bottle fell' has the Value **f** if there are no bottles. But one can, if one wants to, add the stipulation that utterances of the sentence are true (or without truth-value) in situations with no bottles.

## 1.4.  *Plurality Without Plural Values*

Consider (5–9), all of which have "collective" readings.

(5)   They broke seven bottles
(6)   They broke them
(7)   They stabbed them
(8)   Three surgeons stabbed six turnips

For example, (8) can be true if three surgeons *together* stabbed six turnips, with each surgeon stabbing exactly two turnips. And (7) could be used to say what those surgeons did. Similarly, (6) could be used in place of (5), which is naturally heard as implying that seven bottles were broken as a result of some joint activity; compare 'They each broke seven bottles'. I think Conjunctivists can provide an account of collective readings that is superior to the account that Functionists are driven to.[6]

If the Value of 'stabbed' is a function from entities to functions, and 'stabbed' can combine with 'them' to form a phrase as in (7), then the Value of 'them' (in any context) must be an entity of some kind. Given six turnips, there is a six-membered collection of those turnips; call it 'T6'. So an obvious Functionist hypothesis is that if a speaker refers to those turnips with 'them', then in that context, T6 is the Value of 'them'. Similar remarks apply to plural external arguments if the Value of 'stabbed them', like 'stabbed Caesar', is a function from entities to (functions from events to) sentential Values. If the context is one in which the speaker refers to three surgeons by using 'They', and S3 is the three-membered collection of those surgeons, the obvious hypothesis is that the Value of 'They' is S3.

In which case, (7) has the Value t iff S3 stabbed T6. Or if one collection cannot stab another, Functionists can say that S3

---

[6] Specialists may be thinking that anyone who adopts a Tarski-style semantics of quantificational and demonstrative constructions, in terms of relativization to sequences, will also be forced to a plural-entity view. But as we shall see, there is an alternative, given a Boolos-style treatment of plural variables.

stabbed$^{co}$ **T6**; where one collection stabbed$^{co}$ another iff *the elements of* the first stabbed *the elements of* the second. Likewise, one can try to capture the collective reading of (8) in terms of quantification over plural entities: **t** iff *some* three-membered collection of surgeons stabbed, or perhaps stabbed$^{co}$, *some* six-membered collection of turnips. On this view, predication is fundamentally singular: to say that some things collectively satisfy a predicate is to say that a collection, with those things as elements, satisfies a related predicate; see Link (1983, 1987, 1998), Landman (1996), Schwarzschild (1996).

Predicates that seem to be essentially plural, as in (9), pose difficulties for this proposal.

(9)    The rocks rained down on the huts

Moreover, a good account of quantification and plurality should explain why competent speakers hear biconditionals like (10) and (11) as trivialities.

(10)    Every bottle fell if and only if every one of the bottles fell
(11)    If they are the bottles, they fell if and only if the bottles fell

But as Schein (1993) argues, plural-entity theories cannot explain such facts without running afoul of Russell's paradox; see §5. And as the invented term 'stabbed$^{co}$' suggests, Functionists need auxiliary type-shifting hypotheses, even for cases of predicates combining with (plural) arguments. This suggests that we should look for an alternative account of the facts illustrated with (5–11).

Following Schein (1993, 2002, forthcoming), I think speakers understand collective readings of action sentences in terms of events. And a single sentence can be used to report the occurrence of many events. Intuitively, (12) can be true on a collective reading, even if no one event has ten Agents.

(12)    Ten professors wrote fifteen articles

Suppose that Smith wrote two articles with Jones, who wrote another with Bizby and Bloggs, who would never work with Smith, and so on.[7] We could also describe such a situation with (13),

(13)    They wrote some articles

which could also be used to describe a fully cooperative group, or ten authors working alone. Joint effort may sometimes constitute a complex event with many Agents. But plurality does not imply cooperation.

Likewise, 'Brutus stabbed six turnips' is true if Brutus performed *one or more events* of stabbing whose Themes were six turnips. There need not be a single event with six turnips as its Theme. And we need not describe what Brutus did in terms of a six-membered turnip-collection that he stabbed. We can appeal instead to *plural predicates*, given a theory in which meanings are specified in terms of Boolos-style plural quantification. Using capitalized subscripts to indicate plural variables that can be bound by a second-order existential quantifier, *some things*$_O$ have six turnips as their$_O$ Themes iff there are *some things*$_X$ such that: there are six of them$_X$; each of them$_X$ is a turnip; and they$_X$ are the Themes of them$_O$.

More explicitly, and employing restricted universal quantification,

$$\text{Theme(O, six turnips) iff } \exists X[\text{Six}(X) \, \& \, \forall x : Xx(x \text{ is a turnip}) \, \& \, \text{Theme}(O, X)];$$

where '$Xx$' means that $x$ is one of the $X$s, and '$\text{Theme}(O, X)$' means that the $X$s are the Themes of the $O$s. Assuming for simplicity that each noncomposite event has exactly one Theme,

$$\text{Theme(O, X) iff } \forall o : Oo\{\exists x[\text{Theme}(o, x) \, \& \, Xx]\} \, \& \, \forall x : Xx\{\exists o[\text{Theme}(o, x) \, \& \, Oo]\}.$$

The $X$s are the Themes of the $O$s iff the Theme of every $O$ is an $X$, and every $X$ is the Theme of an $O$. This leaves room to add, if appropriate, that the $O$s constitute a composite event (with

---

[7]    See Gillon (1987), Higginbotham and Schein (1989), discussed briefly in §5 below.

multiple Agents and Themes) that satisfies further conditions. But this is not an implication of 'stabbed six turnips'.

The turnips can be six, as the apostles were twelve. To be six, in this plural-predicative sense, is *not* to be a set with six elements; see Yi (1999) for discussion. No one thing is six in the way that six things are six. And a set is one thing, even if *it* has many elements. The predicate 'six' is like 'plural', in this respect, and unlike 'turnip': some things can be six, even if no one of them is six; but if those things are turnips, then each of them is a turnip. So we can say that Theme(O, 'six turnips') iff $\exists X[\text{Val}(X, \text{'six'}) \& \text{Val}(X, \text{'turnip'}) \& \text{Theme}(O, X)]$. And ten professors can be Values of the complex predicate '$\exists O[\text{Agent}(O, X) \& \text{Past-Writing}(O) \& \text{Theme}(O, \text{fifteen articles})]$', even if nobody wrote fifteen articles. Correlatively, 'wrote fifteen articles' has a reading on which it is a plural predicate.

In essence, that's the chapter: the Values of determiners are Frege-Pairs; and this coheres nicely with an independently attractive Conjunctivist conception of plurality. But the proposal is importantly different from more familiar accounts. So some repetition may be welcome, especially with regard to the construal of second-order quantification as plural quantification.

## 2. Interpreting Capitalized Variables

Anyone using '$\exists X$' to state a theory has to say what it means. Any interpretation can be stipulated, but some theories are better than others. After reviewing some concerns about adopting a set-theoretic construal of second-order quantification in semantic theories for natural languages (§2.1), I return to the plural interpretation (§2.2), which lets Conjunctivists say that the Values of determiners are Frege-Pairs (§2.3). Sections 3 and 4 are devoted to details of the compositional semantics, and arguments for it. Collective readings are the topic of §5. But my aim is not to provide a theory that addresses all the aspects of quantification and plurality discussed by semanticists. It is to show that Conjunctivism is better than Functionism with regard to accounting for some basic facts in this domain.

## 2.1. *One or Many: Avoid Counterexamples, Capture Generalizations*

In Chapter 1, I noted that considerations of vagueness make it less than obvious that each predicate has a set as its Value. Some predicates that are not vague also create difficulties for the idea, crucial to Functionist accounts of quantification, that predicates are semantically associated with extensions.

For example, (14) is true, since the empty set is a subset of every set. And (15) is obviously true.

> (14)   Every set has a subset
> (15)   Every set is a set

But if standard (Zermelo-Frankl, or ZF) set theory is correct, there is no *set* of all the sets, just as there is no set of all the nonselfelemental sets.[8] In metalinguistic terms, '{x: x is a set}' does not denote a set given ZF theory, just as 'Vulcan' does not denote a planet given that there is no planet between Mercury and the sun. If there is no set of all the sets, then *nothing* is such that the set of sets bears some relation to it. Similar remarks apply to '{x: x has a subset}'. In which case, the following biconditionals are false, with 'X' and 'Y' ranging over sets:

> (14)   is true iff $\exists X \exists Y[(X \supseteq Y) \& X = \{x: x \text{ has a subset}\} \&$
> $Y = \{x: x \text{ is a set}\}]$;
> (15)   is true iff $\exists X \exists Y[(X \supseteq Y) \& X = \{x: x \text{ is a set}\} \&$
> $Y = \{x: x \text{ is a set}\}]$.

While the left sides of these biconditionals are true if '{x: x is a set}' does not denote a set.

---

[8] An alleged set of all sets would contain—among its *many* elements (including itself, the power set of every other set, and its own power set)—every set $s$ such that $s \notin s$. Given the ZF axioms, there is no such "universal" set, if only because it would follow that there is a set $s^*$ such that $\forall x(x \in s^* \text{ iff } x \notin x)$. See Boolos (1971) for discussion of the "iterative" conception of set (mentioned below), which makes sense of this limitation.

One can try to maintain that *utterances* of (14) and (15) are true, even though these sentences do not have the Value **t** (relative to any context). But, prima facie, (15) is a paradigmatic example of a sentence that (always) has the Value **t**. And if a theory has the consequence that (15) doesn't have the Value **t**, it is hard to see how the theory can explain why (15) is a tautology. Likewise, if a theory has the consequence that (14) doesn't have the Value **t**, it is hard to see how the theory can help explain why utterances of (14) are true (as opposed to false, or without truth-value). So I conclude, tentatively, that the following theory-laden biconditionals are also false:

(14)  has the Value **t** iff $\exists X\exists Y[(X\supseteq Y)$ &
$X = \{x: x\text{ has a subset}\}$ & $Y = \{x: x\text{ is a set}\}]$;

(15)  has the Value **t** iff $\exists X\exists Y[(X\supseteq Y)$ &
$X = \{x: x\text{ is a set}\}$ & $Y = \{x: x\text{ is a set}\}]$.

But these biconditionals are consequences of the first Conjunctivist theory scouted in §1. And while a theory with false consequences may have other virtues, such a theory is still false.

Here is another way of putting the point, emphasizing the difficulty for Functionists, assuming ZF set theory. There is no *set* of all ordered pairs $<x, t>$ such that x is a set. So talking about *the function* that maps each thing x to **t** iff x is *a set* is like talking about the greatest prime number. So a theory according to which $\|\text{set}_\Pi\| = [\lambda x \,.\, \mathbf{t}\text{ iff } x\text{ is a set}]$ is a theory that fails to assign a Value to $\text{set}_\Pi$. In which case, absent special stipulations, the theory won't assign a Value to phrases like $[\text{every}_{\Lambda^*}\ \text{set}_\Pi]_\Lambda$ or sentences like (14) and (15). Conjunctivists can say instead that $\text{set}_\Pi$ has many Values: $\text{Val}(x, \text{set}_\Pi)$ iff x is a set. But the problem resurfaces if one goes on to say that o is a Value of *$\text{set}_\Pi$ as an internal argument* iff the internal participant of o is the set of sets. For if $\text{Val}(o, \text{int-set}_\Pi)$ iff $\text{Internal}(o, \{x: \text{Val}(x, \text{set}_\Pi)\})$, then nothing is a Value of $\text{int-set}_\Pi$; hence, absent special stipulations, (14) and (15) get the Value **f**. So, prima facie, Conjunctivists should not say that $\text{Val}(o, \text{int-}\ldots_\Pi)$ iff

Internal(o, {x: Val(x, . . . $_\Pi$)}). Similar remarks apply to endlessly many examples like (16) and (17).

(16)  Some sets are singletons
(17)  Most sets have members

For many purposes, one can just ignore this and get on with day-to-day semantics. But if we are thinking about our theoretical apparatus (as opposed to just applying it), because the issue before us concerns the interpretation of our metalanguage, then we cannot ignore a tension between ZF set theory and semantic theories formulated in a metalanguage that is interpreted in set-theoretic terms. When thinking about how we *should* construe '∃X' as it appears in semantic theories, the tension cannot be dismissed as a sniggly point with no significance. I can, however, imagine at least three replies to the claim that (14–17) provide counterexamples to Functionist theories and their notational variants.

One might deny that theories of *natural* language apply to (14–17). This insulates the theories, at the cost of restricting their scope. So the motivation for an alternative is clear. Other things being equal, one prefers theories with greater scope. And there is no independent reason for excluding words like 'set' from natural language, while allowing 'number' or 'molecule'. One can grant that (14–17) are in some sense artificial sentences. But facts about such sentences can still bear on theories of natural language. Prima facie, we understand (14–17) compositionally in the way we understand (18–21).

(18)  Every pet has a head
(19)  Every pet is a pet
(20)  Some pets are dogs
(21)  Most pets have whiskers

A theory that applies to (18–21) but not (14–17) thus fails to capture apparent generalizations. Moreover, we need *some* account of how speakers can understand endlessly many expressions like

(14–17). And if understanding (14) does not involve associating (14) with a condition specified in terms of an alleged set of sets, perhaps understanding (18) does not involve associating (18) with a condition specified in terms of an alleged set of pets. Recall that, given vagueness, it isn't obvious that '{x: x is a pet}' denotes a set. And one cannot dismiss this concern, on the grounds that sentences like 'Two precedes three' provide the real paradigms for natural language semantics, while also dismissing concerns about (14–17) on the grounds that (18–21) provide the real paradigms for natural language semantics.[9]

A second response is to reject ZF set theory. One can stipulate that if '{x: x is a set}' denotes anything at all, it denotes the set—or better, the "class"—of all sets, whatever that is (if it is). And one can go on to hypothesize that there is such a thing.[10] So there is room for the following view: 'Every set is a set' has Value **t** iff $\exists X \exists Y[X \supseteq Y \ \& \ X = \{x:\ x\ \text{is a set}\}\ \&\ Y = \{x:\ x\ \text{is a set}\}]$; and the right side of this biconditional is true, since there is a set/class of all the sets. Perhaps there is also a class of the nonselfelemental sets, and this is why 'Every nonselfelemental set is a set' has the Value **t**. But then one has to deal with sentences like 'There are some nonselfelemental classes,

---

[9] If one stipulates that 'x' ranges over a domain that does not include $\|\text{set}_\Pi\|$, one must explain *why* speakers cannot use natural language to quantify over all the sets or talk about $\|\text{set}_\Pi\|$, even if speakers can quantify over all the pets and talk about $\|\text{pet}_\Pi\|$. Perhaps *theorists shouldn't* quantify over all the sets, at least not all at once, and a proper formal language would keep us from doing so; though cf. Williamson (2004). And whatever one says about ideal languages, one cannot *stipulate* that the Value of $\text{set}_\Pi$ is somehow "referentially unavailable" to ordinary speakers. This is an empirical hypothesis about natural language.

[10] For example, one might adopt a (von Neumann–Bernays–Gödel) theory that avoids Russell's paradox by distinguishing sets from classes: every set is a class, but some classes—*proper* classes—are not sets; no proper class is a member of any class; but there is a proper class of all the sets. And a semanticist might say that the Value of 'set' is the *proper class* of sets (i.e. the proper class of improper classes). Of course, this doesn't help if the true set/class theory allows for analogous objections (to standard semantic theories) based on analogous sentences—involving predicates like 'proper class', 'collection', 'abstract thing that satisfies the axioms of ZF set theory', etc. Though perhaps one can argue that any such sentences will be technical enough to make the first reply more plausible.

every one of which is nonselfelemental'. So, at least prima facie, the problem remains. Moreover, this strategy combines tendentious semantics with a tendentious ontology for set theory. And even if it turns out that something has every set as an element, I don't think semantic theories for natural language should depend on this.

Put another way, the worry isn't merely that Functionism makes wrong predictions about (14–17), *given* a certain conception of the set-theoretic universe. It is that, given Functionism, the truth of (14–17) depends on there being something that violates a familiar and plausible conception of sets. Boolos (1971, 1998) discusses the "iterative" view according to which the sets exhibit a stage-like hierarchy: there is the empty set ø; its singleton {ø}; every other set such that each of its elements is one of those "earlier" sets—i.e. {{ø}} and {ø,{ø}}; every other set such that each of its elements is one of those earlier sets; and so on. (For simplicity, focus on the "pure" sets whose elements are all sets.) On this view, there are endlessly many sets; but no set has every other set as an element. This is, in many respects, an attractive conception of what the sets are. So one would expect truistic sentences like (14–17) to have the Value **t** if it turns out that the sets are indeed characterizable in this iterative and ZF-friendly fashion.

This invites a third response: do not interpret '$(X \supseteq Y)$ & $X = \{x: x \text{ fell}\}$ & $Y = \{x: x \text{ is a bottle}\}$' in terms of *sets* when such formalism *figures in semantic theories*. One can hypothesize that, whether or not there is a universal set, there is *some* thing X such that: $\forall x(x \text{ is part of } X \text{ iff } x \text{ is a set})$, with 'is part of' used as a technical locution of semantic theory, perhaps distinct from 'is an element of' as used in the true set theory. Perhaps some such thing is what '$\{x: x \text{ is a set}\}$' denotes when used as device for specifying Values. Of course, if there are set-like things not described by set theory, one will want to know why (and how) this is so; see Boolos (1998). And this third reply may ultimately reduce to the second. Still, one might hope to remain agnostic on this score.

Absent a better alternative, this is a reasonable response to examples like (14–17). But it is not a *defense* of a Functionist theory interpreted in the standard way. It is an admission that another interpretation may be required, coupled with a conjecture: *if* an alternative is required, the best one will preserve the idea that each predicate has some one thing (with parts that satisfy the predicate) as its Value. And the conjecture may be wrong. This illustrates a general point that is worth dwelling on.

If a theorist uses the formal sentence '{x: x fell} $\supseteq$ {x: x is a bottle}' to specify the meaning of 'Every bottle fell', then '$\supseteq$' had better indicate something like inclusion as opposed to intersection. But the interpretation for the metalanguage need not associate '{x: x is a bottle}' with a set *per se*. Perhaps '{x: x fell} $\supseteq$ {x: x is a bottle}' *as it figures in semantic theories* should be viewed as a way of saying that the fallen include the bottles, without implying that 'fell' and 'bottle' have extensions. A semanticist using curly brackets will presumably want to say that '{x: x is a bottle}' and '{x: x is a set}' are meta-linguistic expressions of the same type. This apparently leads to (*a*) rejecting ZF set theory, or (*b*) rejecting the standard interpretation of the formalism. And if (*b*) is the better option, then one should be willing to consider *various* interpretations. One can, of course, interpret a formalism as one likes. But one cannot stipulate that, so interpreted, the formalism is adequate for purposes of explaining relevant facts concerning the semantic properties of natural language expressions.

When we formulate a hypothesis about some expression, the hypothesis is reflected in both the choice of particular formal symbols and the choice of an interpretation for those symbols. If '$\supseteq$' and '$\cap$' signify inclusion and intersection, respectively, then 'Val(o, every$_{\Delta*}$) iff $\exists X\exists Y(o = <X, Y> \& X \supseteq Y)$' is a better proposal about the meaning of every$_{\Delta*}$ than 'Val(o, every$_{\Delta*}$) iff $\exists X\exists Y(o = <X, Y> \& X \cap Y)$'. Different interpretations of the first biconditional, taken as a mere piece of formalism, also correspond to distinct proposals. This is obvious with regard to '$\supseteq$'; construing it as intersection yields a bad hypothesis about every$_{\Pi*}$. Different interpretations of '$\exists X$' can be more subtle but still significant. And facts about natural language, as opposed to sets, should drive theory choice in semantics.

Absent an alternative to a Functionist theory, with second-order quantification interpreted in terms of quantification over sets, it might be reasonable to ignore (14–17) and the reflections they prompt. But once we consider theories that preserve Functionist notation interpreted in some other way, we cannot refuse to consider a Conjunctivist theory with '∃X' interpreted plurally (*à la* Boolos) and *not* in terms of quantification over sets of things that 'x' ranges over. Given this option, one cannot declare (14–17) irrelevant. Perhaps 'Every set is a set' has the Value **t** even if *nothing* has every set as an element (or part). And perhaps the meaning of 'Every bottle fell' is best specified without reference to the alleged set of bottles. Though one wants to hear more about the alleged alternative.

## 2.2. *Plural Quantification*

Prima facie, one can say that some things satisfy a condition—e.g. that they form a triangle, or that each of them fell—without saying anything from which it *follows* that there is a set. And one can interpret '∃X' plurally, with '∃X[∀x(Xx ↔ x is a bottle) & ∀x: Xx(x fell)]' meaning that there are some things$_X$ such that: for each thing$_x$, it$_x$ is one of them$_X$ iff it$_x$ is a bottle, and each one of them$_X$ fell. Here, lower-case and upper-case subscripts indicate (respectively) singular and plural variables, as in Boolos (1998).

It turns out that, given plural quantification, Conjunctivists can provide an attractive account of determiners. Of course, *if* talk of the bottles and being one of them involves covert quantification over collections, then plural interpretations of '∃X' involve appeal to plural entities after all. But *if not*, then on such an interpretation, '∃X[∀x(Xx ↔ x is a bottle)]' does not imply that something has every bottle as an element. If we want to learn whether or not plural noun-phrases have plural entities as Values, we must leave this issue open at the outset, in saying what '∃X' *means*. But one can stipulate that instances of '∃X...X...' are to be understood in terms of plural expressions, whatever such expressions mean, and then *argue* for a theory that specifies the meaning of 'the bottles' in terms of quantification over bottles but not sets. Critics can try to argue that instances of the comprehension schema '$\exists X[\forall x(Xx \leftrightarrow \Phi x)]$' still imply the corresponding instances of '$\exists s{:}set(s)[\forall x(x \in s \leftrightarrow \Phi x)]$'. But (22) suggests otherwise.

(22)   $\exists X[\forall x(Xx \leftrightarrow x \notin x)]$

If we interpret '$\exists X$' as singular quantification over sets, with '$Xx$' meaning that x is an element of X, (22) says falsely that: there is a set$_X$ such that for each thing$_x$, it$_x$ is an element of it$_X$ iff it$_x$ is not an element of itself$_x$.[11] But if we interpret '$\exists X$' as plural quantification over whatever '$x$' ranges over, then (22) means that there *are some* things$_X$ such that for each thing$_x$, it is *one of them*$_X$ iff it$_x$ is not an element of itself$_x$. In which case, (22) is true, given some non-selfelemental things like you and me. And if every thing fails to be an element of itself, (22) is true so long as there are some things to quantify over. Put another way, instead of taking '$Xx$' to mean that x is an element of X, we can let '$Xx$' mean that x is one of the Xs. And there is a difference. The first interpretation makes (22) false, the second makes it true. This in turn suggests that 'is one of' and 'is an element of' are *not* synonymous; see §4.

More generally, instead of taking '$\exists X[\forall x(Xx \leftrightarrow \Phi x)]$' to mean that *the set of* the $\Phi$s exists, we can let '$\exists X[\forall x(Xx \leftrightarrow \Phi x)]$' mean that the $\Phi$s exist. On this view,

---

[11]  This is provably false; see Ch. 1, n. 24. (Likewise, there is no thing whose parts are all and only things that are not parts of themselves.) And since the *reductio* apparently does not rely on any special assumptions about sets, it seems to be immune from any challenges via nonstandard set theory. If there is a person P who likes a person iff that person doesn't like herself, then either P likes herself or not. But if the former, P both does and doesn't like herself; and if the latter, P both doesn't and does like herself. So there is no such person. One can't avoid this conclusion by adopting a nonstandard person theory, or a nonstandard interpretation of '¬Like(Pat, Pat) &=(Pat, Pat*) & Like(Pat, Pat*)' that makes this formal sentence true. While I continue to mix English and Formalese, this is inessential: you are not something that is an element of itself. One can *define* 'element' so that each thing is an element of itself. But that is irrelevant. One can define 'ancestor' (perversely) so that each thing is an ancestor of itself. But this hardly shows that 'Some things are ancestors of themselves' is true, given what the sentence actually means.

[N]either the use of plurals nor the employment of second-order logic commits us to the existence of extra items beyond those to which we already committed . . . We need not construe second-order quantifiers as ranging over anything other than the objects over which our first-order quantifiers range . . . a second-order quantifier needn't be taken to be a kind of first-order quantifier in disguise, having items of a special kind, collections, in its range. It is not as though there were two sorts of things in the world, individuals and collections of them, which our first- and second-order variables, respectively, denote. There are, rather, two (at least) different ways of referring to the same things, among which there may well be many, many collections. (Boolos, 1998: 72)

A priori, there is no reason for thinking that plural reference and second-order quantification can be reduced to singular reference and first-order quantification. Other things equal, one might prefer a theory that provides such a reduction; but other things may not be equal. And this kind of reduction is not the only theoretical virtue, especially if we are talking about theories of *meaning* for natural language. It is a hypothesis that speakers understand plural constructions in terms of singular reference and first-order quantification over plural entities. Many examples, like (14–17) above, tell against this hypothesis.[12] But as the last line in the quote suggests, the point is *not* that we should avoid quantification over sets.

Ontological parsimony is not my concern. There are endlessly many sets, each of which is related in an intimate way to its elements. The question is how to specify the semantic properties of linguistic expressions in a theoretically perspicuous, descriptively adequate way. In my view, we get a better theory by specifying Values in terms of distinctively plural quantification over whatever we quantify over when we employ singular quantification—as opposed to specifying Values in terms of singular quantification over distinctively plural entities whose elements are the things we quantify over when employing singular quantification. But we can

---

[12] I think '$\exists x \exists y (x \neq y \ \& \ x \notin x \ \& \ y \notin y)$' mischaracterizes the semantic structure of 'Some things are not elements of themselves'. But my point *here* concerns the interpretation of (22), not the inadequacy of first-order representations.

quantify, singularly or plurally, over many things: individuals, events, sentential Values, ordered pairs of such things, collections of such things, etc.

A technical matter: we must decide whether or not '$\exists X[\forall x (Xx \leftrightarrow \Phi x)]$' implies that there are *at least two* things$_X$ such that each of them$_X$ is $\Phi$. We could define '$\exists X$' so that '$\exists X[\forall x (Xx \leftrightarrow \Phi x)]$' implies '$\exists x \exists y(\Phi x\ \&\ \Phi y\ \&\ x \neq y)$'. But we can also gloss '$\exists X$' informally as 'there are some things$_X$', and spell this out officially as 'there are one or more things$_X$'. Then we can let 'Plural(X)' mean, nonredundantly, that the Xs are more than one. Like Boolos, I don't think much hangs on this. Though as the formalism is used here, '$\exists X{:}\mathrm{Plural}(X)[\forall x(Xx \leftrightarrow \Phi x)]$' implies '$\exists X[\forall x(Xx \leftrightarrow \Phi x)]$', but not conversely. Correlatively, $\exists X{:}\neg\mathrm{Plural}(X)[\forall x(Xx \leftrightarrow \Phi x)]$ iff $\exists x[\Phi x\ \&\ \forall y(\Phi y \to y = x)]$. Hence, $\exists X[\forall x(Xx \leftrightarrow \Phi x)]$ iff $\exists x\Phi x$; there are one or more $\Phi$s iff there is a $\Phi$. From this perspective, lower-case '$x$' is a variable marked as singular. The restricted upper-case variable '$X{:}\mathrm{Plural}(X)$' is marked as plural. Unrestricted upper-case '$X$' is neutral. But the variable pronounced 'eks' ranges over whatever it ranges over, regardless of font-size. Orthographic distinctions need not reflect ontological distinctions.[13]

## 2.3. *Plural Quantification and Determiners*

Given plural quantification, Conjunctivists can treat determiners as plural predicates. Let 'Internal(O, X)' mean that the Xs are the internal participants of the Os. If only for simplicity, assume that each thing with an internal participant has exactly one, and likewise

---

[13] Even if there are no natural language analogs of neutral '$X$'—cf. Neale (1990) on numberless descriptions—there are analogs of singular and plural variables: the person$_x$ who$_x$ thinks I like him$_x$ admires the people$_X$ who$_X$ think we like them$_X$. One cannot take it as given that 'who$_x$' and 'who$_X$' range over different things, with the latter ranging over collections. Prima facie, it seems wrong to say that 'who$_X$' ranges over people if 'people' indicates a collection. Even if one specifies the meaning of 'ranges over' in terms of a technical locution 'ranges-over*', so that a variable ranges over a collection C iff it ranges-over* the elements of C, one must also specify the meaning of 'elements' in a similar way; etc.

for 'External(O, X)'. Then whatever the Os are—events, or ordered pairs of some kind—

$$\text{External(O, X) iff } \forall o{:}Oo\{\exists x[\text{External}(o, x) \ \& \ Xx]\} \ \& $$
$$\forall x{:}Xx\{\exists o[\text{External}(o, x) \ \& \ Oo]\}; \text{and}$$
$$\text{Internal(O, X) iff } \forall o{:}Oo\{\exists x[\text{Internal}(o, x) \ \& \ Xx]\} \ \& $$
$$\forall x{:}Xx\{\exists o[\text{Internal}(o, x) \ \& \ Oo]\}.$$

So 'Internal' and 'External' do not signify essentially second-order *relations*. And suppose that Val(O, every$_{\Lambda*}$) iff $\forall o{:}Oo[\text{Frege-Pair}(o)$ & External(o, **t**)]. In other words, suppose that some things$_O$ are Values of every$_{\Lambda*}$ iff every one of them$_O$ is a Frege-Pair with **t** as its external participant.

Then a Conjunctivist could say that $\langle[[\text{every}_{\Lambda*} \ \text{int-bottle}_\Pi]_\Lambda \ \text{ext-fell}_\Pi]\rangle$, gets the Value **t** iff

$$\exists O\langle\text{Val(O, every}_{\Lambda*}) \ \& \ \exists X\{\text{Internal(O, X)} \ \& \ \forall x[Xx \leftrightarrow$$
$$\text{Val}(x, \text{bottle}_\Pi)]\} \ \& \ \forall o{:}Oo\{\text{External}(o, \textbf{t}) \leftrightarrow$$
$$\exists x[\text{Internal}(o, x) \ \& \ \text{Val}(x, \text{fell}_\Pi)]\}\rangle.$$

This looks worse than it is. It just says that some things$_O$ are such that: they$_O$ are Values of every$_{\Lambda*}$ —i.e. every one of them$_O$ is of the form $<\textbf{t}, x>$; their$_O$ internal participants are the bottles; and each of them$_O$ has **t** as its external participant iff its internal participant fell. Note that '$\exists X\{\text{Internal(O, X)} \ \& \ \forall x[Xx \leftrightarrow \text{Val}(x, \text{bottle}_\Pi)]\}$' is a predicate of the form '$\Phi(O)$', equivalent to '$\iota X{:} \text{Bottle(X)}[\text{Internal(O, X)}]$', meaning that the bottles are the internal participants of the Os. As we'll see, this corresponds to a plausible hypothesis about the significance of being a determiner's internal argument.

Likewise, '$\forall o{:}Oo\{\text{External}(o, \textbf{t}) \leftrightarrow \exists x[\text{Internal}(o, x) \ \& \ \text{Val}(x, \text{fell}_\Pi)]\}$' is of the form '$\Phi(O)$'. This predicate imposes the condition that each O be of the form $<\textbf{t}, x>$ or $<\textbf{f}, x>$, depending on whether or not x fell. This is important, though it is not yet a satisfactory way of encoding the significance of being a determiner's external argument. The notation suggests that being an external argument differs in kind, and differs in an *ad hoc* way, from being an internal argument. But this appearance will dissipate when we drop the pretense that fell$_{\Pi}$, as opposed to the corresponding open sentence, is the internal argument of every$_{A^*}$. For now, the important point is that '$\exists O[Val(O,$ every$_{A^*}$) & ... O ... ]' can be interpreted as plural quantification over Frege-Pairs, instead of singular quantification over ordered pairs of *extensions*. And as desired, 'Every set is a set' gets the Value $t$, trivially. Given any one of the Frege-Pairs that associates a set with $t$ iff that set is a set, the Frege-Pair associates something with $t$.

For simplicity, let's say that Val(O, every$_{A^*}$) iff $\forall o:Oo[$External $(o, t)]$, suppressing the restriction to Frege-Pairs. (In the end, this restriction would be redundant anyway.) There are, of course, many ways of saying that every O has $t$ as its external participant: $\neg\exists o[Oo$ & $\exists x(o = <f, x>)]$; zero is the number of Os whose external participant is $f$; etc. I take no stand on *how* the meanings of determiners should be specified, so long as their Values are Frege-Pairs. And let me stress: the hypothesis is that, for purposes of *compositional* semantics, every$_{A^*}$ is interpreted as a second-order monadic predicate. But the condition that every$_{A^*}$ imposes on its Values is a condition that can be, and perhaps should be, expressed in first-order terms. Similarly, Val(O, no$_{A^*}$) iff not one of the Os has $t$ as its external participant. But so far as Conjunctivism is concerned, it doesn't matter how we formalize the right side of this biconditional: $\neg\exists o:Oo[$External$(o, t)]$; $\forall o:Oo[$External$(o, f)]$; $|Y: \forall o[Yo \leftrightarrow Oo$ & External$(o, t)]| = 0$, where '$|Y: ... Y ...|$' signifies *the number of* the Ys that satisfy the relevant condition; etc.

Given some Frege-Pairs, they are Values of most$_{A^*}$ iff most of them have $t$ as their external participant. For finite domains, the Os are Values of most$_{A^*}$ iff there is a one-to-one correspondence between *some of* the Os with $t$ as external participant and *all of* the Os with $f$ as external participant. This condition can be described as follows, whether or not this is a good lexical specification:

$$\exists Y \exists N \exists Z \forall o\{[Yo \leftrightarrow Oo \text{ & External}(o, t)] \text{ & } [No \leftrightarrow Oo \text{ & }$$
$$\text{Value}(o, f)] \text{ & } (Zo \rightarrow Yo) \text{ & } \exists x(Yx \text{ & } \neg Zx) \text{ & }$$
$$\text{One-to-One}(Z, N)\}.$$

Infinite domains require appeal to cardinalities: the Os with $t$ as external participant *outnumber* the Os with $f$ as external participant.

Rewriting a "generalized quantifier" treatment of most$_{\Delta^*}$ (cf. Barwise and Cooper (1981)), we can say that the Os are Values of most$_{\Delta^*}$ iff $|Y: \forall o[Yo \leftrightarrow Oo \ \& \ \text{External}(o, \mathbf{t})]| > |N: \forall o[No \leftrightarrow Oo \ \& \ \text{External}(o, \mathbf{f})]|$. But even if the meaning of most$_{\Delta^*}$ is specified in terms of cardinalities, the determiner's Values can be Frege-Pairs.

The hypothesis is that semantic composition treats most$_{\Delta^*}$ and every$_{\Delta^*}$ as plural monadic predicates. But this leaves room for the fact that most$_{\Delta^*}$ imposes a condition on its Values that differs in kind from the condition imposed by 'every'. Given some things$_O$ that are Values of every$_{\Delta^*}$, each and any of them$_O$ are Values of every$_{\Delta^*}$; likewise for no$_{\Delta^*}$. But given some things$_O$ that are Values of most$_{\Delta^*}$, no one of them$_O$ is, and some of them$_O$ can (together) fail to be Values of most$_{\Delta^*}$. In this sense, the proposal is that most$_{\Delta^*}$ is an essentially plural but still semantically monadic predicate.

With regard to 'some', which can combine with a singular or plural noun, multiple strategies may be appropriate. For the sound(s) of 'some'—often pronounced 'sm', as in 'Sm bottles fell'—may reflect more than one sentence-type. And in thinking about what Conjunctivists ought to say, it is worth remembering why we are discussing quantificational constructions: initially, 'Every bottle fell' seems to present a difficulty for the idea that sentential constituents are conjoinable monadic predicates subject to existential closure. But 'Some bottle(s) fell' does not obviously present the same problem. Still, it is worth noting the resources available to Conjunctivists for describing quantificational meanings.

Perhaps 'some' (or at least 'sm') is not a determiner that takes two predicative arguments, but simply an indefinite article that turns a predicate like 'bottle' into an argument, with the article marking number.[14] Conjunctivists can say that $\langle [(\text{sm}_{+\text{pl}} \ \text{bottles}_\Pi)_\alpha$

---

[14] For these purposes, I am using 'determiner' primarily to signify second-order transitive predicates like 'every' that apparently require a pair of predicative arguments. But we are still pretending that the Values of 'fell' are individuals, not events. Compare the treatment of 'Pat is a linguist' in Ch. 1. And note that 'some' is semantically symmetric in a way that 'every' is not: if some bottle fell, then something that fell is a bottle. For relevant discussion, see Kamp (1981), Heim (1982), Higginbotham (1989), and the other essays in Reuland and ter Meulen (1989).

fell$_\Pi$]$_{\Pi P}\rangle$ gets the Value **t** iff $\exists X[\text{Plural}(X)$ & Val$(X,\text{bottle}_\Pi)$ & Val$(X,\text{fell}_\Pi)]$. But we can also treat 'some' as a determiner that takes singular and plural forms: Val$(O,\text{some}_{\Delta^*-\text{pl}})$ iff $\exists o{:}Oo$ [External$(o,\textbf{t})]$; Val$(O,\text{some}_{\Delta^*+\text{pl}})$ iff $\exists o\exists p[Oo$ & $Op$ & $o \neq p$ & External$(o,\textbf{t})$ & External$(p,\textbf{t})]$. And of course, there are many ways of specifying these conditions. For example, Val$(O,\text{some}_{\Delta^*+\text{pl}})$ iff $\exists Y\{\text{Plural}(Y)$ & $\forall o[Yo \leftrightarrow Oo$ & External$(o,\textbf{t})]\}$. Similar remarks apply to 'nine', in 'Nine bottles fell', which could be analyzed as '$\exists X[\text{Nine}(X)$ & ... ]'; where the Xs are (exactly) nine iff $\exists Y\exists Z$ $\{\text{Eight}(Y)$ & $\neg\text{Plural}(Z)$ & $\forall x[Xx \leftrightarrow (Yx \lor Zz)]$ & $\forall x(Yx \rightarrow \neg Zx)\}$. Likewise for 'eight', and so on, with the Xs being one iff $\neg\text{Plural}(X)$.

This doesn't yet deal with the collective/distributive ambiguity of examples like 'Nine boys ate four pizzas'; see §5.[15] The point is simply that some uses of numerals may not *require* plural quantification over Frege-Pairs. If 'nine' can be an indefinite article, perhaps $\langle[(\text{nine bottles}_\Pi)_\alpha \text{ fell}_\Pi]_{\Pi P}\rangle$ gets the Value **t** iff some things$_X$ are such that: they$_X$ are nine bottles, and they$_X$ fell. Likewise, perhaps a thousand rocks rained down iff some things$_X$ are such that: they$_X$ are a thousand rocks, and they$_X$ rained down. The difference being that if some things$_X$ fell, each of them$_X$ fell; but given what 'rained down' means, some things$_X$ can rain down, even though no one of them$_X$ rained down.

That said, 'Nine boys ate four pizzas' does have a distributive reading on which it implies that each of nine boys ate four pizzas. And Conjunctivists can treat 'nine' (sometimes) as a determiner, with $\langle[[\text{nine}_{\Delta^*} \text{ int-bottles}_\Pi] \text{ ext-fell}_\Pi]\rangle$ having the Value **t** iff

$$\exists O\langle\text{Val}(O,\text{nine}_{\Delta^*}) \ \& \ \exists X\{\text{Internal}(O,X) \& \forall x[Xx \leftrightarrow$$
$$\text{Val}(x,\text{bottle}_\Pi)]\} \ \& \ \forall o{:}Oo\{\text{External}(o,\textbf{t}) \leftrightarrow$$
$$\exists x[\text{Internal}(o,x) \ \& \ \text{Val}(x,\text{fell}_\Pi)]\}\rangle;$$

---

[15] Given the simplifying assumption that some things$_X$ are Values of bottle$_\Pi$ iff each of them$_X$ is a bottle, Bottles$(X)$ iff $\forall x{:}Xx[\text{Bottle}(x)]$. Given a similar qualification, Fell$(X)$ iff $\forall x{:}Xx[\text{Fell}(x)]$. But the idea, developed in §4, will be that 'ate four pizzas' can be interpreted as a predicate $\Pi$ such that *some events of eating are Values* of it iff they (together) have four pizzas as their Themes.

where Val(O, Nine$_{\Delta*}$) iff $\exists Y\{\forall o[Yo \leftrightarrow Oo$ & External(o, **t**)] & Nine(Y)\}.

Since '$\exists X:\forall x(Xx \leftrightarrow \Phi x)$' means that there are *the* $\Phi s$, Conjunctivism as developed here allows for more than one way of thinking about expressions like 'the bottles'. We can treat 'the' as a determiner that has the Os as Values iff: each O with a relevant internal participant has the form $<$**t**, x$>$; Val(O, the$_\Delta$) iff $\exists R\langle \forall o$ {Ro $\leftrightarrow$ Oo & $\exists x[$Internal(o, x) & Relevant(x)]\} & $\forall o$:Ro[External (o, **t**)]$\rangle$, adding 'Plural(R)' or '$\neg$Plural(R)' as appropriate. But we can also treat 'the' as a *definite* article, saying that Val(X, [the bottles$_\Pi]_\alpha$) iff Plural(X) & $\forall x[Xx \leftrightarrow$ Relevant(x) & Val(x, bottle$_\Pi$)]. This corresponds to the so-called maximizing effect of definite descriptions, which are obviously like names in many respects.[16] Conjunctivists are thus free to hypothesize that 'the' is a special word often used, not as a monadic predicate, but rather as a device for converting a predicate into an argument.

One might even take the definite article as primitive, and use it to define 'Internal(O, X)' and 'External(O, X)'. I take no firm stand on these issues. My reason for surveying these options is to show that Conjunctivists can treat 'every' and 'most' as determiners, whose Values are Frege-Pairs, without insisting that 'the' and 'some' should always be analyzed in this same way—namely, as expressions that take internal and external arguments.

# 3. Compositional Details

In §4 I offer arguments in favor of treating determiners as predicates of Frege-Pairs. But it still has to be shown that Conjunctivists can adopt this hypothesis while treating verbs like fell$_\Pi$ as predicates of *events*. Specialists will also want to see how the proposal handles sentences with more than one determiner. To address these matters, I must first generalize the treatment of grammatical arguments in

---

[16] See Dowty (1987). For related discussion, see Schwartzschild (1996).

Chapter 1, in order to allow for semantically variable expressions like the demonstratives in (23–5).

(23)   Brutus wrote this

(24)   That fell off that

(25)   They wrote them

The result will be some general claims about the significance of being an internal or external argument. And it is worth being explicit about how the proposal does and does not differ from more familiar alternatives. Readers less concerned with formal issues can skim this moderately technical section.

## 3.1. *Relativizing Values to Assignments*

Tarski (1933, 1944) showed how to assign Values to expressions that contain variables by *relativizing* Values to *assignments* of Values to variables. And given Boolos-style plural quantification, a plural variable can have many Values relative to an assignment.

Recall that $\exists x[Val(x, Brutus_\alpha)]$ iff $\exists X\{\forall x[Xx \leftrightarrow Val(x, Brutus_\alpha)]\}$. Even if $Brutus_\alpha$ has exactly one Value, $\exists X[Val(X, Brutus_\alpha)]$; where $Val(X, \ldots_\alpha)$ iff $\forall x:Xx[Val(x, \ldots_\alpha)]$. In general, given one or more things$_X$, they$_X$ are Values of argument $\alpha$ iff each of them$_X$ is a Value of $\alpha$. Plural demonstratives are obvious candidates for arguments with multiple Values. But to talk sensibly about the Values of demonstratives, we must encode their context-sensitivity. For words like 'this' and 'them' have Values only relative to potential contexts in which things are demonstrated; see §2.3 of the introduction. No thing$_x$ is such that $Val(x, this_\alpha)$. Likewise, no things$_X$ are such that $Val(X, them_\alpha)$. And a sentence may contain more than one occurrence of a demonstrative, as in (24), with the occurrences used to talk about different things. So let's assume (standardly) that in any sentence, each occurrence of a demonstrative has its own index; and that indexed expressions have Values only *relative to assignments*.

The indexed grammatical structures of (23) and (25) are indicated below.

$$\langle[\text{ext-Brutus}_\alpha[\text{wrote}_{\Pi^*}\ \text{int-this}_{\alpha 1}]_\Pi]_{\Pi P}\rangle$$

$$\langle[\text{ext-They}_{\alpha 2}[\text{wrote}_{\Pi^*}\ \text{int-them}_{\alpha 1}]_\Pi]_{\Pi P}\rangle$$

We can encode the relativization of Values by treating 'Val' henceforth as a ternary predicate, with 'Val(X, $\Sigma$, **A**)' meaning that the Xs are Values of expression $\Sigma$ relative to assignment **A**, allowing for the possibility that there is exactly one X. Then we can say that for any assignment **A** and index $i$:

$$\text{Val}(X, \text{this}_{\alpha i}, \mathbf{A}) \text{ iff } \neg \text{Plural}(X) \ \&$$
$$\forall x[Xx \leftrightarrow \text{Associates}(\mathbf{A}, \ i, x)]$$
$$\text{Val}(X, \text{them}_{\alpha i}, \mathbf{A}) \text{ iff } \text{Plural}(X) \ \&$$
$$\forall x[Xx \leftrightarrow \text{Associates}(\mathbf{A}, \ i, x)];$$

where 'Associates(**A**, $i$, x)' means that **A** associates $i$ with x. It follows that Val(X, $\text{this}_{\alpha 1}$, **A**) only if **A** associates the first index with exactly one thing. But by drawing on Boolos (1998), we can allow for assignments that associate an index with many things. For any index $i$, if some things$_X$ can be demonstrated, there is an assignment that associates $i$ with each of them$_X$ (and nothing else). So if some things are Values of them$_{\alpha 1}$ relative to **A**, then **A** associates the first index with more than one thing: Val(X, $\text{them}_{\alpha 1}$, **A**), iff Plural(X) & $\forall x[Xx \leftrightarrow \text{Associates}(\mathbf{A}, 1, x)]$.

This leaves room for a singular relation among assignments, indices, and things. We can say that

$$\exists x\{\text{Anchors}(\mathbf{A}, i, x) \ \& \ \forall y[\text{Anchors}(\mathbf{A}, i, y) \rightarrow y = x \ \&$$
$$\text{Associates}(\mathbf{A}, i, y)]\};$$

where 'Anchors(**A**, $i$, x)' means that **A** anchors $i$ to x. And we can say that **A**$i$ is *the* individual to which **A** anchors $i$. An assignment *anchors* each index to exactly one thing, even if the assignment *associates* the index with additional things. For illustration, consider an assignment **A**$^*$ that anchors each index to an American president: '1' to Washington, '2' to Adams, etc. And suppose that **A**$^*$ associates each index with nothing else. Many assignments are not, in this sense, mere *sequences* of individuals. Let **A**$^{*1(2)}$ be the assignment just like **A**$^*$ except that it associates '1' with both Washington and Adams. Similarly, **A**$^{*1(3)}$ associates '1' with Washington and Jefferson;

$\mathbf{A}^{*1(3,\ 16)}$ associates '1' with Washington, Jefferson, and Lincoln; etc. Let $\mathbf{A}^{*2(16)}$ be the assignment just like $\mathbf{A}^*$ except that it associates '2' with Adams and Lincoln; $\mathbf{A}^{*1(16),\ 2(3)}$ associates '1' with Washington and Lincoln, and '2' with Adams and Jefferson; etc.

Relativizing to (mere) sequences would effectively assume that each variable has exactly one Value relative to each assignment, as in Tarski's (1933) treatment of first-order logic. Relativizing in this singular way is fine as a simplification; for illuminating discussion, see Davies (1981), Larson and Segal (1995). But as Boolos (1998) showed, we can generalize the strategy to plural variables without saying that a plural variable has a collection as its Value relative to each relevant assignment. Intuitively, each occurrence of a demonstrative corresponds to a potential act of *pointing at* one or more things. And a language user can point at some things without pointing at a collection. There is a perfectly fine sense in which one can (intentionally) demonstrate some things without demonstrating the collection of those things. The corresponding idea is that an assignment $\mathbf{A}$ of Values to variables can associate a plural variable $\nu_{+\mathrm{pl}}$ with some Values even if $\mathbf{A}$ does not associate $\nu_{+\mathrm{pl}}$ with any collection.[17]

---

[17] But to repeat an earlier point, the issue is not ontological. There are assignments that anchor indices to plural entities, corresponding to demonstrations of such entities. But a plural variable can have many Values, each of which is a singular entity. We must also leave room for uses of demonstratives that correspond to acts of demonstrating *nothing*. But following Strawson (1950) and Burge (1974), we can say that, if a speaker uses a demonstrative with index $i$ in conversational situation C, then an assignment of A of Values to variables is *relevant to* C only if A associates $i$ with all and only those things demonstrated by the speaker in some act of demonstration corresponding to $i$. In which case, if the speaker demonstrated nothing in C, no assignment is relevant to C. So if a sentential utterance is true or false only if it is true or false relative to some relevant assignment, cases of failed demonstration will correspond to utterances that are neither true nor false, even though the sentence gets the Value **t** or **f** relative to each assignment. Appeal to assignments that associate an index with many things also lets us preserve the idea, defended by Link (1983, 1998) and others, that *lattice structures* are relevant to the semantics of plural noun-phrases (and mass terms). Corresponding to each sequence that associates exactly one thing x with index $i$, there will be many assignments that associate $i$ with x and other things. And these assignments will correspond to the lattice structure involving x and these other things.

Complex predicates like [wrote$_{\Pi^*}$ this$_{\alpha_1}$]$_\Pi$—or, replacing the phrasal subscript with an explicit mark of the grammatical relation, [wrote$_{\Pi^*}$ int-this$_{\alpha_1}$]—inherit semantic variability from their constituents. The corresponding hypothesis is that relative to any assignment, some things$_O$ are Values of an expression *appearing as a potentially indexed internal argument* iff their$_O$ internal participants are (all and only) the Values of the expression. That is, for any index $i$,

$$\text{Val}(O, \text{int-} \ldots {}_{\alpha i}, \mathbf{A}) \text{ iff } \exists X\{\text{Internal}(O, X) \ \& $$
$$\forall x[Xx \leftrightarrow \text{Val}(x, \ldots {}_{\alpha i}, \mathbf{A})]\}.$$

Compare the analogous principle from Chapter 1, which presupposed singular arguments with exactly one (assignment-invariant) argument: Val(o, int-$\ldots{}_\alpha$) iff $\forall$x[Internal(o, x) & Val(x, $\ldots{}_\alpha$)]. Similarly,

$$\text{Val}(O, \text{ext-} \ldots {}_{\alpha i}, \mathbf{A}) \text{ iff } \exists X\{\text{External}(O, X) \ \& $$
$$\forall x[Xx \leftrightarrow \text{Val}(x, \ldots {}_{\alpha i}, \mathbf{A})]\}.$$

Recall that External(O, X) iff the Xs are the external participants of the Os, where there may be exactly one X. And for any assignment $\mathbf{A}$, Val(x, Brutus$_\alpha$, $\mathbf{A}$) iff x is **Brutus**. Hence, Val(O, ext-Brutus$_\alpha$, $\mathbf{A}$) iff $\exists$X{External(O, X) & $\forall$x[Xx $\leftrightarrow$ x = **Brutus**]}. But Val(O, ext-They$_{\alpha 1}$, $\mathbf{A}$) iff $\exists$X{External(O, X) & $\forall$x[Xx $\leftrightarrow$ Associates ($\mathbf{A}$, 1, x)]}. This attributes nontrivial significance to certain grammatical relations. Though as we saw in Chapter 1, attributing significance to some relations is unavoidable; the questions concern which relations. And by treating grammatical arguments as second-order predicates, Conjunctivists significantly increase the empirical scope of their theory.

We could start to describe the context-sensitive semantic contribution of tense in wrote$_{\Pi^*}$ by saying that each assignment is associated with a time, and that Val(O, wrote$_{\Pi^*}$, $\mathbf{A}$) iff each of the Os was an event of writing that occurred prior to the time associated with $\mathbf{A}$. Though for simplicity, let's just say that Val(O, wrote$_{\Pi^*}$, $\mathbf{A}$) iff Past-Writing(O), meaning that every one of the Os was an event of writing. Given second-order variables and relativization to assignments, we need appropriate Conjunctivist composition principles. But these are easily provided:

$$\text{Val}(O, \Phi{}^\wedge\Psi, \mathbf{A}) \text{ iff } \text{Val}(O, \Phi, \mathbf{A}) \ \& \ \text{Val}(O, \Psi, \mathbf{A}); \text{ and}$$

$$\text{Val}(\mathbf{t}, \langle[\ldots]\rangle, \mathbf{A}) \text{ iff } \exists O[\text{Val}(O, \ldots, \mathbf{A})].$$

Relative to $\mathbf{A}$, some things$_O$ are Values of the complex expression $\Phi{}^\wedge\Psi$ iff they$_O$ are Values of each concatenate, and an expression labelled as a sentence gets the Value $\mathbf{t}$ iff the expression has a Value. For example, $\text{Val}(\mathbf{t}, \langle[\text{ext-Brutus}_\alpha \ [\text{wrote}_{\Pi*} \ \text{int-this}_{\alpha 1}]]\rangle, \mathbf{A})$ iff:

$$\exists O\langle\exists X\{\text{External}(O, X) \ \& \ \forall x[Xx \leftrightarrow \text{Val}(x, \text{Brutus}_\alpha, \mathbf{A})]\} \ \&$$

$$\text{Past-Writing}(O) \ \& \ \exists X\{\text{Internal}(O, X) \ \&$$

$$\neg\text{Plural}(X) \ \& \ \forall x[Xx \leftrightarrow \text{Associates}(\mathbf{A}, 1, x)]\}\rangle;$$

some things$_O$ were such that their$_O$ external participants were none other than **Brutus**, they$_O$ were events of writing, and their$_O$ internal participants were none other than the one thing associated with the first index. Likewise, $\text{Val}(\mathbf{t}, \langle[\text{ext-they}_{\alpha 2} \ [\text{wrote}_{\Pi*} \ \text{int-them}_{\alpha 1}]]\rangle, \mathbf{A})$ iff:

$$\exists O\langle\exists X\{\text{External}(O, X) \ \& \ \text{Plural}(X) \ \& \ \forall x[Xx \leftrightarrow$$

$$\text{Associates}(\mathbf{A}, 2, x)]\} \ \& \ \text{Past-Writing}(O) \ \&$$

$$\exists X\{\text{Internal}(O, X) \ \& \ \text{Plural}(X) \ \&$$

$$\forall x[Xx \leftrightarrow \text{Associates}(\mathbf{A}, 1, x)]\}\rangle;$$

some things$_O$ were such that their$_O$ external participants were the "2-associates" of $\mathbf{A}$, they$_O$ were events of writing, and their$_O$ internal participants were the "1-associates" of $\mathbf{A}$.

Given that the external/internal participants of events are Agents/ Themes, $\text{Val}(\mathbf{t}, \langle[\text{ext-Brutus}_\alpha \ [\text{wrote}_{\Pi*} \ \text{int-this}_{\alpha 1}]]\rangle, \mathbf{A})$ iff there was at least one writing whose Agent was **Brutus** and whose Theme was *the* 1-associate of $\mathbf{A}$. Likewise, $\text{Val}(\mathbf{t}, \langle[\text{ext-They}_{\alpha 2} \ [\text{wrote}_{\Pi*} \ \text{int-them}_{\alpha 1}]]\rangle, \mathbf{A})$ iff there were some events of writing whose Agents were the 2-associates and whose Themes were the 1-associates of $\mathbf{A}$.

This leaves room for the possibility that the Agents were ten professors, while the Themes were fifteen articles, each of which may or
may not have been coauthored. This makes it explicit that reports of
collective activity need not involve reference to (or quantification
over) collections. I return to this point.

Let me conclude this subsection, though, by noting that the
generalized Conjunctivist theory also applies to sentential argu-
ments as in ⟨[ext-⟨Pat sang⟩$_\alpha$ [or$_{\Pi^*}$ int-⟨Chris danced⟩$_\alpha$]]⟩; where
the underlining is simply a reminder that the relevant Values are
sentential. Relative to any assignment **A**,

$$\text{Val}(O, \text{ext-}\langle\text{Pat sang}\rangle_{\underline{\alpha}}, \mathbf{A}) \text{ iff } \exists X\{\text{External}(O, X) \ \&$$
$$\forall x[Xx \leftrightarrow \text{Val}(x, \langle\text{Pat sang}\rangle_{\underline{\alpha}}, \mathbf{A})]\};$$

some things$_O$ are Values of ⟨Pat sang⟩ *as an external argument* iff
their$_O$ external participants are the Values of ⟨Pat sang⟩. Since a
sentence has only one Value relative to any assignment, every Value of
ext-⟨Pat sang⟩$_\alpha$ will have the same external participant, **t** or **f**. Likewise
for internal arguments of sentential connectives. And each Value of
or$_{\Pi^*}$ has **t** as its internal or external participant: Val(O, or$_{\Pi^*}$, **A**) iff
∀o:Oo[∃v(o = <**t**, **v**> or o = <**v**, **t**>)]. Thus, Val(**t**, ⟨[ext-⟨Pat sang⟩$_\alpha$
[or$_{\Pi^*}$ int-⟨Chris danced⟩$_\alpha$ ]]⟩, **A**) iff one or more pairs of sentential
Values <**v**, **v'**> are such that: **v** is the Value of ⟨Pat sang⟩; **v** = **t** or
**v'** = **t**; and **v'** is the Value of ⟨Chris danced⟩.[18]

The general principle, which is the Conjunctivist's auxiliary
hypothesis about arguments, is that

$$\text{Val}(O, \text{ext/int-}\ldots_{\alpha i}, \mathbf{A}) \text{ iff } \exists X\{\text{External/Internal}(O, X) \ \&$$
$$\forall x[Xx \leftrightarrow \text{Val}(x, \ldots_{\alpha i}, \mathbf{A})]\}.$$

---

[18] Similarly, Val(**t**, ⟨[ext-⟨She₁ sang⟩$_\alpha$ [or$_{\Pi^*}$ int-⟨He₂ danced⟩$_\alpha$]]⟩, **A**) iff the (female)
1-associate of **A** sang or the (male) 2-associate of **A** danced. One can account for the
gender content in Conjunctivist terms by saying that for any index *i*, Val(x, DEM$_i$, **A**)
iff Val(x, DEM, **A**) & Associates(**A**, *i*, x); where Val(x, 'she', **A**) iff x is female, and Val(x,
'he', **A**) iff x is male. Perhaps one can capture the *joint* significance of a grammatical
relation and a name in first-order terms. But it doesn't follow that the significance of
the grammatical relation can itself be captured in first-order terms.

The advantage of second-order notation lies with plural predicates and arguments that have many Values. But since we can use plural variables without assuming that they range over collections, we are free to use 'O' and 'X' even when characterizing the Values of sentential connectives and singular arguments. And if the Values of determiners are Frege-Pairs, the principle above applies equally well to internal arguments of determiners: Val(O, int-$\ldots$ $_\Pi$, **A**) iff $\exists X\{$Internal(O, X) & $\forall x[Xx \leftrightarrow$ Val(x, $\ldots$ $_\Pi$, **A**)]$\}$. So the next task is to bring external arguments of determiners into the fold.

## 3.2. *Quantifier-Raising*

We can and now should abandon the pretense that [[every$_{\Delta^*}$ int-bottle$_\Pi$] ext-fell$_\Pi$] is an expression of natural language, in favor of a more plausible view: the external argument of a determiner is an *open sentence* from which the determiner (along with its internal argument) has been displaced; and the Value of an open sentence is **t** or **f**, relative to an assignment to Values of variables.

Suppose that the grammatical structure of (2) is as shown in (2G),

(2)    Every bottle fell
(2G)    $\langle$[[every$_{\Delta^*}$ bottle$_\Pi$]$_{\Delta_1}$ $\langle$[t$_1$ fell$_\Pi$]$_{\Pi P}\rangle$]$_{\Delta P}\rangle$

where 't$_1$' indicates the inaudible but indexed trace of a displaced and coindexed determiner phrase, with '$\Delta$P' reflecting grammatical saturation of every$_{\Delta^*}$. Replacing phrasal subscripts with different marks of what is an argument of what, we can rewrite (2G) as follows: $\langle$[[every$_{\Delta^*}$ *int*-bottle$_\Pi$]$_1$ *ext*-$\langle$[int-t$_1$ fell$_\Pi$]$\rangle$]$\rangle$, using italics simply to highlight the determiner's arguments. This makes it explicit that fell$_\Pi$ also takes a grammatical argument—indeed, an internal argument (see §2.4 of Chapter 3). But the main assumption, however we code it, is that sentence (2) is a *transformed* expression (see §2.4 of the Introduction) with a sentential constituent. I won't review the evidence in favor of "quantifier raising" hypotheses with regard to sentences like (2).[19] For present purposes, I assume grammatical structures like (2G). But I will quickly sketch a certain rationale for quantifier raising, since it coheres nicely with the idea that fell$_\Pi$ is a predicate of events.

We cannot represent the grammatical structure of (2) as $\langle$[int-[every$_{\Lambda^*}$ *int*-bottle$_\Pi$] *ext*-fell$_\Pi$]$\rangle$. Even if natural language allows for this kind of "argument circle", in which the argument of the verb has a constituent that takes the verb as an argument, it would be an interpretive mess. Given Conjunctivist principles, the resulting structure would get the Value **t** iff some things$_O$ are such that their$_O$ internal participants are the Values of [every$_{\Lambda^*}$ *int*-bottle$_\Pi$]$_\Lambda$, and their$_O$ external participants are the Values of fell$_\Pi$. So let's assume that each expression consisting of a predicate and an argument is unambiguous with regard to which constituent is grammatically saturated by which.

If the Values of fell$_\Pi$ are events, then semantically, fell$_\Pi$ is not the external argument of every$_{\Lambda^*}$ in (2). Combining [every$_{\Lambda^*}$ bottle$_\Pi$]$_\Lambda$ with fell$_\Pi$ presumably saturates the verb. But the result, [[every$_{\Lambda^*}$ bottle$_\Pi$]$_\Lambda$ fell$_\Pi$]$_{\Pi P}$, may not be an expression. Perhaps every$_{\Lambda^*}$ needs an external argument marked as such, given that the order of its arguments matters semantically. If so, then [[every$_{\Lambda^*}$ bottle$_\Pi$]$_\Lambda$ fell$_\Pi$]$_{\Pi P}$ is not a grammatical way of associating a linguistic signal with a meaning, and neither is $\langle$[[every$_{\Lambda^*}$ bottle$_\Pi$]$_\Lambda$ fell$_\Pi$]$_{\Pi P}\rangle$. On this view, a possible combination of expressions can fail to be an expression. But this particular defect could be repaired, given a *transformational* grammar that allows for the displacement of [every$_{\Lambda^*}$ bottle$_\Pi$]$_\Lambda$ as indicated in (2G).

This line of thought is independent of present concerns; see Higginbotham (1985), Hornstein and Uriagereka (1999). But in Conjunctivist terms, and ignoring details not relevant here, the idea is that the predicate [[every$_{\Lambda^*}$ bottle$_\Pi$] fell$_\Pi$]$_{\Pi P}$ can be labelled as a sentence; though to create something fully interpretable, [every$_{\Lambda^*}$

---

[19] See May (1985), Higginbotham and May (1981), Huang (1982); see Huang (1995) and Hornstein (1995) for reviews. See Pietroski (2003*b*) for discussion in the context of questions about the relation of grammatical form to the traditional notion of logical form, and the relevance of appeals to Frege-Pairs as Values of determiners.

bottle$_\Pi$]$_\Delta$ is displaced, creating the predicate [[every$_{\Delta^*}$ bottle$_\Pi$]$_\Delta$ ⟨[t$_1$ fell$_\Pi$]$_{\Pi P}$⟩]$_{\Delta P}$; and this fully saturated expression can be labelled as a sentence and interpreted as such, via existential closure. On this conception of grammatical/semantic structure, a displaced quantificational subject Δ combines with a sentential expression corresponding to existential closure of the variable associated with the predicate that took Δ as an argument. Independent considerations suggest that raised subjects do indeed take scope over existential closure of "event" variables.[20] But for these purposes, I simply assume that the external argument of a raised subject is indeed sentential in this sense. And at least for now, let's extend this assumption to quantificational direct objects, taking the grammatical structure of 'Pat saw every cat' to be as follows: ⟨[[every$_{\Delta^*}$ int-cat$_\Pi$]$_{\Delta_1}$ *ext*-⟨[ext-Pat$_\alpha$ [saw$_{\Pi^*}$ int-t$_1$]]⟩]⟩; though this assumption is not necessary. (See Pietroski and Hornstein (2002) for discussion in first-order terms.)

With regard to interpretation, ⟨[int-t$_1$ fell$_\Pi$]⟩ invites treatment as an expression with a sentential Value *relative to* an assignment of Values to indices. We can encode this now standard view by saying that for any index *i*, Val(X, t$_i$, **A**) iff ¬Plural(X) & ∀x: Xx[Associates(**A**, *i*, x)]; or put another way, Val(X, t$_i$, **A**) iff ∀x(Xx ↔ x = **A***i*), where **A***i* is the individual to which **A** anchors index *i*. The trace of a displaced determiner phrase is thus interpreted as a singular variable; 't$_1$ fell' is interpreted like 'it$_1$ fell'. Following Boolos, I have simply detached this familiar and good idea from the further assumption that each assignment associates *every* index—even indices on plural demonstratives—with exactly

---

[20] Positing the structure [[every$_{\Delta^*}$ bottle$_\Pi$]$_\Delta$ [t$_1$ fell$_\Pi$]$_{\Pi P}$]$_{\Delta P}$ would yield the wrong interpretation on any account that treats [t$_1$ fell$_\Pi$]$_{\Pi P}$ as a predicate of events; and recall that Functionists must also appeal to existential closure of an event-variable. There are also independent reasons for adopting the following view: the phrase formed by a verb and its argument(s) is a constituent of a larger phrase containing various functional elements associated with tense and agreement features; displaced subjects occupy a 'higher' position than tense; existential closure of the event-variable is somehow associated with tense; and when tense markers appear on verbs, as morphemes, this is because verbs raise or the markers lower. (See Pollack (1989), Chomsky (1995, 2000*b*).)

one thing. So Val(**t**, $\langle$[int-t$_1$ fell$_\Pi$]$\rangle$, **A**) iff $\exists$O$\{\exists$X[Internal(O, X) & $\forall$x(Xx $\leftrightarrow$ x = **A1**)] & Past-Falling(O)$\}$. Given that Val(O, fell$_\Pi$, **A**) iff $\forall$o:Oo[Val(o, fell$_\Pi$, **A**)]—some events$_O$ are Values of fell$_\Pi$ iff each of them$_O$ was an event of falling (i.e. 'fell' differs from 'rained down' in this respect)—we can simplify, saying truly that Val(**t**, $\langle$[int-t$_1$ fell$_\Pi$]$\rangle$, **A**) iff **A1** fell.

Of course, a trace of displacement might not be the only indexed expression in a sentence. In 'Every cat saw it', the external argument of the displaced determiner will be the open sentence $\langle$[ext-t$_1$ [saw$_{\Pi^*}$ int-it$_2$]]$\rangle$, which has the Value **t** relative to assignment **A** iff: **A1** saw **A2**; or more elaborately, $\exists$O$\{\exists$X[External(O, X) & $\forall$x(Xx $\leftrightarrow$ x = **A1**)] & Past-Seeing(O) & $\exists$X[Internal(O, X) & $\forall$x(Xx $\leftrightarrow$ x = **A2**)]$\}$. But $\langle$[ext-It$_1$ [saw$_{\Pi^*}$ int-t$_2$]]$\rangle$, which is the obvious candidate for the external argument of every$_{\Delta^*}$ in 'It saw every cat', also has the Value **t** relative to **A** iff **A1** saw **A2**. And on any theory, we will need some way of indicating that the quantifier is linked to the position indexed with '2', as opposed to the position indexed with '1'. There are various ways of doing this. But for concreteness, let's mark external arguments of determiners as shown below; cf. Heim and Kratzer (1998).

$$\langle[[\text{every}_{\Delta^*} \text{ } \textit{int}\text{-bottle}_\Pi] \text{ } 1\text{-}\textit{ext}\text{-}\langle[\text{int-t}_1 \text{ fell}_\Pi]\rangle]\rangle$$

$$\langle[[\text{every}_{\Delta^*} \text{ } \textit{int}\text{-cat}_\Pi] \text{ } 1\text{-}\textit{ext}\text{-}\langle[\text{ext-t}_1[\text{saw}_{\Pi^*} \text{ int-it}_2]]\rangle]\rangle$$

$$\langle[[\text{every}_{\Delta^*} \text{ } \textit{int}\text{-cat}_\Pi] \text{ } 2\text{-}\textit{ext}\text{-}\langle[\text{ext-}\textit{It}_1[\text{saw}_{\Pi^*} \text{ int-}t_2]]\rangle]\rangle$$

The idea is that an external argument of a determiner is interpreted as the external argument of an expression displaced from a position associated with a certain index. So what we need is a composition principle that deals with phrases like 2-*ext*-$\langle$[ext-It$_1$ [saw$_{\Pi^*}$ int-t$_2$]]$\rangle$ and instances of 'Val(O, *i-ext*-$\langle \ldots \rangle$, **A**)'.

## 3.3. *Interpreting (Indexed) External Arguments*

It is not hard to formulate a suitably general principle according to which some things$_O$ are Values of 1-*ext*-$\langle$[int-t$_1$ fell$_\Pi$]$\rangle$ iff each of them$_O$ has **t** as its external participant iff its internal participant fell.

Given any entity x, the Value of $\langle[\text{int-t}_1 \text{ fell}_\Pi]\rangle$ with x assigned to the variable just is the Value of $\langle[\text{int-t}_1 \text{ fell}_\Pi]\rangle$ relative to an assignment **A** such that $x = \mathbf{A}1$. Correspondingly, we can speak of the Frege-Pairs$_O$ such that each$_o$ of them$_O$ meets the following condition: its$_o$ external participant is the Value of $\langle[\text{int-t}_1 \text{ fell}_\Pi]\rangle$ with its$_o$ internal participant x assigned to the singular variable; that is, its$_o$ external participant is the Value of $\langle[\text{int-t}_1 \text{ fell}_\Pi]\rangle$ relative to an assignment **A** such that $x = \mathbf{A}1$. And given any assignment **A**, we can speak of the Frege-Pairs$_O$ such that for each$_o$ of them$_O$: its$_o$ external participant x is the Value of $\langle[\text{int-t}_1 \text{ fell}_\Pi]\rangle$ relative to some assignment **A'** just like **A** except that $x = \mathbf{A}'1$.

This employs Tarski's (1933) notion of an assignment *variant*, generalized to assignments that associate some indices with many things. Let **A'** be an *i*-variant of **A**—abbreviating, $\mathbf{A}' \approx_i \mathbf{A}$—iff for any index apart from *i*, **A** and **A'** are alike. That is, $\mathbf{A}' \approx_i \mathbf{A}$ iff

$$\forall x \forall j{:}i \neq j\{[\text{Anchors}(\mathbf{A}, j, x) \leftrightarrow \text{Anchors}(\mathbf{A}', j, x)] \,\&$$
$$[\text{Associates}(\mathbf{A}, j, x) \leftrightarrow \text{Associates}(\mathbf{A}', j, x)]\}.$$

Apart from $\mathbf{A}'i$, *i*-associates will not be relevent. So

$$\text{Val}(\text{O}, i\text{-}ext\text{-}\langle\ldots\rangle, \mathbf{A}) \text{ iff}$$
$$\forall o{:}\text{Oo}\{\text{External}(o, \mathbf{t}) \leftrightarrow \exists \mathbf{A}'[\mathbf{A}' \approx_i \mathbf{A} \,\&$$
$$\text{Internal}(o, \mathbf{A}'i) \,\&\, \text{Val}(\mathbf{t}, \langle\ldots\rangle, \mathbf{A}')]\}.$$

After saying what this means, and showing that it delivers the desired results, I'll argue that this generalization about indexed external arguments is a consequence of more basic Conjunctivist principles, given some independently plausible assumptions about indexed expressions.

The generalization implies that some things$_O$ are Values of 1-*ext*-$\langle[\text{int-t}_1 \text{ fell}_\Pi]\rangle$ relative to **A** iff: each of them$_O$ is of the form $<\text{v}, \text{x}>$, with 'v' ranging over the sentential Values **t** and **f**; and **v** is the Value of $\langle[\text{int-t}_1 \text{ fell}_\Pi]\rangle$ relative to some assignment **A'** just like **A** except that $\mathbf{A}'1 = x$. Put another way, in a complex expression where the open sentence $\langle[\text{int-t}_1 \text{ fell}_\Pi]\rangle$ appears as the external argument of a predicate *that has been displaced from a position with index '1'*, some things$_O$ are Values of that sentential argument iff every one$_o$ of them$_O$ is such that: its$_o$ external participant is either **t** or **f**; and its$_o$ external participant is **t** iff its$_o$ internal participant fell. Likewise,

$$\text{Val}(O, 2\text{-}ext\text{-}\langle[\text{ext-it}_1[\text{saw}_{\Pi^*}\ \text{int-t}_2]]\rangle, \mathbf{A})\ \text{iff}$$

$$\forall o\text{:}\ Oo\{\text{External}(o, \mathbf{v}) \leftrightarrow$$

$$\exists \mathbf{A}'[\mathbf{A}' \approx_2 \mathbf{A}\ \&\ \text{Internal}(o, \mathbf{A}'2)\ \&$$

$$\text{Val}(\mathbf{v}, \langle[\text{ext-it}_1[\text{saw}_{\Pi^*}\ \text{int-t}_2]]\rangle, \mathbf{A}')]\}.$$

If $\langle[\text{ext-it}_1\ [\text{saw}_{\Pi^*}\ \text{int-t}_2]]\rangle$ is the external argument of a predicate displaced from a position with index '2', then the Os are Values of that sentential argument relative to **A** iff: every O is of the form $<\mathbf{v}, x>$, where **v** is the Value of $\langle[\text{ext-it}_1\ [\text{saw}_{\Pi^*}\ \text{int-t}_2]]\rangle$ relative to a 2-variant of **A** that anchors '2' to x; or more simply, every O is of the form $<\mathbf{v}, x>$, where $\mathbf{v} = \mathbf{t}$ iff **A1** saw x.

Replacing 'it$_1$' with another trace of displacement makes no difference in this respect. So Val(O, 2-*ext*-$\langle[\text{ext-t}_1\ [\text{saw}_{\Pi^*}\ \text{int-t}_2]]\rangle$, **A**) iff $\forall o\text{:}Oo\{\text{External}(o, \mathbf{t}) \leftrightarrow \exists x[\text{Internal}(o, x)\ \&\ \mathbf{A1}\ \text{saw}\ x]\}$; where **A1** saw x iff **A1** was the Agent of a seeing whose Theme was x. By contrast, Val(O, 1-*ext*-$\langle[\text{ext-t}_1\ [\text{saw}_{\Pi^*}\ \text{int-t}_2]]\rangle$, **A**) iff $\forall o\text{:}Oo\ \{\text{External}(o, \mathbf{t}) \leftrightarrow \exists x[\text{Internal}(o, x)\ \&\ x\ \text{saw}\ \mathbf{A2}]\}$. So the account covers sentences like (26), assuming the grammatical structure in (26G),

(26)    No dog saw every cat

(26G)    $\langle[[\text{No}_{\Delta^*}\ int\text{-}\text{dog}_\Pi]\ 1\text{-}ext\text{-}\langle[[\text{every}_{\Delta^*}\ int\text{-}\text{cat}_\Pi]$
         $2\text{-}ext\text{-}\langle[\text{ext-t}_1\ [\text{saw}_{\Pi^*}\ \text{int-t}_2]]\rangle\rangle]\rangle]\rangle$

with the external argument of 'No' being an open sentence in which the external argument of 'every' is an open sentence that has two variables. Given any assignment $\mathbf{A}'$,

$$\text{Val}(\mathbf{t}, \langle[[\text{every}_{\Delta^*}\ int\text{-}cat_\Pi]\ 2\text{-}ext\text{-}$$

$$\langle[\text{ext-t}_1\ [\text{saw}_{\Pi^*}\ \text{int-t}_2]]\rangle]\rangle, \mathbf{A}')\ \text{iff}$$

every cat is such that $\mathbf{A}'1$ saw it.

I'll spell this out more fully, in terms of Frege-Pairs, in a moment. But for any assignment **A**,

$$\text{Val}(\mathbf{t}, \langle[[\text{No}_{\text{A}*}\textit{int}\text{-dog}_{\Pi}]\ 1\text{-}ext\text{-}\langle\ldots\rangle]\rangle, \mathbf{A}) \text{ iff}$$

$$\exists O\{\text{Val}(O, [\text{No}_{\text{A}*}\textit{int}\text{-dog}_{\Pi}], \mathbf{A})\ \&\ \text{Val}(O, 1\text{-}ext\text{-}\langle\ldots\rangle, \mathbf{A})\}.$$

So (26) has the Value **t** relative to **A** iff some things$_O$ are such that: (i) none of them$_O$ has **t** as its external participant; (ii) their$_O$ internal participants are the dogs; and (iii) each of them$_O$ is of the form $<\mathbf{v}, \text{x}>$, with **v** as the Value of $\langle[[\text{every}_{\text{A}*}\ \textit{int}\text{-cat}_{\Pi}]\ 2\text{-}ext\text{-}\langle[\text{ext-t}_1\ [\text{saw}_{\Pi*}\ \text{int-t}_2]]\rangle]\rangle$ relative to a 1-variant of **A** that anchors '1' to x. Or spelling out clause (iii) explicitly, each of them$_O$ is of the form $<\mathbf{v}, \text{x}>$, where $\mathbf{v} = \mathbf{t}$ iff: relative to some **A'** such that $\text{x} = \mathbf{A'}1$ and $\mathbf{A'} \approx_1 \mathbf{A}$, there are some things$_{O'}$ such that (*a*) each of them$_{O'}$ has **t** as its external participant, (*b*) their$_{O'}$ internal participants are the cats, and (*c*) each of them$_{O'}$ is of the form $<\mathbf{v'}, \text{x'}>$, where **v'** is the Value of $\langle[\text{ext-t}_1\ [\text{saw}_{\Pi*}\ \text{int-t}_2]]\rangle$ relative to some **A''** such that $\text{x} = \mathbf{A''}(2)$ and $\mathbf{A''} \approx_2 \mathbf{A'}$.

By design, this is a minor variation on a Tarskian treatment of '$\forall\text{x}_1\exists\text{x}_2\text{Sx}_1\text{x}_2$', in terms of relativization to sequences.[21]

---

[21] Cf. Larson and Segal (1995). The small twists are that assignments can associate plural variables (but not traces of displacement) with more than one thing; the quantifiers are restricted; and they are treated as monadic predicates with Values. Following Tarski, we could say that '$\forall\text{x}_1\exists\text{x}_2\text{Sx}_1\text{x}_2$' is true relative to a sequence $\sigma$ iff for every 1-variant of $\sigma$, $\sigma'$, there is a 2-variant of $\sigma'$, $\sigma''$, such that '$\text{Sx}_1\text{x}_2$' is true relative to $\sigma''$; where '$\text{Sx}_1\text{x}_2$' is true relative to any sequence iff the first element of that sequence saw the second. But we could also stipulate a semantics for an invented language in which '$(\forall:D)_1(\exists:C)_2[\text{Sx}_1\text{x}_2]$' is true relative to a sequence $\sigma$ iff there are some ordered pairs such that (i) every one of them is of the form $<\mathbf{t}, \text{x}>$, and (ii) their internal participants are the dogs, and (iii) for each of them, $\mathbf{v} = \mathbf{t}$ iff x is the first element of a 1-variant of $\sigma$, $\sigma'$, such that '$(\exists:C)_2[\text{Sx}_1\text{x}_2]$' is true relative to $\sigma'$; where '$(\exists:C)_2[\text{Sx}_1\text{x}_2]$' is true relative to $\sigma'$ iff there are some ordered pairs such that (*a*) at least one of them is of the form $<\mathbf{t}, \text{x}>$, and (*b*) their internal participants are the cats, and (*c*) for each of them, $\mathbf{v} = \mathbf{t}$ iff x is the second element of a 2-variant of $\sigma'$, $\sigma''$, such that '$\text{Sx}_1\text{x}_2$' is true relative to $\sigma''$. And similarly, *mutatis mutandis*, for '$(\exists:C)_2\ (\forall:D)_1[\text{Sx}_1\text{x}_2]$'. But since (26) has no reading according to which every cat is such that no dog saw it, I assume that (26) is *not* ambiguous as between (26G) and the following structure: $\langle[[\text{every}_{\text{A}*}\ \textit{int}\text{-cat}_{\Pi}]\ 2\text{-}ext\text{-}\langle[[\text{No}_{\text{A}*}\ \textit{int}\text{-dog}_{\Pi}]\ 1\text{-}ext\text{-}\langle[\text{ext-t}_1\ [\text{saw}_{\Pi*}\ \text{int-t}_2]]\rangle]\rangle]\rangle$. (See Pietroski and Hornstein (2002) for related discussion.)

Conjunctivists, like anyone else, are free to use Tarski's apparatus in stating hypotheses about natural language. This matters, because initially (26) might have seemed like an obvious counterexample to the claim that concatenation signifies conjunction. But in fact, it is not at all obvious. While Conjunctivism may be false, it is not refuted by cases of predicates combining with quantificational subjects and objects. Given the availability of Tarskian tools, one can provide a compositional semantics that treats determiners and their arguments as conjoinable monadic predicates.

Still, one might object that the alleged generalization for indexed external arguments

$$\text{Val}(O, \textit{i-ext-}\langle \ldots \rangle, \mathbf{A}) \text{ iff}$$
$$\forall o\colon Oo\{\text{External}(o, \mathbf{v}) \leftrightarrow \exists \mathbf{A}'[\mathbf{A}' \approx_i \mathbf{A} \ \& \ \text{Internal}(o, \mathbf{A}'\mathbf{i}) \ \& \\ \text{Val}(\mathbf{v}, \langle \ldots \rangle, \mathbf{A}')]\}$$

is an *ad hoc* addition to a Conjunctivist theory. But the idea is simply that if $\langle \ldots \rangle$ is the external and sentential argument of a determiner linked to index $i$, then relative to $\mathbf{A}$: some things$_O$ are Values of *ext-*$\langle \ldots \rangle$ iff their$_O$ external participants are the Values of $\langle \ldots \rangle$ relative to the relevant variants of $\mathbf{A}$. And this makes perfect sense from a Conjunctivist perspective. Or so I'll argue in the rest of this section.

It would be wrong, in several ways, to interpret *i-ext-*$\langle \ldots \rangle$ as a predicate $\Pi$ such that some things$_O$ are Values of $\Pi$ relative to $\mathbf{A}$ iff their$_O$ external participants are the Values of $\langle \ldots \rangle$ relative to $\mathbf{A}$ itself. For each of those$_O$ things would have the *same* external participant, $\mathbf{t}$ or $\mathbf{f}$, since $\langle \ldots \rangle$ has only one Value relative to $\mathbf{A}$. This would make it impossible to assign genuinely quantificational meanings to determiners. And '$t_1$' in $\langle \ldots \rangle$ would be treated as a demonstrative with the Value $\mathbf{A}i$, despite the absence of an accompanying act of demonstration. So another interpretation is required.

Given a system that interprets concatenation as conjunction, one expects it to interpret indices so that indexed expressions can be coherently interpreted as predicates conjoinable with others, much as one expects such a system to interpret grammatical relations so that predicate–argument combinations can be coherently interpreted as conjunctions of predicates. But there are constraints. Given that

$$\text{Val}(O, \text{int-} \ldots, \mathbf{A}) \text{ iff } \exists X\{\text{Internal}(O, X) \ \&$$

$$\forall x[Xx \leftrightarrow \text{Val}(x, \ldots_\alpha, \mathbf{A})]\},$$

and assuming that the external argument of a determiner (is an open sentence that) has the Value **t** or **f** relative to any assignment, a Conjunctivist system must interpret determiners accordingly—in effect, as predicates whose Values are Frege-Pairs. This limits the interpretive possibilities for indexed external arguments. But it also suggests a possibility, given that Values are relativized to assignments in any case: treat *i-ext-*⟨...⟩ as a predicate $\Pi$ such that some things$_O$ are Values of $\Pi$ relative to **A** iff their$_O$ external participants are the Values of ⟨...⟩ relative to *relevant variants* of **A**.

Bear in mind that the notion of an assignment variant is a formal analog of something intuitive. In a context where a speaker points at one thing, she could have pointed at something else. And there is a natural way of determining relevance if the Values of determiners are Frege-Pairs. Given an index *i* and a Frege-Pair o, the obvious candidates for *relevant* variants of **A** are the assignments that anchor *i* to the internal participant of o. In this sense, the proposal about indexed external arguments is a natural relativization of the basic Conjunctivist principle for external arguments

$$\text{Val}(O, \text{ext-} \ldots, \mathbf{A}) \text{ iff } \exists X\{\text{External}(O, X) \ \&$$

$$\forall x[Xx \leftrightarrow \text{Val}(x, \ldots_\alpha, \mathbf{A})]\}$$

to indices, which mark variables in sentential arguments. This point is important enough to restate.

Imagine a Conjunctivist system that ignored the distinction between *ext-*⟨...⟩ and *1-ext-*⟨...⟩. Such a system would treat 1-*ext-*⟨[int-t$_1$ fell$_\Pi$]⟩ like the external argument of a sentential connective. For relative to **A**, 1-*ext-*⟨[int-t$_1$ fell$_\Pi$]⟩ would be interpreted as a predicate that has the Os as Values iff the external participants of the Os are the Values of $\langle[\text{int-t}_1 \text{ fell}_\Pi]\rangle$ relative to **A**. In which case, every O would have the same external participant: **t** if **A1** fell, **f** otherwise. And so $1\text{-}ext\text{-}\langle[\text{int-t}_1 \text{ fell}_\Pi]\rangle$ would be equivalent to the external argument of or$_{\Pi^*}$ in expressions like $[ext\text{-}\langle[\text{ext-That}_{\alpha 1}$ fell$_\Pi]\rangle$ $[\text{or}_{\Pi^*} int\text{-}\langle\ldots\rangle]]$; where arguments of the connective are highlighted. If these implications are incompatible with other systemic constraints—due to the interaction of experience and innate capacities—then the distinction between $ext\text{-}\langle\ldots\rangle$ and $1\text{-}ext\text{-}\langle\ldots\rangle$ will have to be interpreted as semantically significant, like some other indicators of grammatical relations. (Otherwise, the system would not provide any coherent interpretation of expressions formed by combining determiners with their grammatical arguments.)

This raises a twofold question: what significance *could* be assigned to the distinction, given constraints imposed by Conjunctivism; and if there is a natural interpretation, given these constraints, is the net result independently plausible? If so, that is an indirect argument for Conjunctivism. And if we really want to, we can specify the posited significance of the distinction between 'ext' and '1-ext', revealing the latter as a special case of the former. The principle for indexed arguments can be rewritten, to make it look more like the principle for unindexed arguments, by adding the first line of the formalism below to the earlier formulation (in paragraph three of this subsection): Val(O, $i\text{-}ext\text{-}\langle\ldots\rangle$, **A**) iff

$$\exists X\{\text{External}(O, X) \ \& \ \forall x[Xx \leftrightarrow \exists A' \exists o: Oo\{A' \approx_i A \ \&$$
$$\text{Internal}(o, A'i) \ \& \ \text{Val}(x, \langle\ldots\rangle, A')\}] \ \&$$
$$\exists o: Oo\{\text{External}(o, \mathbf{t}) \leftrightarrow \exists A'[A' \approx_i A \ \& \ \text{Internal}(o, A'i) \ \& \ \overset{.}{}$$
$$\text{Val}(\mathbf{t}, \langle\ldots\rangle, A')]\}\}.$$

This says that the Os are Values of $i\text{-}ext\text{-}\langle\ldots\rangle$ relative to **A** iff there are some things$_X$ such that: they$_X$ are the external participants of the Os; and each$_x$ thing is one of them$_X$ iff (i) it$_x$ is the Value of $\langle\ldots\rangle$ relative to an $i$-variant of **A** that anchors $i$ to the internal participant of an O, and (ii) for each one of the Os, its external participant is the Value of $\langle\ldots\rangle$ relative to some i-variant of **A** that anchors $i$ to its internal participant. Condition (i) just says that the Xs include not only the Value of $\langle\ldots\rangle$ relative to **A** itself, but also the Value of $\langle\ldots\rangle$ relative to any **A′** such that **A′** $\approx_i$ **A** and **A′**$i$ is the internal participant of some O. This does not yet impose the condition that for each one$_o$ of the Os, the relevant $i$-variants of **A** anchor $i$ to its$_o$ internal participant. But this is the condition imposed by (ii), making (i) otiose.

Let's come up for air. By talking about how a Conjunctivist system could "make sense of" indexed arguments, I invite charges of speculation about matters far removed from currently available data. But what sustains my interest in Conjunctivism, through the hack work, is the thought that it might help explain *why* expressions get interpreted in ways roughly described by the more familiar accounts. The accounts suggested here are surely wrong at interesting levels of detail. But they illustrate a *kind* of explanation we should be looking for. On any extant view, the semantic primitives are embarrassingly many: individuals, **t** and **f**, ordered pairs, and events; assignments of Values to (singular and plural) variables; conjunction, existential closure, and a mechanism for assigning significance to certain grammatical relations. I see no way to eliminate any of these, and so hope for future reduction. But we can ask whether we need still *more*—like a general notion of function-application, or quantification over extensions—to account for the meanings of quantificational phrases. The suggestion is that we do not, so long as a Conjunctivist system can naturally assign certain significance to the (complex) grammatical relation of being an external argument of a determiner displaced from an indexed position.

## 3.4. *Comparison with Functionism*

If the proposal still seems unduly complicated, it is worth comparing it with a more standard one that accommodates sentences with multiple determiners. Given any expression $\Sigma$, let $\|\Sigma\|^{\mathbf{A}}$ be the Functionist Value of $\Sigma$ relative to **A**. And assume that $\|\text{every}_{\mathbf{A}^*}$ bottle$_\Pi\|^{\mathbf{A}} = \lambda X$ . **t** iff $\{x: X(x) = \mathbf{t}\} \supseteq \{x:\ x\ \text{is a bottle}\}$, while $\|\langle[\mathbf{t}_1\ \text{fell}_\Pi]\rangle\|^{\mathbf{A}} = \mathbf{t}$ iff there was a falling of **A1**. (As we saw in

Chapter 1, Functionists also posit covert quantification over events.) Initially, this looks like a type mismatch. For one expects Functionists to say that $\|[\text{every}_{\text{A*}} \text{ bottle}_\Pi]_1 \langle[t_1 \text{ fell}_\Pi]\rangle\|^{\text{A}} = \|\text{every}_{\text{A*}}$ $\text{bottle}_\Pi\|^{\text{A}}(\|\langle[t_1 \text{ fell}_\Pi]\rangle\|^{\text{A}})$. But $\|\text{every}_{\text{A*}} \text{ bottle}_\Pi\|$ maps *functions* to sentential Values, and $\langle[t_1 \text{ fell}_\Pi]\rangle$ is of type $<t>$. On the other hand, the Value of $\langle[t_1 \text{ fell}_\Pi]\rangle$ is assignment-relative; and for each entity x in the domain, there is an assignment **A** such that **A**1 = x. So there is an intimate relation between (i) having the assignment-relative Value *t iff* **A**1 *fell*, and (ii) having the assignment-invariant Value $\lambda x \cdot t$ *iff x fell.*

There are various ways to exploit this relation in a compositional semantic theory. But one way or another, Functionists can represent an open sentence like $\langle[t_1 \text{ fell}_\Pi]\rangle$ in two ways that are effectively notational variants of each other: as a variable expression of type $<t>$, whose Value depends on an assignment of some entity x to '$t_1$'; or as an invariant expression of type $<\textbf{x, t}>$. For concreteness, consider a theory with an axiom according to which for any assignment **A** and index *i*:

$$\|[\ldots]_{\text{A}i}\langle\ldots t_i\ldots\rangle\|^{\text{A}} = \|[\ldots]_{\text{A}}\|^{\text{A}}(\lambda i\text{-}\|\langle\ldots t_i\ldots\rangle\|^{\text{A}}); \text{ where}$$

$$\text{if } \|\langle\ldots t_i\ldots\rangle\|^{\text{A}} = F(\textbf{A}i), \text{ then } \lambda i\text{-}\|\langle\ldots t_i\ldots\rangle\|^{\text{A}} = \lambda x \cdot F(x).$$

Sliding between use and mention, the idea is that $\lambda i\text{-}\|\langle\ldots t_i\ldots\rangle\|^{\text{A}}$ is the function of type $<\textbf{x, t}>$ corresponding to substitution of a variable for **A**$i$ in $\|\langle\ldots t_i\ldots\rangle\|^{\text{A}}$, which will be of type $<t>$. Since $\|\langle[t_1 \text{ fell}_\Pi]\rangle\|^{\text{A}} = \textbf{t}$ iff there was a falling of **A**1, $\lambda 1\text{-}\|t_1 \text{ fell}_\Pi\|^{\text{A}} = \lambda x \cdot \textbf{t}$ iff there was a falling of x. So

$$\|[\text{every}_{\text{A*}} \text{ bottle}_\Pi]_{\text{A}1}\langle[t_1\text{fell}_\Pi]\rangle\|^{\text{A}} = \|\text{every}_{\text{A*}}\text{bottle}_\Pi\|^{\text{A}}$$
$$(\lambda x \cdot \textbf{t} \text{ iff there was a falling of x}).$$

In which case, $\|[\text{every}_{\text{A*}} \text{ bottle}_\Pi]_{\text{A}1} [t_1 \text{ fell}_\Pi]\|^{\text{A}} = \textbf{t}$ iff {x: x is a bottle} $\subseteq$ {x: there was a falling of x}. Likewise, $\|\langle[\text{it}_1 [\text{saw}_{\Pi*} t_2]]\rangle\|^{\text{A}} = \textbf{t}$ iff: there was a seeing by **A**1 of **A**2; or more briefly, **A**1 saw **A**2. Hence, $\lambda 2\text{-}\|\langle[\text{it}_1 [\text{saw}_{\Pi*} t_2]]\rangle\|^{\text{A}} = \lambda x \cdot \textbf{t}$ iff **A**1 saw x. In which case,

$\|[every_{\Delta^*} cat_{\Pi}]_{\Delta_2} \langle[it_1 [saw_{\Pi^*} t_2]]\rangle\|^A = \|every_{\Delta^*} cat_{\Pi}\|^A(\lambda x . \mathbf{t}$ iff $\mathbf{A1}$ saw x$) = \mathbf{t}$ iff $\{x: x$ is a cat$\} \subseteq \{x: \mathbf{A1}$ saw x$\}$.

Correspondingly, $\|[every_{\Delta^*} cat_{\Pi}]_{\Delta_2} \langle[t_1 [saw_{\Pi^*} t_2]]\rangle\|^A = \{y: y$ is a cat$\} \subseteq \{x: \mathbf{A1}$ saw x$\}$. So

$$\lambda 2\text{-}\|[every_{\Delta^*} cat_{\Pi}]_{\Delta_2}\langle[t_1[saw_{\Pi^*} t_2]]\rangle\|^A = \lambda x . \mathbf{t} \text{ iff}$$

$$\{y: y \text{ is a cat}\} \subseteq \{y: x \text{ saw } y\}; \text{hence,}$$

$$\|[No_{\Delta^*} dog_{\Pi}]_1[[every_{\Delta^*} cat_{\Pi}]_1\langle[t_1[saw_{\Pi^*} t_2]]\rangle]\|^A =$$

$$\|No_{\Delta^*} dog_{\Pi}\|^A(\lambda x . \mathbf{t} \text{ iff } \{y: y \text{ is a cat}\} \subseteq \{y: x \text{ saw } y\}).$$

So if $\|No_{\Delta^*} dog_{\Pi}\|^A = \lambda X . \mathbf{t}$ iff $\{z: z$ is a dog$\} \not\cap \{z: X(z) = \mathbf{t}\}$, then relative to any assignment, the sentence gets the Value $\mathbf{t}$ iff: $\{z: z$ is a dog$\} \not\cap \{z: [\lambda x . \mathbf{t}$ iff $\{y: y$ is a cat$\} \subseteq \{y: x$ saw y$\}](z) = \mathbf{t}\}$; or more briefly, $\{z: z$ is a dog$\} \not\cap \{z: \{y: y$ is a cat$\} \subseteq \{y: z$ saw y$\}\}$; that is, no dog saw every cat. While this introduces an extra degree of complexity for indexed arguments, it is not *ad hoc*. But nor is it any simpler than the Conjunctivist treatment.

Functionists can say that their principle for indexed arguments reflects the significance of indices in a system that interprets concatenation as function-application. How else should such a system interpret the external and sentential argument of a determiner? But as discussed in Chapter 1, true Functionists also hypothesize that natural language deals with predicate–adjunct combinations by type-shifting: if two predicates of type $<\mathbf{x}, \mathbf{t}>$ are combined, one of them is interpreted as being of type $<<\mathbf{x}, \mathbf{t}>, <\mathbf{x}, \mathbf{t}>>$. This leaves various entailment facts unexplained. And if it is better to say that concatenating predicates signifies predicate-conjunction, one cannot just *assume* a Functionist interpretation of indices.

This leaves room for the mixed view according to which saturating predicates with arguments still signifies function-application. While external arguments of determiners introduce a further twist, this does not undermine the mixed view. But nor does this twist undermine Conjunctivism. So if a Conjunctivist account of determiners is as good as a Functionist account, that tells against the mixed view, which posits the resources that Conjunctivists need *and more.* If the extra resources are also unwanted, because of the implication that every predicate has an extension, then determiners actually tell *against* the hypothesis that combining predicates with arguments signifies function-application.

The mixed view does, however, have virtues. An especially nice feature, highlighted by Heim and Kratzer (1998), is that it offers an attractive conception of relative clauses. For independent reasons, it has become standard to say that the grammatical structure of a phrase like 'bottle that fell' involves extraction of an unpronounced element like the wh-element in questions like 'What did Pat see'. On this view, 'bottle that fell' is a complex predicate whose grammatical structure is roughly as follows: [bottle$_\Pi$ [w̶h̶$_1$ [that$_{C\text{-}rel}$ $\langle$[int-t$_1$ fell$_\Pi$]$\rangle$]]$_\Pi$]$_\Pi$; where that$_{C\text{-}rel}$ is a complementizer that relativizes a sentence. Functionists can say that the extracted wh-element converts the open sentence, whose Value is **t** relative to assigment **A** iff **A**1 fell, into a predicate of type $<$**x**, **t**$>$; and on a mixed view, this predicate is conjoined with bottle$_\Pi$. From this perspective, that$_{C\text{-}rel}$ is semantically inert, but it provides "grammatical space" for the typological conversion.

The mixed view thus provides a coherent account of determiners, relative clauses, predicate-argument concatenation, and predicate–adjunct concatenation. But Conjunctivists can also provide a unified account. Suppose that w̶h̶$_1$ is an unpronounced plural variable that can—like 'them'—have many Values relative to an assignment, and likewise for the trace of w̶h̶$_1$. Then Val(**t**, $\langle$[int-t$_{1+pl}$ fell$_\Pi$]$\rangle$, **A**) iff

$$\exists O \langle \exists X \,\{\text{Internal}(O, X) \,\&\, \forall x[Xx \leftrightarrow \text{Associates}(\mathbf{A}, 1, x)]\} \,\& $$
$$\text{Past-Falling}(O)\rangle.$$

The open sentence gets the Val **t** relative to **A** iff there are some events$_O$ whose$_O$ Themes were the 1-associates of **A**. Likewise, Val(X, w̶h̶$_{1+pl}$, **A**) iff $\forall x[Xx \leftrightarrow \text{Associates}(\mathbf{A}, 1, x)]$. Thus,

$$\text{Val}(X, [\text{w̶h̶}_{1+pl}[\text{that}_{C\text{-}rel}\langle[\text{int-t}_{1+pl}\text{fell}_\Pi]\rangle]]_\Pi, \mathbf{A}) \text{ iff}$$
$$\forall x[Xx \leftrightarrow \text{Associates}(\mathbf{A}, 1, x)] \,\&$$
$$\text{Val}(X, [\text{that}_{C\text{-}rel} \langle[\textit{int}\text{-t}_{1+pl} \text{ fell}_\Pi]\rangle], \mathbf{A}).$$

So given the following generalization,

$$\text{Val}(X, [\text{that}_{C\text{-rel}}\langle \ldots \rangle], A) \text{ iff Val}(t, \langle \ldots \rangle, A)$$

we get the desired result: $\text{Val}(X, [\text{wh}_{1+\text{pl}} [\text{that}_{C\text{-rel}} \langle [\text{int-t}_{1+\text{pl}} \text{ fell}_\Pi ]\rangle ]]_\Pi, A)$ iff

$$\forall x[Xx \leftrightarrow \text{Associates}(A, 1, x)] \ \& \ \text{Val}(t, \langle [\text{int-t}_1 \text{ fell}_\Pi]\rangle, A).$$

That is, relative to **A**, some things are Values of the relative clause iff the 1-Associates of **A** fell.

Initially, the generalization 'Val(X, [that$_{C\text{-rel}}$ $\langle \ldots \rangle$], **A**) iff Val(**t**, $\langle \ldots \rangle$, **A**)' might look like an *ad hoc* principle designed to avoid conjoining wh$_{1+\text{pl}}$ with an open sentence, whose assignment-relative Value is **t** or **f**. One might reply that it is just a Conjunctivist way of saying that that$_{C\text{-rel}}$ relativizes a sentence—i.e. that$_{C\text{-rel}}$ turns a sentence into a conjunct of a complex predicate. But more can be said. Many theorists treat complementizers, one way or another, as devices that let a recursive system mark a sentential clause for some "higher" purpose. This is especially common with regard to complementizers that introduce arguments of verbs used to report thought and speech, as in 'The mayor thinks that Batman said that Bruce is at home'. I return to these special complementizers in Chapter 3. For now, I just want to note that Conjunctivists can employ a variant on an idea associated with "paratactic" theories, according to which a complementizer is a device for making reference to its sentential complement.

Instead of adopting a principle that assigns Values to complementizer phrases without assigning Values to complementizers, Conjunctivists can say that

$$\text{Val}(X, [\text{that}_{C\text{-rel}}\langle \ldots \rangle], A) \text{ iff Val}(X, \text{that}_{C\text{-rel}}, A); \text{ and}$$

$$\text{Val}(X, \text{that}_{C\text{-rel}}, A) \text{ iff Relativizes}(\text{that}_{C\text{-rel}}, \langle \ldots \rangle) \ \&$$

$$\forall x[Xx \leftrightarrow \text{Val}(t, \langle \ldots \rangle, A)];$$

where 'Relativizes' signifies a *grammatical* relation that a complementizer bears to the sentence it introduces. The idea is that relative to any assignment, no matter what the Xs are, they are Values of [that$_{C\text{-rel}}$ $\langle \ldots \rangle$] iff $\langle \ldots \rangle$ gets the Value **t**; either everything is a Value of that$_{\text{C-rel}}$, or nothing is. So if Val(t, $\langle$[int-t$_1$ fell$_\Pi$ ]$\rangle$, A), then everything is a Value of [that$_{\text{C-rel}}$ $\langle$[int-t$_1$ fell$_\Pi$ ]$\rangle$] relative to A; and so the Values of [~~wh~~$_1$ [that$_{\text{C-rel}}$ $\langle$[int-t$_1$ fell$_\Pi$ ]$\rangle$]]$_\Pi$ are the 1-Associates of A. But if Val(f, $\langle$[int-t$_1$ fell$_\Pi$ ]$\rangle$, A), then nothing is a Value of [~~wh~~$_1$ [that$_{\text{C-rel}}$ $\langle$[int-t$_1$ fell$_\Pi$ ]$\rangle$]]$_\Pi$ relative to A.

On this view, a complementizer phrase is not really a con-catenation of expressions, at least not in a sense that matters for compositional semantics. Rather, a phrase like [that$_{\text{C-rel}}$ $\langle$[int-t$_1$ fell$_\Pi$ ]$\rangle$] is a device for "summing up" with regard to the embedded sentence, which is a constituent of a still larger phrase. Chomsky (2000*b*) and others speak of a complementizer phrase as a "phase" in a derivation of a more complex expression; where a displaced ele-ment like ~~wh~~$_1$, on the "periphery" of the phrase headed by that$_{\text{C-rel}}$, is "visible" to the next phase of the derivation.[22] And in any case, Conjunctivists are free to adopt the hypothesis that relative clauses have the semantic character just described. So they can provide an account of relative clauses and determiners that is at least as unified as the mixed view.

It may have been obvious to some readers that Conjunctivists can use the (Tarskian) formal techniques employed in this section. But following Montague and one strand of thought in Frege, semanticists often use these techniques to specify alleged sets cor-responding to sentences with variables. Relative to assignment A, one appeals to the function $\lambda x . t$ iff $\exists A'[A' \approx_i A \,\&\, \|S\|^A]$, or the set $\{x: \exists A'[A' \approx_i A \,\&\, \text{Val}(t, S, A') \, x = Ai]\}$. Even Larson and Segal (1995), whose theory is otherwise Conjunctivist in spirit, adopt this strategy by taking the Values of determiners to be ordered pairs of sets.

---

[22] See also Uriagereka (1999, 2002), who argues that complementizer phrases (among other complex sentential constituents) are "spelled out"—marked as ready for phonological and semantic interpretation—and effectively treated as units in sub-sequent phases of the derivation. This is, as he notes, a way of preserving much older ideas about cyclicity. If tense also marks a phase, as Chomsky (2000*b*) suggests, this invites the speculation that existential closure is a reflection of "spelling out" a tensed phrase, and perhaps not a grammatical formative.

This is understandable. For it can seem that the only alternative is a refusal to theorize. Although inspired by Davidson, and a different strand of Frege's thought, those skeptical of appeals to sets might opt for a syncategorematic account that specifies Values for sentences containing determiners *without* assigning Values to determiners. One can say that relative to assignment $A$, any sentence of the form $\langle [\text{every}_{A^*} \ldots _{\Pi}]_{A_i} \langle \ldots t_i \ldots \rangle \rangle$ gets the Value $t$ iff every Value$_x$ of the predicate $\ldots _{\Pi}$ is such that for some $A'$: $A' \approx_i A$, $A'$ anchors $i$ to it$_x$, and the open sentence $\langle \ldots t_i \ldots \rangle$ gets the Value $t$ relative to $A'$. But this generalization about sentences with every$_{A^*}$ isn't much of a theory. There is a thin sense in which it explains how certain semantic properties are determined by others; though as discussed in the introductory chapter, accounting for the (mere) compositionality of meaning is just one explanatory task among many. One would like a compositional semantics that reveals something about why the generalization is true, why it patterns with other generalizations about sentences with other quantificational expressions, and why such expressions have the (essentially conservative semantic character they do), see Larson and Segal (1995) for helpful discussion.

Higginbotham (1985) offers a more sophisticated account that supplements his mixed view, which replaced function-application and type-adjustment with theta-binding and theta-linking, by adding a third composition principle for expressions of the form $\langle [\ldots _{A^*} \ldots _{\Pi}]_{A_i} \langle \ldots t_i \ldots \rangle \rangle$. Heim and Kratzer's (1998) framework is, in many ways, similar. But I think this misses an underlying conjunctive unity across the posited composition principles, making it look like concatenation can signify multiple operations in natural language. (If three, one wonders, why not four or seventeen? And this raises questions about why children don't treat concatenation as more ambiguous than it is.) That said, my proposal is a relatively minor variation on these others. My main point in this section has been to show that Conjunctivists can deal with quantificational constructions, in detail, since the needed tools are not essentially tied to any one conception of what concatenation signifies in natural language. But I turn now to some reasons for saying that the Values of determiners are indeed Frege-Pairs, and hence, that determiners have Values.

# 4. Explanatory Virtues

I argued above that one should expect a Conjunctivist system to treat determiners as predicates whose Values are Frege-Pairs. In this section, I argue that, given this conception of determiners, Conjunctivism can help explain two important and related facts: determiners combine with predicates to form *restricted* quantifiers; and as noted in §1, determiners are *conservative*. Moreover, unlike Functionist accounts, the proposal on offer preserves some independent virtues of a Boolos-style construal of second-order quantification.

## 4.1. *Restricted Quantifiers and Conservativity*

If the Values of determiners are Frege-Pairs, then a determiner imposes a semantic constraint on the external participants of its Values. For example, $\text{Val}(O, \text{every}_{\Delta^*}, A)$ iff $\neg\exists o[Oo\ \&\ \text{External}(o, f)]$. And as I have been stressing, the sentential/external argument of a determiner specifies a sentential Value relative to each assignment. So in a Conjunctivist system, the predicative/internal argument specifies the relevant constraint on internal participants of relevant Frege-Pairs. This corresponds to a constraint on *which* entities matter for purposes of evaluating the relevant indexed variable. In one sense, this is obvious. But Functionism offers no rationale for why natural languages lack primitive expressions of type $<<\mathbf{x}, \mathbf{t}>, \mathbf{t}>$, analogs of '∀' and '∃', that can combine with a predicate of type $<\mathbf{x}, \mathbf{t}>$ to form a sentence.

Why *isn't* there a noncompound word 'Ev', with 'Ev is red or blue' meaning that every thing is red or blue? And why isn't there a word 'Pers' such that 'Pers fell' gets the Value **t** iff every person fell? Conjunctivism suggests an answer. Such an expression would be displaced, taking a sentential argument.[23] And if it took just one argument, as sentential negation does, then a Conjunctivist system couldn't assign the intended interpretation. But such a system can treat 'everything' as a phrase, whose values are Frege-Pairs, that has a constituent whose Values are individuals.

The relativized nature of natural language quantification is connected with many linguistic phenomena; see, for example, Kamp (1981), Heim (1982, 1983), Diesing (1992). Especially important here is the fact that if determiner phrases are interpreted as restricted quantifiers, then determiners are conservative; see Barwise and Cooper (1981), Higginbotham and May (1981), Westerståhl (1984), Keenan and Stavi (1986). Recall from §1 that biconditionals like (27–9) are trivial.

(27)   Every bottle fell iff every bottle *is a bottle that* fell
(28)   No bottle fell iff no bottle *is a bottle that* fell
(29)   Most bottles fell iff most bottles *are bottles that* fell

The generalization seems to be that instances of (30) are sure to be true.

(30)   Determiner Noun Verb iff Determiner Noun (copula) Noun that Verb

In more theoretical terms, a sentence of the form indicated in (31*a*) is sure to have the same Value as the corresponding sentence of the form indicated in (31*b*).

(31*a*)   $\langle [\text{Det}_\Delta {*} \text{Pred1}_\Pi]_i \, \langle [t_i \, \text{Pred2}_\Pi] \rangle \rangle$
(31*b*)   $\langle [\text{Det}_\Delta {*} \text{Pred1}_\Pi]_i \, \langle [t_i \, (\text{copula}) \, [\text{Pred1}_\Pi \, [\text{w̶h̶}_j \, [\text{that}_{\text{C-rel}} \, \langle [t_j \, \text{Pred2}_\Pi] \rangle ]]]] \rangle \rangle$

---

[23] Otherwise, 'Pers' would be interpreted as a potential argument of a verb, and thus the sort of expression that can have an individual (or individuals) as its Value(s). In which case, 'Pers wrote ten papers' would not mean that every person wrote ten papers.

Biconditionals like (32–3) suggest that the relevant generalization is productive, not an idiosyncratic fact about a handful of expressions.

(32)   More than eleven but fewer than eighty-nine bottles are red iff more than eleven but fewer than eighty-nine bottles *are bottles that* are red

(33)   None of the bottles except for the red ones fell iff none of the bottles except for the red ones are bottles that fell

This calls for explanation. We can say that such biconditionals are logical truths. But then one wants a semantic theory to explain why reproducing the internal argument within the external argument results in a logical truth. One can easily imagine a compositional semantics for a language in which an instance of (31*a*) typically differs in Value from the corresponding instance of (31*b*). So one wants to know why natural language is, in this respect, the way that it is. Given that the internal argument of a determiner restricts the domain of quantification, it does indeed follow that instances of (31*a*) are equivalent to instances of (31*b*). But merely deriving the conservativity generalization from another true generalization is not yet an explanation. We need an independent account of why determiner phrases are interpreted as restricted quantifiers—or using Barwise and Cooper's metaphor, why determiners "live on" their internal arguments. And Functionism offers no help here. On the contrary, Functionism makes it hard to see why the generalizations are true. I'll spend the rest of this subsection saying why. In §4.2, I offer a Conjunctivist explanation according to which the conservativity of determiners follows from deeper facts that also explain why determiner phrases are interpreted as restricted quantifiers.

Functionists effectively treat determiners as devices for expressing relations between extensions. From this perspective, the explanandum is that determiners are semantically associated with set-theoretic relations that satisfy the following condition: $\mathfrak{R}(X, Y)$ iff $\mathfrak{R}(Y \cap X, Y)$; where Y corresponds to the internal argument,

'$\mathfrak{R}(X, Y)$' means that X bears $\mathfrak{R}$ to Y, and the intersection sign corresponds to the intuitively conjunctive meaning of combining a noun with a restrictive relative clause.[24] Trivially, intersection is conservative: $X \cap Y$ iff $(Y \cap X) \cap Y$. Inclusion is also conservative, given that each set includes itself as a subset: $X \supseteq Y$ iff $(Y \cap X) \supseteq Y$. Likewise for the relation associated with most$_{A*}$: $|Y - X| > |Y \cap X|$ iff $|Y - (Y \cap X)| > |Y \cap (Y \cap X)|$. So *if* Functionism is correct, then the Values of determiners correspond to conservative relations. But this way of describing conservativity makes it hard—and perhaps impossible—to explain.

For if determiners express conservative relations between sets, then natural language permits words that (i) combine with predicates to form phrases, and (ii) express relations between sets. More precisely, given Functionism, the Values of determiners are functions of type $<<\mathbf{x}, \mathbf{t}>, <<\mathbf{x}, \mathbf{t}>, \mathbf{t}>>$. In which case, it is hard to see why any principle of natural language should be violated by words semantically associated with various nonconservative relations. Consider equinumerosity. It is false that the bottles are equinumerous with the things that fell iff the bottles are equinumerous with the bottles that fell. But corresponding one-to-one is a conceptually simple relation, and intuitively simpler than the relation indicated with 'more than eleven but fewer than eighty-nine', or the relation of corresponding *more than* one-to-one. So we want to know why natural language seems to preclude a determiner 'Equi' such that 'Equi bottles fell' would mean that the bottles are equinumerous with the bottles that fell.

Similarly, given that speakers can understand claims like 'the women *outnumber* the men', why can't we have a corresponding determiner 'Numby'? The intent would be that 'Numby women are men' gets the Value **t** iff $|\{x: x \text{ is a woman}\}| > |\{x: x \text{ is a man}\}|$. This would be a counterexample to (30), since it isn't generally true that the Ys outnumber the Xs iff the Ys outnumber the Ys that are Xs.

---

[24] Since linear order does not matter, [[*Predicate* Internal] External] is equivalent to [External [*Predicate* Internal]]. So 'Every bottle fell' corresponds to $\mathfrak{R}(\{x: \text{fell}\}, \{x: x \text{ is a bottle}\})$.

But this does not keep us from saying that there are the men, and there are more women—or that most people are women.[25] Why can't we say the same thing with a sentence in the form 'DETER-MINER women are men', where the determiner's Value is $\lambda Y . \lambda X .$ $t$ iff $|\{x: Y(x) = t\}| > |\{x: X(x) = t\}|$? Or consider the invented term 'gre', which would impose a uniqueness condition on its *external* argument: $\|gre_{\Delta^*}\| = \lambda Y . \lambda X . t$ iff $\exists x\{Y(x) = t \ \& \ X(x) = t \ \&$ $\forall y[X(y) = t \rightarrow y = x]\}$; cf. Montague's (1970) Russellian analysis according to which $\|the_{\Delta^*}\| = \lambda Y . \lambda X . t$ iff $\exists x\{Y(x) = t \ \& \ X(x) = t$ $\& \ \forall y[Y(y) = t \rightarrow y = x]\}$. Why can't we say 'Gre bottle fell', meaning that exactly one thing fell, and it is a bottle?

One might deny the explanandum, holding that natural language does permit determiners that express nonconservative relations. In particular, one might cite 'only', since (34) can easily be false.

(34)    Only bottles fell iff only bottles *are bottles that* fell

Suppose that some nonbottles fell, and hence, that the left side of this biconditional is false. The right side is still true, since trivially, only bottles are bottles that fell. Correlatively, nonbottles are relevant to the truth of 'Only bottles fell'. But this is not a counterexample to (30) if 'only' is not a determiner. Moreover, it is not a datum that 'bottle' is the internal argument of 'only' in (34); perhaps there is a relevant transformation. And these escape clauses are not mere wishful thinking. For as the medievals recognized, 'only' seems to be a kind of sentential operator.

Unlike 'every' and 'most', 'only' can appear before any word in (35),

(35)    The student said that his teacher likes her job

with roughly the meaning that (35) is true, *and* that some contrasting claim is false; where the contrasting claim—that someone else said the same thing, that there was more than one

---

[25] A character like Yoda could say 'Outnumbered by the women, the men are' and be understood.

student, that what was said may be false (or unjustified), or whatever—is determined by the constituent of (35) that is "focused" by its association with 'only'. Herburger (2001) offers an independently attractive account, friendly to Conjunctivism, in which the focused expression is displaced—leaving an open sentence as the argument of 'only'. But the distributional facts alone suggest that 'only' is not a determiner, and so not a counterexample to the conservativity generalization.[26]

Still, 'only' is important. For it reminds us that the converse of inclusion, the *subset* relation, is not conservative. It isn't generally true that $X \subseteq Y$ iff $(Y \cap X) \subseteq Y$; for trivially, $(Y \cap X) \subseteq Y$, but it doesn't follow that $X \subseteq Y$. So if there *were* a determiner 'ryev' such that $\|\text{ryev}_{\Delta *}\| = \lambda Y . \lambda X . \mathbf{t}$ iff $\{x: X(x) = \mathbf{t}\} \subseteq \{x: Y(x) = \mathbf{t}\}$, it really would be a counterexample to (30).

(30) Determiner Noun Verb iff Determiner Noun (copula) Noun that Verb

Thus, Functionists owe an account of why natural languages *don't* include logically possible expressions like: 'ryev', the semantic converse of 'every'; 'gre', which is like 'the' except for imposing a uniqueness condition on external arguments; 'equi' and 'numby', which indicate conceptually simple relations between sets. To take one last example, let 'Nall' signify the relation $\Re$ such that $\Re(X, Y)$ iff $\neg(Y \supseteq X)$. It isn't generally true that $\neg(Y \supseteq X)$ iff $\neg[Y \supseteq (Y \cap X)]$; and 'Not all Xs are Ys' is not equivalent to 'Not all Ys that are Xs are Ys', since the latter is surely false. But no natural language has 'Nall' as a determiner. Even if it would be useful to introduce such a word, we evidently cannot. From a Functionist perspective, this is puzzling, since we can use 'No Ys are Xs' to deny that some Ys are Xs.

One can put the question this way: why don't kids grow up to be adults who speak a language with nonconservative determiners? Functionism provides no answer, and it makes the question harder.

---

[26] See Herburger (2001) for discussion building on Schein (1993).

Why wouldn't some Functionist children become adults who use some nonconservative determiners?

One can speculate that all natural language determiners are defined, in a way that preserves conservativity, from "basic" determiners that express conservative relations; see Keenan and Stavi (1986). But even if this proves correct, one wants to know why the mechanism for defining determiners has the character it does, and why the basic determiners do not include 'ryev' or 'equi'. (As noted in §4.3 below, the notion of one-to-one correspondence seems to be foundational for arithmetic reasoning.) Perhaps natural language somehow "filters out" candidate determiners that express nonconservative relations. But again, one wants to know why 'most' is a possible determiner, while 'numby' is not.

One can say that 'equi' is not a possible determiner because it would not combine with a noun to form a restricted quantifier: when evaluating 'Equi bottles fell', each fallen thing would be potentially relevant, whether or not it is a bottle. But not only does this raise the question of why determiners are interpreted as constituents of restricted quantifiers, it effectively admits that determiners are *not* devices for expressing relations between sets. When evaluating 'Every bottle fell', we need not—and intuitively, we do not—consider {x: x fell}. We can consider the bottles$_X$, and ask whether or not they$_X$ all fell. In general, we can evaluate '...$_{\Lambda^*}$ bottle(s) fell' by sorting the bottles$_X$ into those$_X$ that fell and those$_X$ that did not, and asking whether or not the former are suitably "related" to the latter. From a Conjunctivist perspective, determiner meanings are not even relations in this restricted sense. But on any view that treats '...$_{\Lambda^*}$ bottle(s)' as a restricted quantifier, it is gratuitous to associate 'fell' with {x: x fell}. Correlatively, it seems wrong to characterize negative facts about determiners in terms of a constraint on *which* second-order relations determiners can express.

## 4.2. *Conservativity and Frege-Pairs*

There is a simpler explanation. Determiners do not express relations; a fortiori, they do not express nonconservative relations.

And if determiners impose restrictions on Frege-Pairs, a sentence of the form 'Determiner Noun Verb' must have the same Value as the corresponding sentence of the form 'Determiner Noun copula Noun that Verb'. For the shared Value will be as described in (36a) and (36b);

(36a)    $\exists O\{\Delta(O)$ & $\exists X[\text{Internal}(O, X)$ & $\forall x(Xx \leftrightarrow \Phi x)]$ &
         $\forall o:Oo\{\text{External}(o, t) \leftrightarrow \exists x[\text{Internal}(o, x)$ & $\Psi x]\}\}$

(36b)    $\exists O\{\Delta(O)$ & $\exists X[\text{Internal}(O, X)$ & $\forall x(Xx \leftrightarrow \Phi x)]$ &
         $\forall o:Oo\{\text{External}(o, t) \leftrightarrow \exists x[\text{Internal}(o, x)$ &
         $\Phi x$ & $\Psi x]\}\}$

where '$\Delta$' indicates the contribution of the determiner, '$\Phi$' corresponds to the noun, and '$\Psi$' to the verb. Or more precisely, '$\Psi$' corresponds to the relevant open sentence, whose Value is **t** or **f** relative to each relevant assignment of Values of variables. Thus, the external participant of each O is either **t** or **f**.

The only difference is that the third conjunct in (36a) imposes the condition that each O be of the form $<\mathbf{t}, x>$ iff $\Psi x$, while the third conjunct in (36b) imposes the condition that each O be of the form $<\mathbf{t}, x>$ iff $\Phi x$ & $\Psi x$.[27] The shared second conjunct imposes the condition that x is the internal participant of an O iff $\Phi x$. So the condition imposed by the *second and third* conjunct is the same in each case: the Os are the Frege-Pairs that associate each $\Phi$ with **t** iff that $\Phi$ is $\Psi$; trivially, the Frege-Pairs that associate each$_x$ $\Phi$ with **t** iff it$_x$ is $\Psi$ *just are* the Frege-Pairs that associate each$_x$ $\Phi$ with **t** iff it$_x$ is a $\Phi$ that is $\Psi$. So an instance of (36a) is sure to have the same Value as the corresponding instance of (36b), whatever condition the determiner imposes. Conjunctivists can thus account for the absence of nonconservative determiners without positing constraints that block unwanted determiner meanings.

---

[27] For example, if $\langle[\text{int-}t_1, \text{fell}_\Pi]\rangle$ is the external argument of a determiner, it imposes the condition that each O be of the form $<\mathbf{t}, x>$ iff x fell. And if $\langle[t_1$ is a $[\text{bottle}_\Pi [\text{wh}_2[\text{that}_{\text{C-rel}} \langle[\text{int-}t_2 \text{ fell}_\Pi]\rangle]]]]\rangle$ is the external argument, it imposes the condition that each O be of the form $<\mathbf{t}, x>$ iff x is a bottle *and* x fell.

From this perspective, the conservativity generalization isn't itself very interesting. It doesn't show that natural languages are Functionist languages limited by a substantive constraint. Rather, the generalization tells against Functionism. If concatenation signifies conjunction, with sentencehood indicating second-order/plural existential closure, we can explain why the trivial biconditionals are trivial. The otherwise puzzling generalization can be viewed as a spandrel of the underlying Conjunctivist semantic architecture, which requires that determiners and their grammatical arguments be interpreted as predicates of Frege-Pairs. Correlatively, it is a virtue of the proposed compositional semantics that it predicts the absence of nonconservative determiners.[28]

---

[28] One might worry that this proves too much. How can Conjunctivists deal with 'Only bottles fell', given the essentially conservative character of predicates whose Values are Frege-Pairs? But, in fact, Conjunctivism makes a plausible prediction about 'only' that leaves room for various more specific options: either 'only' is not a predicate of Frege-Pairs, or its internal argument is marked as such at a level of grammatical structure reflecting displacement, or both. Herburger (2001) argues that 'only' is interpreted as a universal quantifier whose internal argument may be a predicate whose Values are events. With respect to 'Only bottles fell', the idea is that displacement of 'bottles' results in a sentence whose Value is **t** iff all *events of falling* (are events of falling that) have bottles as their Themes. Likewise, 'Only Pat fell' has the Value **t** iff each event of falling (is an event of falling that) has Pat as its Theme; cf. Lewis (1975) and Kratzer (1989) on quantificational adverbs like 'always'. Spelling out Herburger's proposal in detail, and casting it in explicitly Conjunctivist terms, would take us far afield. And my aim here is not to incorporate a serious theory of 'only'. But it is worth considering an especially simple option with the same effect as Herburger's account, at least for a wide range of cases.

In general, only $\Phi$s are $\Psi$s iff some $\Phi$s are the—and hence, the only—$\Psi$s. And if a focused expression '$\Phi$' is displaced to the periphery of a phrase, then given Conjunctivism, some things$_X$ will be Values of that phrase iff they$_X$ are Values of '$\Phi$' that meet a further condition. For example, if [bottles$_\Pi$ 1-$\langle$[int-t$_1$ fell$_\Pi$]$\rangle$] is a possible expression, it would be interpreted as a predicate $\Pi$ such that some things$_X$ are Values of $\Pi$ iff they$_X$ are bottles that are also Values of 1-$\langle$[int-t$_1$ fell$_\Pi$]$\rangle$. This invites the thought that 'only' does not impose its own restriction: Val(X, [only$_{Foc}$ $i$-$\langle$ . . . $\rangle$], A) iff Val(X, $i$-$\langle$ . . . $\rangle$, A). Perhaps 'only' is, at least sometimes, a focus operator that simply creates the grammatical space needed to say that (sm) bottles are the things that fell. Conjunctivists can say that Val(X, 1-$\langle$[int-t$_1$ fell$_\Pi$]$\rangle$, A) iff: $\forall x[Xx \leftrightarrow$ for some **A**′ such that $\mathbf{A}' \approx_1 \mathbf{A}$ , Val(**t**, $\langle$ . . . $\rangle$ **A**′)]; that is the Xs are the (only) potential Values of the variable relative to which $\langle$[int-t$_1$ fell$_\Pi$]$\rangle$ gets the Value **t**.

## 4.3. *Meaning and Second-Order Quantification*

The virtues of Conjunctivism would be lost—or at least greatly obscured—within a theory whose second-order variables range over collections. Such a theory would lead back to the idea that the Values of determiners are ordered pairs of sets. So in the next (and final) section, I return to the concern that a Boolos-style construal of '∃X' smuggles in quantification over sets. But it is worth reviewing some independent virtues of the plural construal, which is less familiar among linguists. Any theorist using a second-order metalanguage must eventually think generally about second-order quantification, since lapsing into incoherence is all too easy. Moreover, whatever we say about the semantics of plural and quantificational constructions, the capacity to understand them is connected somehow with the logical/arithmetical reasoning that interested Frege; and if the enterprise of semantics is continuous with the enterprise of logic, in any interesting way, then we must consider both when thinking about either.

For any condition Φ, ∃X[∀x(Xx ↔ Φx)] iff ∃xΦx; see §2. Given the plural construal, instances of comprehension are as trivial as they seem, since they do not embody the assumption that each condition corresponds to a thing that includes each satisfier of the condition. But monadic second-order quantification remains

---

If this seems contrived, note that the result of focusing 'Pat' in 'Pat fell' is plausibly a structure that has something$_x$ as a Value iff it$_x$ is a Value of Pat$_\alpha$ that is also the Theme of a falling, while the result of focusing 'fell' is plausibly a structure that has something$_x$ as a Value iff it$_x$ is an event of falling whose Theme is the Value of Pat$_\alpha\langle$[int-t$_1$ fell$_\Pi$]$\rangle$. On this view, (indexed) open sentences are indeed interpreted as predicates of individuals. But one can say that in 'Only bottles fell', 'fell' corresponds to a predicate whose Values are the things that fell *without* saying the same about 'Every bottle fell'. The difference between 'every' and 'only' may run deep, despite superficial similarities. Alternatively, one could treat 'only' as an expression that takes an indexed open sentence as its internal argument and a noun as its external argument, positing the structure [*ext*-bottles$_\Pi$[only 1-*int*-$\langle$[int-t$_1$ fell$_\Pi$]$\rangle$]]. Given Conjunctivism, this would amount to saying that the Values of 'only' are "inverse Frege-Pairs" of the form <x, **v**>, with the sentential Value as the internal participant; cf. Horn's (1997) suggestion that 'only' is a neo-conservative determiner, associated with a relation ℜ such that ℜ(X, Y) iff ℜ(X, X ∩ Y).

distinctive and powerful. For example, we can define 'ancestor' in terms of 'parent': Axy iff $\neg\exists X\{\forall z(Pzy \rightarrow Xz)$ & $\forall w[\forall z(Xw$ & $Pzw) \rightarrow Xz]$ & $\neg Xx\}$; x is an ancestor of y iff it *isn't* true that some things$_X$ are such that each parent of y is one of them$_X$, and every one$_w$ of them$_X$ is such that each of its$_w$ parents is one of them$_X$, but x *isn't* one of them$_X$.

These points bear on the study of logic and its relation to arithmetic.[29] For while Frege (1893, 1903) adopted a paradoxical assumption about Concepts and their extensions, he used it only to derive a generalization now known as "Hume's Principle": the number of the Xs is also the number of the Ys iff the Xs correspond one-to-one with the Ys; see Wright (1983), Heck (1993), Boolos (1998), Demopolous (1994). Frege proved that the Dedekind-Peano axioms follow from this biconditional, given his second-order logic *without* his infamous Axiom V.[30]

This remarkable result was obscured by Frege's conception of second-order quantification as quantification over Concepts, given his stipulation that each Concept has an extension (or Value-Range);

[29] We can also define '$\forall X$' (read as 'whatever the Xs are') in terms of '$\neg\exists X\neg$', and say that x is an ancestor of y iff: $\forall X[\forall z(Pzy \rightarrow Xz)$ & $\forall z\forall w(Xz$ & $Pwz \rightarrow Xw) \rightarrow Xx]$; whatever the Xs are, *if* every parent of y is one of them, and every one of them is such that each of its parents is one of them, *then* x is one of them. More about '$\forall X$' shortly; see also Lewis (1991). But let me stress that one can adopt this construal for purposes of natural language semantics without endorsing more tendentious claims about logic— e.g. that it just *is* second-order monadic predicate logic.

[30] Letting 'X' and 'Y' range over Concepts (or predicates), Axiom-V implied that X has the same extension as Y iff $\forall x(Xx \leftrightarrow Yx)$. This is trivial if the Concepts in question *have* extensions. But it isn't true in general that *if* $\forall x(Xx \leftrightarrow Yx)$, then X has an extension that it shares with Y; and given Frege's logic, one can prove that Concepts like *is not selfelemental* do and don't have extensions. Frege recognized that Axiom-V was not *as* self-evident as his other basic assumptions. He introduced it because he could see no other way to derive Hume's Principle (HP), understood as a claim about how the *things* described by the Dedekind-Peano axioms are related to equinumerosity of Concepts, from claims he regarded as axiomatic. Given HP and a Boolos-contrual, one can say (without presupposing a set of all things) that o is the number of *(the) nonselfidentical things*; 1 is the number of things identical with o; 2 is the number of things identical with o or 1; etc. Luckily, we need not address the further questions of whether HP is itself analytic, true, or compatible with ZF set theory. (See Wright (1983), Boolos (1998).)

see §2 of Chapter 1. But the relevant fragment of Frege's logic is evidently consistent, and it can be interpreted plurally. Of course, the interest of Frege's proof is reduced if what we *call* second-order logic turns out to be part of mathematics *and not* part of logic— with the latter understood (in Fregean terms) as the general principles governing truth and falsity as such, without regard to particular branches of knowledge like mathematics, physics, and psychology. And given the standard interpretation of '∃X', it can seem that any generalizations of second-order logic belong to set theory, understood as a branch of mathematics; see Quine (1970). But at least in so far as second-order logic admits of a Boolos-style interpretation, it has a good claim to being part of *logic*, as opposed to set theory.

This is a good thing, and not just because it lets us frame interesting questions about how logic is related to set theory. Sentences of natural language exhibit logical relations not characterizable in first-order terms. And a semantic theory should reflect this, preferably without implausible assumptions about logic or sets. For example, there seems to be a pattern across examples like (37–9),

(37)  Nothing is both a linguist and not a linguist
(38)  Nothing is both a philosopher and not a philosopher
(39)  Nothing is both an avocado and not an avocado

which are tautologies. This suggests a second-order generalization: $\forall X \neg \exists x[Xx \;\&\; \neg Xx]$. And one might try to explain the truistic character of (37–9) by saying that such sentences *must* get the Value **t** because: each gets the Value **t** iff certain things$_X$—the linguists, philosophers, or avocados—are such that nothing is both one of them$_X$ and not one of them$_X$; so it follows as a matter of *logic* that (37–9) get the Value **t**; and since the relevant logical principle is so simple, it is plausible that any competent speaker will (tacitly) recognize instances of it as logical truths. But a set-theoretic interpretation of '$\forall X$' fosters a kind of Quinean skepticism, about the prospects for any such explanation, that might be voiced as follows.

If 'X' ranges over sets, '∀X¬∃x[Xx & ¬Xx]' is really shorthand for '∀s¬∃x[(x ∈ s) & ¬(x ∈ s)]'. But this truism—for each set, nothing is both a member of it and not—is not a *law of logic*. One can call it a logical truth because of its form. But the "Law of Noncontradiction" is not a claim about *sets*. No claim about sets, it seems, can explain why nothing is both a linguist and not a linguist. On the contrary, one expects a principle of noncontradiction to explain why nothing *is and isn't* an element of any set. And if '∀s¬∃x[(x ∈ s) & ¬(x ∈ s)]' can somehow explain its own instances, why can't (23)? What does quantification over sets add to the explanation, apart from potential trouble? But if '∀X¬∃x[Xx & ¬ Xx]' is *not* a basic principle governing truth and falsity, then revealing (37–9) as instances of this generalization does not yet explain why such sentences are truistic, or why they are heard as truistic. Semanticists would have to say that (37–9) exemplify a set-theoretic generalization whose instances are, and are recognized by ordinary speakers to be, trivial. This is less parsimonious than the explanation hoped for, since we must assume in any case that speakers have a minimal grasp of logic. Ascribing tacit grasp of some set theory is more tendentious.

Worse, as we'll see in §5, one cannot consistently state set-theoretic generalizations that explain the facts. In my view, this is another reason for not saying that 'X' ranges over sets: it spoils the idea of capturing patterns across first-order tautologies in second-order terms; cf. Putnam (1971). One can say instead that '∀X¬∃x[Xx & ¬Xx]' is equivalent to '¬∃X∃x[Xx & ¬Xx]', which is the negation of '∃X∃x[Xx & ¬Xx]', which means that: *some things*$_X$ are such that some thing$_x$ is both one of them$_X$ and not one of them$_X$. That is a contradiction. So its negation is a logical truth. Hence, it is a truth of *logic* that ∀X¬∃x[Xx & ¬Xx]. Whatever the Xs are, nothing is both one of them and not.[31]

---

[31] There may be a more "basic" form of noncontradiction. But perhaps being one of the Xs just *is* being one of Xs *and not* one of the other things (if any). Leibniz's Law, '∀x∀y[x = y ↔ ∀X(Xx ↔ Xy)]', is also truistic on a plural interpretation: x = y iff no matter what the Xs are, x is one of them iff y is.

There also seems to be a pattern across (37–9) and (40), which can be rendered as (40*a*).

(40)   Nothing is both a successor of something and not a successor of it

(40*a*)   $\neg\exists x\exists y[Sxy \ \& \ \neg Sxy]$

And (40*a*) is not an instance of '$\forall X\neg\exists x[Xx \ \& \ \neg Xx]$'. But there is an obvious move: introduce a new monadic predicate '$\underline{S}$' such that for any o, where 'o' ranges over a domain that includes ordered pairs of individuals, o satisfies '$\underline{S}$' iff $\exists x\exists y[o = <x, y> \ \& \ Sxy]$. Then (40*a*) is equivalent to (40*b*),

(40*b*)   $\neg\exists o[\underline{S}o \ \& \ \neg\underline{S}o]$

assuming that the existence of x and y ensures the existence of $<x, y>$. No ordered pair is such that its external element both is and isn't a successor of its internal element. So for relations characterizable in terms of predicates of ordered pairs, or events and a pair of thematic roles, we can capture the relevant generalization as follows: $\neg\exists O\exists o(Oo \ \& \ \neg Oo)$; where 'O' ranges over the same things that 'o' ranges over. There are no things$_O$ such that some thing is both one of them$_O$ and not one of them$_O$.[32]

Boolos thus provides a construal of monadic second-order quantification that lets us state various generalizations we want to state—candidate laws of logic, and a principle that connects arithmetic to logic—without thereby quantifying over extensions in

---

[32] This trick, together with others for keeping us out of trouble when we introduce a *little* more impredicativity, can be extended beyond relations definable in first-order terms (as the previous characterization of the ancestral function suggests). As Hartry Field has noted, this still doesn't provide everything that every logician wants. And for purposes of logic, one might object to the quantification over ordered pairs; though see Hazen (1997) and the appendix to Lewis (1991), cowritten with Hazen and Burgess. (My thanks to Richard Heck for a discussion about these issues.) In any case, we are concerned here with the semantics of natural languages, which already distinguish external from internal arguments; and semanticists may not need all the expressive power logicians might want.

illicit ways. This presupposes that words like 'nothing' ('everything', etc.) are *not* to be analyzed as predicates satisfied by ordered pairs of things, like sets, on analogy with 'successor' in (40); otherwise, the point of the plural construal is undermined. But given plural quantification over Frege-Pairs and their participants, Conjunctivists can specify the Values of determiners without quantifying over pairs of extensions. In this sense, we can restrict ourselves to the minimal Fregean apparatus discussed in Chapter 1: entities, sentential Values, and ways of pairing the former with the latter. And we should not reify ways as Concepts with extensions, since the Values of a predicate may not form a set. Functionists, following Montague (1974), retain the problematic aspects of Frege's view.

Conjunctivism and the plural interpretation of '∃X' thus form a coherent package: each provides resources for rebutting an objection to the other. And the package view lets us capture the second-order character of quantificational constructions, while preserving an independently attractive conception of what second-order quantification is. It is a virtue of Conjunctivism that it can be combined in this way with a good interpretation of '∃X'.

## 4.4. *Expressive Power*

I said that sentences of natural language exhibit logical relations not characterizable in first-order terms. But a critic might say that semanticists should adopt a second-order metalanguage only if there are sentences whose semantic properties *cannot* be represented in a first-order metalanguage. And a critic with no brief for Functionism might say that semantic properties can be adequately represented in first-order terms, so long as we allow for mismatches between grammatical form and "logical" form. My own view is that semanticists should not have an a priori preference for first-order representations, much less one that trumps considerations in favor of minimizing mismatches between grammar and meaning. But the preference is common enough in philosophy to warrant a reminder that endlessly many sentences of natural language are not firstorderizable.[33] Geach–Kaplan examples, like 'Some critics admire only one another' are well known. Rescher (1962) and Wiggins (1980) discuss sentences like (21).

(21)   Most pets have whiskers

But I don't want the point to hang on examples with 'only' or 'most', which might be regarded as somehow special.[34] So let me mention a few other more illustrative cases.

While '$\forall x[Fx \rightarrow \exists y(Gy)]$' does not imply that there are at least as many Fs as Gs, speakers hear 'For every pleasure there is a pain' as having this kind of pessimistic implication; see Boolos (1998). We

---

[33] See Pietroski (2003b) for further discussion. If one viewed semantics as a project of "regimenting" natural language, as opposed to an empirical investigation of natural facts, one might try to regiment as much as possible into formal languages for which there are completeness proofs; see Quine (1950, 1951, 1960). But as Boolos notes, completeness is one virtue among many, even when assessing formal languages. Why not say that semanticists should adopt a metalanguage with formulae like '$\forall x \exists y(Fx \rightarrow Rxy)$', which may figure in undecidable inferences, only if there are sentences whose semantic properties *cannot* be adequately represented (even allowing for considerable discrepancies between logical form and grammatical form) in a metalanguage without such sentences? A more general methodological point, stressed by Quine but largely ignored in his discussions of language, is that reasons for theory choice can come from anywhere. For example, Boolos (1987, 1998) discusses a class of intuitively valid arguments with the following character: they have firstorderizable premises and conclusions; but the shortest proof of their validity in any familiar first-order system would be fantastically beyond astronomically long; whereas they are easily shown to be valid when represented in second-order terms. Semanticists might well prefer second-order representations on such grounds; see also Evans (1981).

[34] One might think that 'Most' is an irreducible but first-order quantifier in addition to '$\exists$' (or '$\forall$'), with 'Most Fs are Gs' being true iff most *sequences* with an F in the relevant position have an F that is G in that position. This yields the wrong result given infinitely many sequences but finitely many Gs. And while the Logic-English expression 'Every x such that x is a pet is such that x has fleas' seems acceptable, 'Most x such that x is a pet is such that x has fleas' does not; cf. 'Most Xs that *are pets are* Xs that *have* fleas'. But put this aside. Similarly, a critic might analyze 'The women outnumber the men' as follows: $\exists s \exists n \exists s' \exists n'[\forall x(x \in s \leftrightarrow Wx) \& n = |s| \& n > n' \& \forall x(x \in s' \leftrightarrow Mx) \& n' = |s'|]$. Of course, even if the determiner phrases indicate sets, one might wonder what *in the natural language sentence* indicates quantification over numbers. Correlatively, one might wonder if the sentence really implies (by virtue of its meaning) that there are at least two numbers. But put these issues aside as well.

can grasp the intended thought, which would be false given many pleasures and just one pain; yet this thought, which could be true no matter how many pleasures there are, cannot be represented in first-order terms. So it seems that firstorderizability does not even extend to instances of 'For every F, there is a G', which is relevantly like 'There are more Fs than Gs'. Similarly, given a hundred submissions, 'For every paper accepted, we rejected nine' is not a claim compatible with ninety-one acceptances.[35]

Plural pronouns and relative clauses provide endlessly many examples of nonfirstorderizability, like the following truism: my ancestors were [those people]$_X$ who$_X$ include my parents and the parents of [each person]$_x$ who$_x$ they$_X$ include. And it is often useful, for theorists and speakers, to talk about the things$_X$ such that each thing$_x$ is one of them$_X$ iff it$_x$ bears a certain relation to one of them$_X$. Given some thing$_x$, we might want to talk about the things that are at least as large as it$_x$. And given some things$_X$, we might want to talk about the big ones$_X$. I mention this in part because it suggests an alternative to saying merely that x is a Value of 'big ant' iff x is a Value of both 'big' and 'ant'; cf. Kamp (1975).

A particular ant, Adam, is a big one iff the ants$_Y$ are such that Adam is one of the big ones$_Y$. One might formalize this as follows: $\exists Y\{\forall x(Yx \leftrightarrow x \text{ is an ant}) \,\&\, \exists X[BIG(X, Y) \,\&\, Xa]\}$, with 'BIG(X, Y)' meaning that the Xs are big Ys. But this suggests that 'BIG' indicates a second-order *relation* that holds between some things$_X$ and some

---

[35] One can insist, implausibly, that these are pragmatic effects. But then the following argument is not valid: for every paper accepted, nine were rejected; finitely many papers were accepted; hence, most papers were rejected. And why insist that meanings are first-order if pragmatic implications are not? It is also worth noting that a first-order treatment of 'Every bottle fell' will be syncategorematic; determiners will not themselves be assigned Values. But semanticists need a second-order metalanguage to capture the conservativity generalization about determiners—and to report the fact that there is no determiner 'Equi' such that 'Equi dogs are cats' is synonymous with 'The dogs are equinumerous with the cats'. And one might be suspicious of a theory that describes the semantic role of determiners syncategorematically for purposes of ascribing Values to expressions (and characterizing the semantic competence of ordinary speakers in first-order terms) but resorts to a second-order characterization to capture generalizations about sentences (and human semantic competence).

things$_Y$. And intuitively, the Xs are big Ys iff the Xs *are* Ys that are significantly bigger than average (for the Ys). So x is a big ant iff $\exists Y\{\forall y(Yy \leftrightarrow y$ is an ant$)$ & $\exists X\{\forall y[Xy \leftrightarrow Yy$ & Significantly-Bigger-than-Average$(y, Y)]$ & $Xx\}\}$. This characterizes the meaning of 'big' in terms of a relation that an individual$_x$ bears to some things$_Y$ such that it$_x$ may be one them$_Y$.[36]

I won't try to defend a particular grammatical analysis here. But consider the complex sentence 'Those$_1$ are ants$_2$, and (they$_1$ are) big ones$_2$,', which has the Value **t** relative to assignment **A** iff:

$$\exists X\{\forall x[Xx \leftrightarrow \text{Associates}(\mathbf{A}, 1, x)] \text{ \& Plural}(X) \text{ \& } \forall x:Xx(x \text{ is an ant}) \&$$

$$\forall x[\text{Associates}(\mathbf{A}, 2, x) \leftrightarrow x \text{ is an ant}] \text{ \& } \exists Y\{\forall x[Yx \leftrightarrow$$

$$\text{Associates}(\mathbf{A}, 2, x)] \text{ \& } \forall x:Xx[Yx \text{ \& Significantly-}$$

$$\text{Bigger-than-Average}(x, Y)]\}\};$$

there are some things$_X$ such that they$_Y$$_X$ are the 1-associates of **A**, each of them$_X$ is an ant, the ants$_Y$ are the 2-associates of **A**, and they$_Y$ are big ones$_Y$. So if the underyling structure of 'That is a big ant' is more like 'That is an ant, and a big one'—or perhaps 'There are the ants, and that is a big one'—Conjunctivists have an account ready to hand. (Plausibly, 'That is big' is elliptical for 'That is a big one'; and speakers easily understand locutions like 'For ants, they are big'.) The point of these brief remarks is to illustrate resources

---

[36] If this seems strange, note that a student who gets an 'A' in a class with a 'B' average bears the following relation to the students in the class: her grade is above the average of their grades. Perhaps it is a context-sensitive matter, even given some things$_X$, which ones$_X$ are the big ones$_X$; and perhaps a theory of meaning should reflect this. One might say that 'Adam is a big ant' is true relative to some contexts, but false relative to others, without varying the time, or Adam, or the ants. For one might say that whether or not Adam counts as a *big* ant depends on the context. And in so far as vague terms admit of various precisifications, there is surely something right about this; see Graff (2000) for discussion. Maybe it is also true that whether or not Adam counts as big *for an ant* depends on the context, even if one controls for vagueness. And *maybe* a theory of meaning should reflect this by allowing for the possibility that 'Adam is a big ant' gets the Value **t** relative to some but not all assignments, even controlling for vagueness. But for simplicity and at least for now, let's assume that, whatever the Xs are, it is (modulo vagueness) a context-invariant fact which Xs are big Xs.

available to Conjunctivists, not to offer a theory of comparative adjectives. But it is also worth noting that for simple cases like 'big ant', plural quantification over Values of nouns is sufficient. Quantification over abstracta—like scales, or functions from ants to numbers—is not required.

Returning now to the main theme of this section, whatever we say about words like 'big' and 'ancestor' must cohere with the fact that many arithmetically inspired sentences are *provably* non-firstorderizable (given a technique due to David Kaplan). Consider the following examples discussed by Boolos: there are some horses that are all faster than Zev and also faster than the sire of any horse that is slower than all of them; and there are some gunslingers each of whom has shot the right foot of at least one of the others. By using such sentences, speakers can express thoughts whose structures cannot be fully reflected with sentences of a first-order language. Hence, semanticists need a more expressive metalanguage; see also Higginbotham (1998). But it does not follow that to capture the meanings of such sentences, semanticists must quantify over things besides horses and gunslingers.

The plural construal of '∃X' provides enough expressive power for purposes of constructing reasonable theories of meaning, without going beyond the spare Fregean assumptions discussed in Chapter 1; see also Lewis (1991). Conjunctivism lets us preserve this virtue of the plural construal. And this is an argument in favor of the proposed package—Conjunctivism about natural language, with a Boolos-style interpretation of second-order quantification in our metalanguage.

## 5. Plural Noun-Phrases as Second-Order Predicates

Let's descend from these logical heights and recall the dialectic. I want to defend Conjunctivism without assuming that the Values of determiners are ordered pairs of sets. So I have been urging an interpretation of second-order formalism according to which 'Xx' means that x is one of the Xs. We have seen some reasons for thinking that 'is one of' does not mean *is an element of*, prima facie, 'x is one of the Xs' does not imply that the Xs form a set. But specifying the meanings of plural expressions in terms of plural entities can seem so natural, and the idea is so prevalent, that one wants to see many arguments in favor of the alternative. I take this demand seriously. But skeptics must also take care not to beg the question.

In particular, one does not object by noting that *if* speakers covertly quantify over plural entities when using 'it is one of them', then a plural construal of 'Xx' does not avoid such quantification. While the conditional is true, the proposal is that the antecedent is false. This does involve a kind of circularity: one stipulates what instances of '∃X(...X...)' mean by using plural expressions, like 'some things' and 'one of them', that we already understand; then one uses instances of '∃X(...X...)' to state hypotheses about (*inter alia*) the meanings of plural expressions, like 'one of the dogs' and 'uno de los perros', in a natural language that we may also understand. But this is not an objection.

We also stipulate what instances of '∃x(...x...)' mean by using singular expressions, like 'something' and 'it'. Then we use instances of '∃x(...x...)' to specify the meanings of sentences like 'Something is brown and furry'. And this kind of circularity is not an objection to singular construals of first-order quantification. It might seem different with regard to '∃X'. For if one expects a *reduction* of plural reference and second-order quantification to singular reference and first-order quantification, one expects a stipulation about what instances of '∃X(...X...)' mean in terms of singular expressions like 'is an element of'. But one cannot object that a proposal fails to provide this kind of reduction, when it is part of the proposal that such a reduction would *mis*characterize the meanings of plural expressions.

That said, such expressions appear in many contexts besides 'one of ___'. Consider (41) and (42),

(41)    The surgeons stabbed the turnips
(42)    Nine boys ate four pizzas

which have collective readings. This raises two questions. *Can* one account for collective readings without quantifying over collections? And are there independent reasons for *preferring* such an account to one that specifies the relevant meaning of (42) as follows: **t** iff a nine-membered collection of boys ate a four-membered collection of pizzas? I address the second question in §§5.2–4 below. But one can quickly reply to the first, affirmatively, by drawing on Schein (1993, 2001, forthcoming); see also Higginbotham and Schein (1989), Higginbotham (1998).[37]

## 5.1. *Collective Readings without Quantifying over Collections*

Conjunctivists can represent the collective reading of (42) with (42*a*).

(42*a*)   $\exists$O[External(O, nine boys) & Past-Eating(O) & Internal(O, four pizzas)]

Recall that the Values of ate$_\Pi$ are events whose external and internal participants are, respectively, Agents and Themes.[38] On this view, (42) has a reading on which it gets the Value **t** iff some things$_O$ were such that: nine boys were their$_O$ Agents; they$_O$ were events of eating; and four pizzes were their$_O$ Themes. Instead of interpreting 'External(O, nine boys)' as a predicate satisfied by some thing$_O$ iff a nine-membered collection of boys is its$_O$ external participant, one

---

[37] One can treat '$\exists$X:{Nine(X) & $\forall$x:Xx(x is a boy)}[External(e, X)]' as a monadic predicate satisfied by e iff $\exists$O{Nine(O) & $\exists$X:$\forall$x(Xx $\leftrightarrow$ x is a boy)[Internal(O, X)] & $\forall$o:Oo[External(o, **t**) iff $\exists$x[Internal(o, x) & Agent(e, x)]]}; where Nine(O) iff nine of the Os have **t** as their external element. Of course, appeal to events hightlights the need for an account of 'Every bottle fell' that treats the verb 'fell' as a predicate satisfied by events; see §4.

[38] This leaves room for the possibility that some events$_O$ are Values of ate$_{\Pi*}$ because they$_O$ together counted as eating, even though at least one of them$_O$ was not itself an event of eating. Perhaps a chewing and a swallowing, along with some other events, can together be Values of ate$_{\Pi*}$—in something like the way many events of a raindrop falling can count as a downpour. I take no firm stand on this issue here. But if only for simplicity, let's assume that each Value of ate$_{\Pi*}$ was itself an event of eating.

can interpret it as a predicate satisfied by some things$_O$ iff nine boys are their$_O$ external participants. That is,

External(O, nine boys) iff

$\exists$X[External(O, X) & Nine(X) & $\forall$x:Xx(x is a boy)].

This doesn't yet show *how* (42) supports the reading indicated in (42*a*). The details depend on the grammatical structure, which is not obvious. So it is worth considering a few related suggestions based on ideas already discussed: we can distinguish an eventish predicate like [ate$_{\Pi*}$ them$_{\alpha2}$]$_\Pi$ from the homophonous open sentence, whose Value is **t** or **f** relative to an assignment; we can distinguish a saturated phrase like [They$_{\alpha1}$ [ate$_{\Pi*}$ them$_{\alpha2}$]$_\Pi$]$_{\Pi P}$ from the homophonous closed sentence; and 'nine boys' can be a plural argument of a verb, as in $\langle$[(nine$_{+pl}$ boys$_\Pi$)$_\alpha$ [ate$_{\Pi*}$ (four$_{+pl}$ pizzas$_\Pi$)$_\alpha$]$_\Pi$]$_{\Pi P}$$\rangle$— or rewriting to make the grammatical relations explicit, $\langle$[ext-(nine$_{+pl}$ boys$_\Pi$)$_\alpha$ [ate$_{\Pi*}$ int-(four$_{+pl}$ pizzas$_\Pi$)$_\alpha$]]$\rangle$.

Suppose the plural arguments raise, leaving traces as indicated below:

$$\langle[(\text{nine}_{+pl}\ \text{boys}_\Pi)_{\alpha1}\langle[(\text{four}_{+pl}\ \text{pizzas}_\Pi)_{\alpha2}$$
$$\langle[\text{ext-t}_1[\text{ate}_{\Pi*}\text{int-t}_2]]\rangle]\rangle]\rangle.$$

Then the sentence gets the Value **t** relative to **A** iff:

$\exists$Z$\langle$Val(Z, (nine$_{+pl}$ boys$_\Pi$)$_\alpha$, **A**) & $\forall$x[Zx $\leftrightarrow$ Associates(**A**, 1, x)] &

$\exists$Y$\langle$Val(Y, (four$_{+pl}$ pizzas$_\Pi$)$_\alpha$, **A**) & $\forall$x[Yx $\leftrightarrow$ Associates(**A**, 2, x)] &

$\exists$O$\langle\exists$X{External(O,X) & $\forall$x[Xx $\leftrightarrow$ Associates(**A**, 1, x)]} &

Past-Eating(O) & $\exists$X{Internal(O,X) &

$\forall$x[Xx $\leftrightarrow$ Associates(**A**, 2, x)]}$\rangle\rangle\rangle$;

or more briefly, and as desired,

$\exists$Z$\exists$Y$\exists$O{Nine(Z) & $\forall$x:Zx[Boy(x)] & Four(Y) & $\forall$y:Yy[Pizza(y)] &

External(O,Z) & Past-Eating(O) & Internal(O,Y)}.

This reflects the idea that 'nine' and 'four', unlike 'boy' and 'pizza', are plural predicates: $Val(Z, nine_{+pl}, \mathbf{A})$ iff the Zs are nine; $Val(Z, boys_\Pi, \mathbf{A})$ iff each of the Zs is a boy, and the Zs are plural.

Alternatively, suppose the plural arguments do not raise. If we apply the proposed semantics' grammatical relations directly to $[ext\text{-}(nine_{+pl}\ boys_\Pi)_\alpha\ [ate_{\Pi^*}\ int\text{-}(four_{+pl}\ pizzas_\Pi)_\alpha]]$, we get the following:

$Val(O, [ext\text{-}(nine_{+pl}\ boys_\Pi)_\alpha[ate_{\Pi^*}\ int\text{-}(four_{+pl}\ pizzas_\Pi)_\alpha]], \mathbf{A})$ iff

$\exists X\{External(O, X)\ \&\ \forall x[Xx \leftrightarrow Val(x, (nine_{+pl}\ boys_\Pi)_\alpha, \mathbf{A})]\ \&$

$Past\text{-}Eating(O)\ \&\ \exists X\{Internal(O, X)\ \&$

$\forall x[Xx \leftrightarrow Val(x, (four_{+pl}\ pizzas_\Pi)_\alpha, \mathbf{A})]\}\}.$

This raises questions about how to interpret expressions like '$\forall x[Xx \leftrightarrow Val(x, (nine_{+pl}\ boys_\Pi)_\alpha, \mathbf{A})]$'. While this is not a type mismatch in the traditional sense, since 'x' and 'X' range over the same domain, a single boy x can be a Value of a phrase like 'nine boys' only in a derivative sense: he$_x$ and eight other boys are (together) Values of the phrase.[39] But we get the right result if we say that

$External(O, ext\text{-}(nine_{+pl}\ boys_\Pi)_\alpha, \mathbf{A})$ iff
$\exists X\{External(O, X)\ \&\ \exists Y[Val(Y, nine_{+pl}, \mathbf{A})\ \&\ Val(Y, boys_\Pi, \mathbf{A})\ \&$
$\forall x(Xx \leftrightarrow Yx)]\}.$

That is, some things$_O$ are Values of 'nine boys' appearing as an external argument iff: their$_O$ external participants are nine boys; that is, [their$_O$ external participants]$_Y$ are such that nine boys are them$_Y$.

---

[39] We don't want to say that $Val(x, (nine\ boys_\Pi)_\alpha, \mathbf{A})$ iff $\exists Y\{Yx\ \&\ Val(Y, nine, \mathbf{A})\ \&\ Val(Y, boys, \mathbf{A})\}$. For then the mere existence of nine boys would guarantee that every boy is a Value of 'nine boys', and '$External(O, nine\ boys, \mathbf{A})$' would imply that the Os have *all* the boys as their external participants.

Perhaps a Conjunctivist should just leave matters here, saying that a plural quantificational argument like 'nine boys' is understood as taking scope *over* the relevant instance of comprehension '$\forall x(Xx \leftrightarrow \Phi x)$'. But if unraised arguments are indexed, one could say that relative to **A**, x is a Value of (nine boys)$_{\alpha 1}$ iff **A** associates the first index with nine boys$_X$, one of whom$_X$ is x. More formally,

$$\text{Val}(O, \text{ext-}(\text{nine}_{+\text{pl}} \text{ boys}_\Pi)_{\alpha 1}, \mathbf{A}) \text{ iff}$$
$$\exists X\{\text{External}(O, X) \;\&\; \forall x[Xx \leftrightarrow \text{Associates}(\mathbf{A}, 1, x) \;\&\;$$
$$\text{Val}(X, (\text{nine}_{+\text{pl}} \text{ boys}_\Pi)_\alpha, \mathbf{A})]\}$$

This reflects the hypothesis that an indexed expression may impose a semantic restriction of its own, apart from the index. If them$_{\alpha 1}$ indicates that the 1-Associates are plural, perhaps (nine boys)$_{\alpha 1}$ indicates that the 1-associates are nine boys.

For present purposes, I take no stand on exactly which conception of grammatical structure Conjunctivists should adopt with regard to collective readings. But given any plausible conception, it seems that Conjunctivists will be able to say that (42) has a reading on which: there are some things$_X$, and there are some things$_Y$ such that they$_X$ are nine boys, they$_Y$ are four pizzas, and there were some eatings$_O$ whose Agents were them$_X$ and whose Themes were them$_Y$. The more interesting question is whether we *should* characterize collective readings in these terms.

## 5.2. *Semantic Noncommitment*

If nine boys ate together, sharing a common meal, there may be a single event divisible along its "Agent-axis" into nine parts, and divisible along its "Theme-axis" into four parts corresponding to the pizzas eaten. This is compatible with a collective reading of (42).

(42) Nine boys ate four pizzas

But we should not assume that, whenever some events are Values of a predicate, they are parts of *an* event. (Is there an event whose parts are all and only the Values of 'event that is not part of itself'?)

*Given* an event with multiple Agents, a natural thought is that such an event has parts each of which has at most one Agent, and likewise for other thematic relations.[40] But four pizzas could have been eaten by nine boys, with no independent reason for thinking there was a single event with the nine boys as Agents; see Higginbotham and Schein (1989), Gillon (1987), Schein (1993, 2002).

The boys may have formed three groups of sworn enemies who would never share a meal. And the pizzas may have been served over the course of a day, with some of the boys coming back for another slice. Yet (42) could still be used by the restaurant manager to report the day's pizza consumption due to boys. While (12) may invite thoughts of collaboration,

(12)    Ten professors wrote fifteen articles

replacing 'wrote' with 'refereed' suggests that cooperation is not required. And it seems that (12), read collectively, implies *neither* that there was an event with ten professors as Agents; *nor* that there were ten events of professors working alone. Plural quantification over events seems to be exactly what is wanted, in order to capture this lack of semantic commitment. For we can say that (12) gets the Value **t** iff

$$\exists O\{\exists X[\text{External}(O, X) \ \& \ \text{Ten}(X) \ \& \ \forall x: Xx(x \text{ is a professor})] \ \& $$
$$\text{Past-Writing}(O) \ \& \ \exists X[\text{Internal}(O, X) \ \& \ \text{Fifteen}(X) \ \& $$
$$\forall x: Xx(x \text{ is an article})]\}.$$

This leaves open the possibility that the relevant Os constitute one or more collaborative efforts; see n. 38 above. And *perhaps* there are

---

[40] For discussion, see Carlson (1984), Taylor (1985), Davies (1989, 1991), Parsons (1990), Schein (2001, 2002). Letting ' $\succeq$ ' indicate a whole-to-part relation, one could say that $\forall x: \text{Agent}(e, x)\exists f:\{\succeq (f, e) \ \& \ \text{Agent}(f, x) \ \& \ \forall y: \text{Agent}(f, y)[y = x]\}$. This would not require collections as participants for events that are the Values of predicates like 'rained'. We could say that Val(O, rained$_\Pi$, **A**) iff the Os constituted rain(ing). The idea would be that two drops of water falling do not constitute rain, and two rocks falling are not rocks raining down. But when enough things of the right sort fall in the right way, it raineth.

distinctive collective readings that actually imply cooperation; if so, Conjunctivists can specify special cases with predicates like '∃o[Comprise(O, o)]'. Though one should not assume that different "ways of making a sentence true" correspond to different readings; see Pietroski and Hornstein (2002) for related discussion in a first-order framework.

As Gillon (1987) discusses, a plural-entity theorist can build in the relevant lack of semantic commitment by appealing to possible partitions of collections. Perhaps nine boys (collectively ate) four pizzas iff: a collection of nine boys is divisible into one or more subgroups, each of which ate some pizza, and a collection of four pizzas is the sum of the pizza eaten by each subgroup. This may be the Functionist's best strategy. For if nine boys who never share a meal still constitute a collection that can eat four pizzas, one cannot maintain that talk of collections eating things is just an innocuous way of describing what happens when Agents do things *together*. But quantifying over partitions of collections seems like an unnecessarily baroque alternative to quantifying plurally over individuals. Put another way, Functionists end up positing singular/first-order quantification over individuals, events, collections, and partitions of collections; whereas plural/second-order quantification over events and their participants delivers the desired results more directly and economically.

At this point, we should ask again whether collections can do what individuals together do. Four people can share a meal, move some pianos, and play the Beethoven quartets. But can a *collection* do all this? It may be tempting to read 'Agent(E, four people)' as the claim that a collection of four people is *the* Agent of *the* composite event E, which has four single-agent *parts*. But does this really make sense? Does it posit too many Agents? Reasonable people disagree. And given type-shifting, Functionists can describe the basic facts while avoiding unwanted implications; see Landman (1996) for discussion building on Link (1983) and others. But if Functionism requires auxiliary type-shifting hypotheses to handle cases of verbs combining with plural *arguments*, this tells against the claim that concatenating predicates with arguments signifies function-application. Predicate–argument combinations are supposed to be the poster cases for Functionism. If plural arguments are treated as special cases, like adjuncts in this respect, Functionist accounts of semantic composition become more complex and less explanatory.[41]

In my view, this is another reason for saying that the Values of transitive action verbs are simply *events*, as opposed to functions of type $<x, <x, <e, t>>>$, from individuals to functions from individuals to *functions from events to* sentential Values. If we say that $\|ate\| = \lambda y . [\lambda x . [\lambda e . t$ iff Agent(e, x) & Past-Eating(e) & Theme(e, y)]]$, then we need to say that the variables range over collections; and then we need auxiliary hypotheses to correctly describe collective readings in terms of collections. Still, one would like to see further reasons for preferring a Conjunctivist account that employs plural quantification over events to a Functionist account that employs singular quantification over collections. So in the remainder of this section I'll argue, following Schein, that the Functionist/plural-entity apparatus is both insufficient and unwanted.

## 5.3. *Collections are Not Enough*

Verbs like 'give' can combine with *three* arguments. Consider 'Pat gave Chris the puppy', which can be paraphrased with the indirect object 'Chris' in a prepositional phrase, as in 'Pat gave the puppy to Chris'. Similarly, 'Pat taught a student the theory' can be paraphrased with 'Pat taught the theory to a student'. Given three plural arguments, we get multiple ambiguity, if only because

---

[41] If one adopts a theory according to which a collection can eat$^{co}$ something without eating it, one has to say what 'eat$^{co}$' means. If $c_1$ ate$^{co}$ $c_2$ iff the elements of $c_1$ (together) ate the elements of $c_2$, then one has to say what it is for the elements of $c_1$ to eat the elements of $c_2$ without using 'eat$^{co}$' or appealing to a Schein-style account. And consider 'The dogs are equinumerous with the cats'. One can say that a collection $c_1$ has the same numerosity as a collection $c_2$. But if this is not just to say that $1 = 1$, the claim is evidently that the elements of $c_1$ *are* equinumerous with (i.e., *they* correspond 1-to-1 with) the elements of $c_2$.

each noun-phrase can be understood collectively or distributively. For example, (43) has many readings.

(43)  Three linguists taught five students four theories

Schein (1993) stresses that, in particular, (43) seems to have a reading according to which the subject is understood collectively, while the indirect object ('five students') is understood distributively with respect to the direct object ('four theories'). On this reading, (43) implies that each of five students was taught four theories, but it does not say how the linguists divided the work. Perhaps each theory was team-taught, and perhaps not. It may be that no student encountered all three linguists. Indeed, the linguists might not have been working as a team. One could use (43), on the reading in question, to describe what happened during a theory-teaching contest in which each linguist was competing against the others. Similar examples include (44) and (45).

(44)  Three quarterbacks threw five receivers four passes
(45)  Three parents read five children four stories

The relevant reading of (44) leaves it open how many passes each quarterback threw, and which receivers each quarterback threw to; though each quarterback had to throw at least one of the twenty passes, four to each of five receivers. On the "Schein-reading" of (45), three parents together made it the case that (one way or another) each of five children was read four stories. Likewise, the Schein-reading of (43) is *not* captured by saying that for each of five students, three linguists together taught that student four theories. For this implies that each linguist was involved in the teaching of each student.[42] But one can capture the Schein-reading, without glossing collective readings in terms of collections, as an essentially

---

[42] One can stipulate that a collection of linguists (all of whom did some teaching) can teach—or at least teach*—a student some theories even if some members of the collection never encountered that student. But then if three linguists taught Pat four theories, and there are a hundred linguists (who did some teaching, but never encountered Pat), a hundred linguists taught Pat four theories. And that seems wrong.

plural claim about some events: three linguists were the Agents of those events, which were events of teaching; and in those events, each of five students received a certain amount of instruction (namely, four theories' worth).

We can think about this reading of (43) as follows: the grammatical subject 'three linguists' is understood collectively as a (plural) predicate; and 'taught five students four theories' is understood as another predicate that has some events$_O$ as Values iff they$_O$ are events of teaching with five students as the "Recipients" and four Themes *per* Recipient, with each Theme being a theory. (For these purposes, I take no stand on whether 'Recipient' corresponds to a covert preposition or a distinctive grammatical relation that ditransitive verbs bear to indirect objects.) Crucially, the grammatical subject imposes no conditions on the Themes or Recipients, and the (complex) verb-phrase imposes no conditions on the Agents of relevant events. Schein speaks of "thematic separation"; each argument of the verb imposes its condition independently. And this captures the right degree of commitment and noncommitment with regard to what (43–5) imply on the readings in question.

Such examples constitute an argument for Conjunctivism. To restate the point from two paragraphs back, the Schein-reading of (43) is *not* captured with the Functionist-friendly (43F).

(43F)    for each of five students z, there are four theories y such that for some event e and some collection x of three linguists, e was a teaching by x of y to z

One can hypothesize that the Value of 'teach' is $\lambda z . [\lambda y. [\lambda x . [\lambda e . \mathbf{t}$ iff e was a teaching by x of y to z]]], letting the variables range over individuals and collections. This allows for a mixture of distributive and collective quantification, as in (43F). But on any such view, individuals are connected to events *via the Value of the verb itself.* This excludes the possibility that each argument is an independent predicate (whose Values are events) because of that argument's specific *grammatical relation to* the verb. And given Schein-readings, it seems that arguments can indeed be independent predicates in just this way.

Given two arguments, it is hard to make this point, since Functionists can appeal to collections and scope ambiguities. But with three arguments, appeal to collections and scope does not provide a simulacrum of thematic separation. There is a difference between saying that o is a Value of 'teach' iff o was an event of teaching—leaving the rest to grammatical relations, thematic roles, and conjunction—and saying that a certain (four-place) function is the Value of 'teach'. Given the Functionist view, (43) implies that the relevant arguments of the function are related (by virtue of being arguments of the same function) in ways *not* implied by the more agnostic Conjunctivist view. This leaves no room for Schein-readings. But if each grammatical argument indicates a logically independent predicate/conjunct, and the indirect object in (43) can be understood as taking scope over the direct object, then one expects the reading indicated below:

$$\exists O\{\exists X[\text{External}(O, X) \,\&\, \text{Three}(X) \,\&\, \forall x : Xx(x \text{ is a linguist})] \,\&$$
$$\text{Past-Teaching}(O) \,\&\, \exists X[\text{Five}(X) \,\&\, \forall x : Xx(x \text{ is a student}) \,\&$$
$$\forall x : Xx(x \text{ was a Recipient of four theories in the Os})]\};$$

there were some things$_O$ such that their$_O$ Agents were three linguists, they$_O$ were events of teaching, and each of five students was taught four theories in (the course of) them$_O$.

To say that *x was a recipient of four theories in the Os* is to say that some of the Os were events in which x was a Recipient of four theories. More formally,

$$\exists E\{\forall o : Eo(Oo) \,\&\, \exists Z[\text{Recipient}(E, Z) \,\&\, \forall y(Zy \leftrightarrow y = x)] \,\&$$
$$\exists Y[\text{Internal}(E, Y) \,\&\, \text{Four}(Y) \,\&\, \forall y : Yy(y \text{ is a theory})]\}.$$

Taken out of context, this might seem like notational overkill. But (43F), which *fails* to capture the relevant reading, isn't much less complicated. And the point is not that these readings are especially simple on a Conjunctivist account. The claim is that (43) can have an essentially plural meaning not captured in terms of functions and plural entities. Schein (forthcoming) extends this point to a wide range of constructions in various languages. If correct, this is a powerful empirical argument for the hypothesis that grammatical arguments are interpreted as conjoinable monadic predicates.

At a minimum, this suggests that it is question-begging to ignore examples like (43) and (9).

   (9)   The rocks rained down on the huts

Or consider Schein's (1993) example 'The elms are clustered in the middle of the forest'. Even if one insists that a collection of elms can be clustered somewhere, what could this mean, except that the collection's *elements are* clustered somewhere? And if the semantic architecture of natural language is revealed in these essentially plural constructions, then appeals to collections really do not capture the collective readings of simpler constructions like (42).

   (42)   Nine boys ate four pizzas

## 5.4. *Collections Get in the Way*

Still, one might think that a good Functionist theory will capture the facts about collective readings. Perhaps Schein and I have mischaracterized the phenomena in a way unfriendly to Functionism, and appealing to collections in the right way will capture the real phenomena. So let me turn to Schein's argument that some very simple facts go unexplained, given a theory that interposes plural entities between the individual satisfiers of a predicate like 'dog' and the Values of sentences like (46) and (47).

   (46)   Every dog barked
   (47)   Every one of the dogs barked

Speakers of English know that (46) is true iff (47) is true, and likewise for endlessly many similar pairs of sentences. Correlatively, speakers know that, if the dogs barked, there was a dog that barked.

One expects a semantic theory to account for such implications. Given a theory that associates plural noun-phrases with plural entities, the desired explanations will presumably be based on generalizations about how individuals are related to plural entities. But the obvious candidates are false.

Suppose we have a theory according to which: 'There is a dog' has the Value **t** iff some singular individual$_x$ meets a certain condition—namely, that it$_x$ is a dog; and 'The dogs barked' has the Value **t** iff some plural individual$_X$ meets a certain condition—namely, that every (relevant) dog is an element of it$_X$, nothing else is an element of it$_X$, and every element of it$_X$ barked. This does not yet explain why the latter implies the former. We need the further assumption, not guaranteed by logic alone, that nothing meets the relevant condition if there are no dogs. But one can make it part of the semantic theory that the "empty" collection does not meet the relevant condition. So this is not, by itself, a serious objection. Though it is worth noting that given a Boolos-interpretation, *no further assumption is needed*.

If 'X' ranges over whatever 'x' ranges over, then trivially: $\exists X[\forall x(Xx \leftrightarrow x$ is a dog$)] \rightarrow \exists x(x$ is a dog$)$; if there are the dogs, there is a dog. Likewise, given a Boolos-interpretation, generalizations like the following are truistic: x is a dog iff $\exists X[\forall y(Xy \leftrightarrow y$ is a dog$)$ & $Xx]$; that is, x is a dog iff x is one of the dogs. So trivially, every dog barked iff every one of the dogs barked, and every thing that is a Value of 'dog' barked iff every one of the things that is a Value of 'dog' barked. And this is important. For suppose we have a theory according to which (47) gets the Value **t** iff some plural individual$_X$ is such that every dog (and nothing else) is an element of it$_X$; and every element of it$_X$ barked. Then (46) semantically implies (47) only if (46) semantically implies that some thing$_X$ is such that for each thing$_x$, it$_x$ is an element of it$_X$ iff it$_x$ is a dog. And at least prima facie, logic alone does not guarantee that given a dog or two, there is a collection **c** such that every dog barked iff every element of **c** barked.

Logic seems to leave room for the possibility that, while each dog barked, *there is no collection* of the dogs. This is not to deny the existence of collections. I readily grant that, given some dogs, there is something whose elements are all and only those dogs. And for purposes of this argument, I even grant that '{x: x is a dog}' specifies a set whose elements are all and only the dogs. The issue is how we should *explain* certain implications. Putting the point in psychological terms, speakers *recognize* that (46) and (47) are truth-conditionally equivalent, and arguably synonymous. But is this in part *because* speakers tacitly know (or at least assume) that, given a dog or two, there is a collection such that every dog barked iff every element of the collection barked? An alternative is to characterize speakers' semanatic competence in terms of a theory whose second-order quantifiers are interpreted *à la Boolos*. Then the inference from (46) to (47) would be seen as trivial; and the inference would not be enthymematic, with a suppressed premise about collections.

So we have to ask if candidate premises about collections are plausible additions to a semantic theory. One might be tempted to adopt, as Frege (1893, 1903) did, something like the following principle that links plural entities to more "basic" singular things:

every thing that satisfies $\Phi$ satisfies $\Psi$ iff

for some plural entity $c$, $\forall x(x \in c \leftrightarrow x$ satisfies $\Phi)$ &
$\forall x: x \in c(x$ satisfies $\Psi)$;

or in more explicitly Functionist terms,

every thing that $\|\Phi\|$ maps to $t$ is a thing that
$\|\Psi\|$ maps to $t$ iff

for some plural entity $c$, $\forall x[x \in c \leftrightarrow \|\Phi\|(x) = t]$ &
$\forall x: x \in c(\|\Psi\|(x) = t)$.

But prima facie, these "naive comprehension" principles are false, given at least one predicate such that there is no entity whose elements are all and only the things that satisfy the predicate. And there seem to be many such predicates, like 'is not an element of itself'.[43]

This was part of the motivation for a Boolos-style interpretation of '$\exists X[\forall x(Xx \leftrightarrow \Phi x)]$'. But now the point is not just that Functionists have a hard time assigning Values to a certain range of unusual predicates. It is that false generalizations cannot provide correct explanations of facts concerning typical predicates like 'dog'. So the objection is not merely that a plural-entity/Functionist account is *descriptively* limited, leaving us wondering how speakers can understand sentences like 'Some sets are nonselfelemental'. A plural-entity/Functionist account is also *explanatorily* inadequate, since it leaves us unable to account for some elementary implications.

As theorists, we want to know *why* (47) is sure to get the Value **t** if (46) gets the Value **t**. But we have a problem if our semantic theory "interposes" collections between the entities that satisfy a predicate $\Phi$ and the Values of sentences containing a clause of the form 'one of the $\Phi$s'. For in that case, our theory must also include a suitably *general* principle—a principle that does not make reference to idiosyncratic features of $\Phi$ itself—according to which the $\Phi$s form a collection such that something is one of the $\Phi$s iff it is in that collection. But the theory is *false* if the principle applies to any predicate that (on pain of contradiction) does not correspond to a collection with the right membership.

I cannot prove that there is no suitably general yet suitably restricted principle. (I cannot here even survey the many responses to Russell's paradox.) Suffice it to say that all extant proposals face serious difficulties. And even given a coherent linking principle, one would have to argue that it is a plausible component of a semantic theory for *natural* languages. This will be difficult, given that no suitably restricted principle will preserve the following attractive idea: the explanation for why (46) implies (47) applies, equally well

---

[43] To take another example, an adjective is heterological iff it does not describe itself. So assuming that any word of less than six letters is a short word, 'long' is heterological and 'short' is not. But while there are some heterological words, there is no entity **p** such that $\forall x(x \in p$ iff x is heterological); for if there were such an entity, 'heterological' would be one of it, and 'heterological' would not be one of it.

and without type-adjustment, to apparently similar pairs like 'The set of prime numbers is a nonselfelemental set' and 'The set of prime numbers is one of the nonselfelemental sets'. By contrast, on a Boolos-style interpretation, there is no need to link the things that 'X' ranges over to things that 'x' ranges over. So there is no need for a dubious linking principle—just as there is no need for an independent constraint to capture the "conservativity" facts.

One might reply that principles of a semantic theory don't have to be *true*, they just have to be principles that speakers tacitly (and perhaps incorrectly) assume. Perhaps a semantic theory should be understood as if prefixed by an operator like 'Speakers of the language tacitly (and perhaps incorrectly) assume that . . .'. I agree that semantic theories should be construed as psychological theories. But I don't think this dispels the difficulty for Functionist/plural-object theories. For one thing, it's hard to see how a principle of semantic composition assumed by all speakers could be *false*. How could it be true that speakers tacitly assume that the meanings of complex linguistic expressions are related to the meanings of simpler expressions in certain ways, but false that the complex meanings are related to the simpler ones in those ways? What other facts determine the facts about semantic composition? Functionists presumably think it is true—and not *merely* something speakers assume—that $\|\Pi^\wedge \alpha\| = \|\Pi\|(\|\alpha\|)$. And it seems like cheating to insist on a distinction between truth and tacit assumption precisely when the hypothesized principles appear to be false.

Moreover, speakers who explicitly believe that there is no set of all the sets still find the inference from (48) to (49) impeccable.

(48)   Some set has no members
(49)   One of the sets has no members

But one would expect these speakers to *reject* (49), even if they accept (48), if all speakers tacitly assume a naive comprehension principle for purposes of understanding sentences like (49). If a speaker understands a sentence S as having the Value **t** iff p, and the speaker thinks that p is not the case, then one expects the speaker to reject S. If you think that there are infinitely many primes, and understand a sentence S as having the Value **t** iff there are finitely many primes, you will presumably reject S.

A plural-entity theorist might reply in one or both of two ways: even sophisticated speakers *tacitly assume that* there is some $x^*$ such that $\forall x(x$ is one of $x^*$ iff $x$ is a set), and this assumption drives their acceptance of (49); or in so far as sophisticated speakers bring their sophisticated knowledge to bear on (49), their acceptance of (49) is driven by a *reinterpretation* according to which (48) is correct even though (49) gets the Value **f** on its "natural" interpretation. In my view, these are *ad hoc* maneuvers. If a theory requires them, that is a point against the theory. But let's take them in turn.

If (49) has a meaning according to which it implies a nonexistent plurality, why doesn't (49) seem paradoxical to those who think there is no set of all the sets? Why don't sophisticated speakers at least feel *pulled* to reject (49)? By contrast, we do feel pulled to accept naive comprehension principles, even when we know that they are false. But our inclination to accept such principles does not seem to be part of how we *understand* plural noun-phrases. We may have a mistaken "folk set-theory" as well as a mistaken "folk probability-theory" and other liabilities to error; see, for example, Kahneman and Tversky (1972). But there are many false generalizations that humans are disposed to believe, though not disposed to assume for purposes of understanding speech. Naive comprehension principles would seem to be overgeneralizations of this sort, since (49) remains an obvious truth.

Let me put this another way. Sentences (50) and (51) seem to be parallel truisms.

> (50)   There is no barber who shaves all and only the barbers who do not shave themselves
>
> (51)   There is no set that includes all and only the sets that do not include themselves

Ordinary speakers can be brought to see that (50) is true by supposing (in order to derive a contradiction) that there is such a barber. This is compatible with there being a plural entity $x^*$ such that $\forall x(x$ is one of $x^*$ iff x is a barber & x does not shave x). So no trouble yet. But similar reasoning shows that (51) is true. And how can one see that (51) is provably true yet still *understand* (51) so that it implies the existence of a plural entity $x^*$ such that $\forall x(x$ is one of $x^*$ iff x is a set & x does not include x)? If sophisticated speakers reinterpret (51), why and how does the reinterpretation preserve the provable truth of (51)?

This doesn't prove that plural-object theories face insuperable difficulties. But I do think that Functionism faces a foundational difficulty, familiar from discussions of Frege's logic and Russell's paradox. The following condition cannot be generally true: if $\Pi$ is a predicate satisfied by x iff x satisfies a certain condition, then *there is a function* F such that for every x, $F(x) = \mathbf{t}$ iff x satisfies the condition. There are the Values of $\Pi$, but they may not form a unity. It is tempting to think that this limitation—there cannot be as many functions as Frege's (naive) comprehension principle implied— does not bear on empirical hypotheses about natural language. So I have stressed, perhaps past the point of belaboring, that the limitation is indeed relevant. Functionists will keep bumping up against it, in ways that frustrate explanation, with the consequent need for independently motivated remedies or admissions that certain (apparently semantic) facts cannot be explained in Functionist terms. If Functionism were the only game in town, it might be reasonable to put this concern aside; though conceptual incoherence is a bad trait for a theory to have, even in the absence of better theories. And given an alternative, we must at least consider the possibility that Functionism—like Frege's comprehension principle—should be replaced with something that yields similar results in most cases without also yielding undesirable results. Boolos (1998) and Schein (1993) show how to do this.

I hope it is now clear why I wanted to deal with quantification and plurality together. Since the first section of this "double" chapter was an overview, which can also serve as a summary, I won't recapitulate. But I have tried to show that Conjunctivists can provide a compositional semantics for quantificational and plural constructions, that this account has explanatory virtues, and that it is actually preferable to a Functionist account. If this is correct, then quantification and plurality tell *against* the idea that concatenating predicates with arguments corresponds to function-application. If the apparent virtues of Functionism dissipate, once we turn from simple cases of predicates combining with singular arguments to cases involving determiners and plural arguments, this suggests that Functionism does not provide a theoretically illuminating conception of semantic architecture. In the next chapter, I extend this point to a range of cases involving singular nonquantificational arguments. If this line of thought is correct, we will have to ask what, if anything, Functionism actually explains.

# 3

## Causal Verbs and Sentential Complements

Functionism implies that if a verb combines with $n$ grammatical arguments to form a sentence, the Value of the verb is a function from $n$ arguments to Values of some kind—sentential Values, or functions (say, from events to sentential Values). The virtues of Functionism lie with its treatment of predicate–argument combinations. So if verbs that take more than one argument can be treated as semantically monadic predicates, and a Conjunctivist account of such verbs is often *better*, this tells against the hypothesis that concatenating predicates with arguments signifies function-application. We have seen some reasons for thinking that ditransitive verbs, as in 'Three linguists taught five students four theories', are semantically monadic. But perhaps Functionism provides the best account of verbs that combine with *two* arguments, at least if we ignore plural/quantificational arguments.

In this chapter, I review some evidence that verbs like 'melted' and 'boiled' in (1–4)

> (1)   Hilary melted the ice
> (2)   The ice melted
> (3)   Pat boiled the soup
> (4)   The soup boiled

are semantically monadic. I argue that the same is true for "serial verbs", as in the Edo sentence (5),

> (5)   Òzó ghá lé èvbàré ré     [Ozo will cook food eat]

meaning roughly that Ozo will cook some food and eat it—with a further implication discussed below. Given some assumptions about the syntax, defended by Baker and Stewart (1999, 2002), one can offer an attractive Conjunctivist semantics for sentences like (5). But sentences like (1–5) tell against Functionism, and not just because of questions about the number of arguments per verb. If the Value of each verb is a function, one needs auxiliary hypotheses that effectively treat concatenation as a sign of predicate-conjunction. So it seems that Conjunctivism is preferable to Functionism, even for many cases of verbs combining with singular arguments. In practice, this point is often granted. But if it is correct, the empirical scope of Functionism is further reduced.

Finally, I discuss predicates that take sentential arguments, focusing on speech-act verbs like 'explain' and psychological verbs like 'doubt', as in (6).

(6) Nick doubted that Fido barked, but Nora explained that a cat had gone by.

Functionism fails to account for some interesting facts about such verbs, which are better viewed as conjoinable monadic predicates that bear a distinctive grammatical relation to their sentential arguments. But verbs that take sentential complements provide the most interesting cases of *recursive* predicate–argument concatenation. If these cases also suggest that concatenation signifies conjunction, perhaps we should abandon the idea that function-application is a basic principle of natural semantic composition.

# 1. Causatives

Sentences like (1–4) are related in ways that confirm a hypothesis suggested by surface appearances: each word in (2) is a constituent of (1). This turns out to be good news for Conjunctivists. And the hypothesis is widely accepted. But it has been challenged by Fodor (1970), Fodor and Lepore (1998, 2002); although Fodor and Lepore—henceforth, F&L—have no brief for Functionism. The resulting dialectic is complicated enough to merit a review of some much discussed facts, in order to be clear that these facts do indeed favor Conjunctivist analyses, like the specific proposal in §1.2 below.

## 1.1. *Notation and Stage Setting*

We can distinguish intransitive and transitive "forms" of a verb—say, 'melt$_I$' vs 'melt$_T$'. But instances of 'β melted$_I$ if α melted$_T$ β' are sure to be true; and, prima facie, this is because *the* verb 'melt' appears twice, in some form or other. By contrast, instances of 'β melted$_I$ if α moved$_T$ β' may well be false. Many verbs are like 'melt' in this regard, especially if alternations like 'raised$_T$'/'rose$_I$' in (7–8) count as forms of the same verb.[1]

> (7)    Chris raised the flag
> (8)    The flag rose

I think this pattern tells in favor of analyses like (7M) and (8M);

> (7M)    ∃O{Agent(O, Chris) & ∃O'[Terminater(O, O') & Past-Rising$_I$(O') ] & Theme(O, the flag)}
>
> (8M)    ∃O[Past-Rising$_I$(O) & Theme(O, the flag) ]

where 'Terminater' indicates a relation that causal *processes* can bear to *final parts* of themselves.[2]

For simplicity, I assume that some things$_O$ are Values of 'raised$_T$' iff each of them$_O$ is a Value of 'raised$_T$'; for each assignment **A**, Val(O, raised$_{\Pi^*}$, **A**) iff ∀o:Oo[Val(o, raised$_{\Pi^*}$, **A**) ]. At some point, we may want to say that some events can *together* be Values of raised$_{\Pi^*}$ even if no one of them$_O$ was a Value of the transitive verb. Maybe an Agent can, by performing a series of actions, raise

---

[1] For example, if 'rose$_I$' = 'rise$_I$' + 'past', and 'raised$_T$' also has 'rise$_I$' as a part, then every part of (8) is a part of (7). I assume that (8) is true whenever (7) is true; although (8), which can be true if nobody raised the flag, might be an infelicitous description of a context in which someone raised it. Many verbs fit this pattern. But it takes care (and the right theory) to state the generalization properly, since not all instances of 'y V$_I$ if x V$_T$ y' are true. If x counted$_T$ y, then x counted, while y need not have. So 'counted$_T$' must be treated differently.

[2] *Being a Terminater of* will be understood as a kind of thematic relation: ∀O∀Z{Terminater(O, Z) ↔ ∀o:Oo[∃z(Zz & z is a final part of o)] & ∀z:Zz[∃o(Oo & z is a final part of o)]}.

something without there being any *one* event/process that was a raising of that thing. But if we abstract away from this potential source of complexity, the central idea of this section can be expressed as follows: 'raised$_T$' is a complex monadic predicate such that each of its Values has a final part that is a Value of 'rose$_I$'. Suppressing relativization to assignments for further simplicity, Val(o, raised$_{\Pi^*}$) iff ∃o'[Terminater(o, o') & Val(o, rose$_\Pi$) ]; likewise for boiled$_{\Pi^*}$, melted$_{\Pi^*}$, etc. As we'll see, the Theme of a process is also the Theme of any Terminater of that process. So (7M) implies (7M'), which implies (8M).

(7M')　∃O{Agent(O, Chris) & ∃O'[Past-Rising$_I$(O') &
　　　　Theme(O', the flag) ]}

In my view, plural examples like 'Chris raised six flags' provide further support for Conjunctivism. But my aim in this chapter is to argue, independently of considerations already adduced, for the claim that verbs are semantically monadic. So the focus will be on singular arguments. And since '∃O' means that there are *one or more* Os, (7M) is true iff ∃o{Agent(o, Chris) & ∃o'[Terminater(o, o') & Past-Rising$_I$(o')] & Theme(o, the flag)}. Thus, for purposes of this chapter, we can pretend without loss that '∃O{ ... O ... }' is equivalent to '∃o{ ... o ... }'. Correlatively, my aim is not to establish a *specific* Conjunctivist analysis. I have argued elsewhere (1998, 2000*a*, 2003*c*) for appeal to notions like 'Terminater' in the semantics of action reports, drawing on Thomson (1971, 1977) and others to provide a variant of Parson's (1990) version of a much older view. But on any account of this sort, (7) semantically implies that Chris acted, and that there was a rising of the flag (caused by Chris's action). This is really all I need for the argument in favor of Conjunctivism; though it is also what F&L deny.

So in §1.2, I present my favored version of a traditional view in an explicitly Conjunctivist form, in a way that speaks to F&L's concerns—but otherwise suppressing details (and comparison with alternatives) not directly relevant to questions about the significance of concatenation. This leaves room for a reply: perhaps investigation of a broader range of facts will show that the best Functionist account is superior to the best Conjunctivist account. But that is a debate we can and should have.

## 1.2. *A Proposal (that does not Derive 'Boil*$_T$*' from 'Cause to Boil*$_I$*')*

So much by way of preparation. For simplicity, let's assume that in (3) and (4),

(3)   Pat boiled the soup
(4)   The soup boiled

'the soup' is semantically like a name, in that the Value of 'the soup' (relative to any given context) is simply the soup in question. On many views, (3) has a covert constituent that contributes a "causative" aspect of meaning; see Lakoff (1970), McCawley (1968), Williams (1981). Following Baker (1988) and others, I adopt a version of this hypothesis according to which the overt verb moves and combines with a covert verbal element to form a grammatical unit as shown below.

$$[\text{Pat}_\alpha[[\textbf{\textit{v}}^\wedge\text{boiled}_\Pi]_{\Pi^*}[\_\_\text{(the soup)}_\alpha]]_\Pi]_{\Pi P}$$

The blank indicates the pre-displacement position of the fundamentally intransitive 'boiled$_\Pi$', which takes an internal argument. The grammatical argument Pat$_\alpha$ can be viewed in two ways: as the sole argument of $\textbf{\textit{v}}$, to which Pat$_\alpha$ bears a distinctive structural relation associated with external arguments; or as the external argument of the grammatically complex predicate $[\textbf{\textit{v}}^\wedge\text{boiled}_\Pi]_{\Pi^*}$, which inherits the internal argument of boiled$_\Pi$. Assuming that boiled$_\Pi$ makes its lexical contribution in the post-displacement position, Conjunctivists can treat $[\textbf{\textit{v}}^\wedge\text{boiled}_\Pi]_{\Pi^*}$ as a semantically monadic predicate by treating $\textbf{\textit{v}}$ as a device for creating a certain grammatical relation that influences interpretation, much as the relation between a verb like fell$_\Pi$ and its grammatical argument influences interpretation.

Given Conjunctivism, when a name N is suitably related to a verb, N is interpreted as a predicate whose Values are things that *bear a certain relation to* the Value of N. Likewise, one can say that when a verb V is suitably related to *v*, V is interpreted as a predicate whose Values *bear a certain relation to* the Values of V. Put another way, one can hypothesize that displacing boiled$_\Pi$ creates a predicate such that some things$_O$ are Values of that predicate iff they$_O$ *end with* Values of boiled$_\Pi$. That is, Val(O, *v*^boiled$_\Pi$) iff ∃O'[Terminater (O, O') & Val(O', boiled$_\Pi$)]. Or in explicitly first-order terms, Val(O, *v*^boiled$_\Pi$) iff ∀o: Oo[Val(o, *v*^boiled$_\Pi$)], and Val(o, *v*^boiled$_\Pi$) iff ∃o'[Terminater(o, o') & Val(o, boiled$_\Pi$)]. Formally, 'Terminater' is like 'Agent' and 'Theme': it indicates a relation between Values of a predicate and things that are somehow "involved in" those Values; although 'Terminater' indicates a kind of mereological rather than participatory involvement.

On this view, which differs slightly from other event analyses, each Value of 'boiled$_T$' has a Value of 'boiled$_I$' as a final part. So (3) has the Value **t** iff at least one thing$_O$ was such that: its$_O$ Agent was Pat, *and* its$_O$ Terminater was an event of boiling$_I$, *and* its$_O$ Theme was the soup. The idea is not new. Appeal to *processes*, which start when an Agent acts but end later, are familiar in discussions of action; see, for example, Feinberg (1965), Vendler (1967), Goldman (1970), Thalberg (1972), Thomson (1977), Costa (1987), Wilson (1989). Presumably, to be the Agent of a process o is to perform an action that is a first part—an Initiater—of o; and to be the Theme of o is to be the thing affected at the end of o. (See Tenny, 1994.) While a Terminater of a boiling$_T$ is distinct from the corresponding Theme, a boiling$_T$ and its Terminater will have the same Theme: any thing boiled$_T$ by someone is something that boiled$_I$. Correlatively, (3) means roughly that Pat performed an action that began a process that ended with a boiling$_I$ of the soup; see Pietroski (1998, 2000c, 2003c) for elaboration and defense. In which case, (3) implies that there was a boiling$_I$ of the soup, and this semantic fact mirrors the hypothesized structural fact that boiled$_I$ is a constituent of (3).

Causation plays a role in this account, since the parts of processes are causally related. If an Agent did something that started a process that ended with a boiling$_I$, the process began with an action that caused the boiling$_I$. If event o is a Terminater of a process p, then an Initiater of p caused o. In this sense, 'Terminater' indicates a relation that is not *merely* mereological. An event o of boiling$_I$ can be an effect of some action without there being a boiling$_T$ that starts with the action and ends with o. Put another way, a Value of 'boiled$_T$' exhibits a kind of *unity* not guaranteed by the mere fact that someone's action caused something to boil$_I$. If this is correct, then (3) is not synonymous with (9) or (10),

(9)    Pat caused the soup to boil

(10)   Pat did something that caused a boiling of the soup

even though (3) implies at least one of these.

This bears on cases of the sort discussed by F&L, and familiar from earlier discussions of action and responsibility; see Hart and Honoré (1959), Feinberg (1965), Davidson (1967b). Suppose Pat set fire to a house that (unbeknownst to Pat) contains a pot of cold soup. Then (9) and (10) might be true while (3) is false. One can cause a boiling$_I$ of something without boiling$_T$ it. In general, if x boiled$_T$ y, then x brought about a boiling$_I$ of y *in the right way*. But x can bring about a boiling$_I$ of y in a way that doesn't count as boiling$_T$ y. What counts as a right way is presumably a vague, context-sensitive, and verb-sensitive matter; though as Hart and Honoré discuss, the distinction between killing and merely causing a death is entrenched in both common sense and common law. And the distinction is not simply a matter of some causal chains being "indirect". A murderer can kill by *very* circuitous means. Likewise, one can invent a Rube-Goldberg device for boiling$_T$ soup.

As F&L stress, the history of philosophy is strewn with illustrations of the general point. There is a difference between hearing a dog bark, and seeming to hear a dog bark because a dog barked; between raising one's arm, and having one's arm rise because one intended to raise it; etc. In each case, the effect has to be caused *in the right way*, where the qualifier excludes many but not all intuitively indirect chains. (Spies can hear things via satellite, and astronomers can see things using lots of apparatus.) Often, we don't care about the difference between boiling$_T$ something and merely causing it to boil$_I$. But there is a distinction. And when it matters, judges and juries can be exquisitely sensitive to it.

This suggests that we should reject theories according to which (3) has the Value **t** iff $\exists o\{Agent(o, Pat)$ & $\exists o'[Cause(o, o')$ & $Boiling_I(o')$ & $Theme(o', the soup)]\}$. It might seem that there is an easy fix: replace 'Cause' with a technical term 'Cause*', meaning *caused in the right way*. But one has to say what 'in the right way' means for purposes of determining what the theory predicts. And even given an adequate specification of what caused* what, worries remain. For given *any* relation R, (3R)

> (3R)   $\exists o\{Agent(o, Pat)$ & $\exists o'[R(o, o')$ & $Boiling_I(o')$ &
> $Theme(o', the soup)]\}$

fails to represent Pat and the soup as coparticipants in some event. But one expects Conjunctivists to say that (3) gets the Value **t** iff $\exists o[Agent(o, Pat)$ & $Boiling_T(o)$ & $Theme(o, the soup)]$, just as 'Pat hugged Chris' gets the Value **t** iff $\exists o[Agent(o, Pat)$ & $Hugging(o)$ & $Theme(o, Chris)]$. Correspondingly, (3R) is not really a Conjunctivist analysis, despite the appeal to ampersands and thematic roles. Conjunctivism predicts that Values of 'boiled$_T$ the soup' are Values of 'boiled$_T$', which have Agents *and* Themes.

This bears on F&L's point that (3) and (10) differ in the scope of temporal modifiers.

(3)   Pat boiled the soup

(10)   Pat did something that caused a boiling of the soup

(11)   On Monday, Pat boiled the soup.

(12)   On Monday, Pat did something that caused
the soup to boil.

Suppose Pat turned a dial on the stove, thereby creating a flame beneath a pot of soup at 11:55 p.m. on Monday, but the soup did not boil until after midnight. Then (12) is true on one reading, while

(11) is not. And even if one rejects this diagnosis of the intuitions, one has to explain why (11) and (12) *seem* to differ if (3) and (10) are relevantly similar. In the envisioned situation, there was indeed an event on Monday done by Pat (namely, Pat's turning of the dial) that caused a boiling$_I$ of the soup—and caused it in the right way, since Pat boiled$_T$ the soup. That is, $\exists o\{On(o, Monday)$ & $Agent(o, Pat)$ & $\exists o'[R(o, o')$ & $Boiling_I(o')$ & $Theme(o', the\ soup)]\}$. But this is not a good analysis of (11), which is false if the boiling$_I$ occurred on Tuesday. So (3R) is not a good analysis of (3).

By contrast, suppose that a process occurs on a given day only if the *whole* process occurred on that day. Then if o is a process that TERMINATES in an event of boiling$_I$, o occurred on Monday only if the relevant boiling$_I$ occurred on Monday. So we can specify the meaning of (11) as follows: something that occurred on Monday was done by Pat, was a boiling$_T$ (i.e. a process that Terminated in a boiling$_I$), and was done to the soup. This shows how taking Conjunctivism seriously, treating a verb like 'boiled$_T$' and its arguments as conjoinable monadic predicates, helps avoid an objection to more traditional causative analyses. As another illustration of this point, suppose that Nora melted some candy by moving a lens between the candy and the sun. Then (13–16) can be true, while (17–18) are not; see Pietroski (1998).

(13)    Nora melted$_T$ the candy
(14)    Nora moved$_T$ the lens
(15)    Nora melted$_T$ the candy with her lens
(16)    Nora moved$_T$ the lens with her hand
(17)    Nora melted$_T$ the candy with her hand
(18)    Nora moved$_T$ the lens with her lens

Since (15) and (17) imply (13), while (18) and (16) imply (14), the adjuncts 'with her lens' and 'with her hand' are presumably to be analyzed as conjuncts of complex event descriptions. Given (13R),

(13R)    $\exists o\{Agent(o, Nora)$ & $\exists o'[R(o, o')$ & $Melting_I(o')$ & $Theme(o', the\ candy)]\}$

this yields two possibilities for (15):

∃o{Agent(o, Nora) & ∃o'[R(o, o') & Melting$_I$(o') &

   Theme(o', the candy)] & With(o, her lens)};

∃o{Agent(o, Nora) & ∃o'[R(o, o') & Melting$_I$(o') &

   Theme(o', the candy) & With(o', her lens)]}.

The latter analysis seems wrong. There is no intuitive sense in which the melting$_I$ of the candy—the salient *effect* of Nora's action—was with her lens. As Parsons (1990) notes, instrumental adjuncts seem to modify *things Agents do* rather than effects of Agents' actions.[3] If (15) is analyzed the first way, then parallel reasoning suggests the following analysis of (17):

∃o{Agent(o, Nora) & ∃o'[R(o, o') & Melting$_I$(o') &

   Theme(o', the candy)] & With(o, her hand)}.

And if (15) has the Value **t** while (17) has the Value **f**, then Nora was the Agent of something that was with her lens but not with her hand. Similarly, if (16) has the Value **t** while (18) has the Value **f**, Nora was the Agent of something that was with her hand but not with her lens. In which case, Nora was the Agent of at least *two* distinct things, even though she melted the candy *by* moving her lens—and even though there is some sense in which she performed just one action.

   By itself, this is not a problem. Indeed, I think it is correct. But it strongly suggests that Agents are the Agents of things other than

---

[3] If one insists that the melting$_I$ was (brought about) with her lens, why isn't the melting$_I$ also with her hand? One can insist that (17) is true. But this seems unmotivated, given the proposed alternative. See Taylor (1985), citing Christopher Arnold, and Pietroski (1998) for arguments against the idea that something was with her hand *for a melting* and with her lens *for a moving*—but not with her hand *for a moving* or with her lens *for a melting*. It is also worth noting that, absent a specification of what 'R(o, o')' means, (13R) is compatible with (13) having the Value **t** even though Nora's action was irrelevant to the candy melting$_I$; suppose 'R' stands for 'is *not* causally related to'. One can add the following stipulation: R(o, o') → o caused o'. But this takes us back to the idea that 'R' means *caused in the right way*.

"basic actions". A person can do several things—like moving her hand, moving a lens, and melting some candy—by performing exactly *one* basic action (say, the action of moving her hand) in the right circumstances; see Anscombe (1957), Davidson (1967*b*), Goldman (1970). Once we grant this, there is no reason to insist on interpreting 'R' as 'caused' or 'caused in the right way', as opposed to 'Terminater'. For as Thomson (1977) and many others have suggested, it seems that an Agent like Nora can be the Agent of several *overlapping processes* as indicated in the diagram. Here, *a* is

$$
\begin{array}{l}
a \text{———} e_1 \text{———} e_2 \\
p_1 = \lfloor\text{\_\_\_\_\_}\rfloor \\
p_2 = \lfloor\text{_____}\rfloor
\end{array}
$$

Nora's basic action, whatever that is; $e_1$ is the moving$_I$ of her lens; $e_2$ is the melting$_I$ of the candy; $p_1$ is the process of Nora moving$_T$ her lens; $p_2$ is the distinct process of Nora melting$_T$ the candy, which has $p_1$ as a part; and Terminater($p_1$, $e_1$), while Terminater($p_2$, $e_2$). The idea is that $p_1$ was (done) with Nora's hand, while $p_2$ was (done) with her lens.

For present purposes, we can set aside disputes about what basic actions *are*, and whether processes like $p_1$ count as (nonbasic) actions; see Pietroski (2000*a*) for discussion. The more important point is that, while sentences like (13) do indeed involve a double quantification over events—as with perceptual idioms like 'Nora heard Fido bark', discussed in §3 of Chapter 1—we need not specify the meaning of (13) in terms of one thing *causing* another. We can speak of one thing having another *as a final part*, as in (13M), which represents Nora and the candy as coparticipants in something.

(13M)   $\exists o\{\text{Agent}(o, \text{Nora})\ \&\ \exists o'[\text{Terminater}(o, o')\ \&\ \text{Melting}_I(o')]\ \&\ \text{Theme}(o, \text{the candy})\}$

On this view, the semantic structure of (13) parallels the apparent gramatical structure; 'melted$_T$' corresponds to '$\exists o'[\text{Terminater}(o, o')\ \&\ \text{Melting}_I(o')]$'. Likewise, 'moved$_T$' corresponds to '$\exists o'[\text{Terminater}(o, o')\ \&\ \text{Moving}_I(o')]$'. But the process of moving$_T$ the lens differs from the process of melting$_T$ the candy. For example, they have different Themes and different temporal properties.

Suppose that $a$ and e1 occurred on Monday, while e2 occurred on Tuesday. Then (all of) p1 occurred on Monday, but not so for p2. And we can adopt the following partial definition of 'Agent': Agent(o, x) if $\exists a$[Action($a$, x) & Initiater($a$, o)]; an individual$_x$ is the Agent of something$_o$ if she$_x$ performed an action that Initiated it$_o$, where an action is an Initiater of a causal process if the action is a first part of the process. If we combine this thesis with the claim that Nora (by moving her hand) performed an action that Initiated both p1 and p2, then it follows that Nora was the Agent of both, even though there is a sense in which she "did just one thing". Abbreviating, if $\exists$a[Action(a, Nora) & Initater(p1, $a$) & Initater(p2, $a$)], then Agent(p1, Nora) & Agent (p2, Nora). I have argued elsewhere that this conception of Agency has independent virtues; see Pietroski (2000$a$).

A closely related point is that an overtly causative construction like (20) seems to be ambiguous in a way that (19) is not.

(19)   Pat boiled the soup on Monday
(20)   Pat caused the soup to boil on Monday

On one reading, (20) implies that the soup boiled on Monday, but not that Pat's action occurred on Monday. But (19) has no such reading. And even if one rejects this diagnosis of the intuitive difference between (19) and (20), it seems clear that (19) and (11) are equivalent in a way that (20) and (21) are not.

(11)   On Monday, Pat boiled the soup
(21)   On Monday, Pat caused the soup to boil

This tells against analyzing (19) as (20). But the facts are predicted by a Conjunctivist account that treats 'boiled$_T$' as a predicate of processes.[4]

---

[4] A similar kind of contrast is exhibited by 'Pat boiled the soup without getting burnt' and 'Pat caused the soup to boil without getting burnt'. Only in the latter can 'without getting burnt' describe the soup, implying that *the Theme* didn't get burnt.

### 1.3. *Caveat and Confirmation*

Questions remain. I have no detailed theory of what marks the difference between (i) cases in which an Agent's action merely causes something to boil$_I$ and (ii) cases in which the action Initiates a process of boiling$_T$. But this hardly shows that there is no distinction. Likewise, it may be hard to say exactly what the hypothesized covert verb in (11) means, except by subtraction: '*v*' is what you add to 'boil$_I$' to get 'boil$_T$'. But this difficulty cannot show that 'boil$_I$' is not a constituent of (11). It is hard to say what *overt* causative morphemes mean in languages that have them. Consider Baker's (1988) example from Chichewa, with the causative morpheme in bold (ignoring morphology indicating aspect or agreement).

(22)    Mtsuko u-na-gwa-a

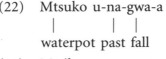

　　　　waterpot past fall

(23)    Mtsikana u-na-u-gw-**ets**-a mtsuko

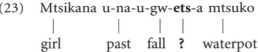

　　　　girl　　　past  fall  **?**　waterpot

Sentence (23) implies more than just that the girl caused a falling of the waterpot; her action must have caused the falling in the right way. And the pattern is evidently productive: 'bwer-a' means *come*, while 'bwer-**ets**-a' means *bring* (not merely *cause to come*); 'on-a' means *see*, while 'on-**ets**-a' means *show* (not merely *cause to see*); etc.[5] The one-way entailments are like those exhibited by

---

Compare 'Pat wanted the soup to boil on Monday', which has one reading where Pat's desire is satisfied only if the soup boiled on Monday, and another reading where Pat had on Monday a desire for the soup to boil. It may help, in this regard, to imagine that, on Sunday, Pat wanted the soup to boil on Monday; but when Monday came around, Pat wanted the soup to boil on Tuesday. Examples like (20–1) are closer to Fodor's own: 'x killed y by swallowing his tongue', which lacks a reading had by 'x caused y to die by swallowing his tongue'. But such cases are complicated by the empty subject of the 'by'-clause: x caused y to die by '—' swallowing his tongue; perhaps '—' cannot have 'y' as its antecedent, even if the covert-verb hypothesis is true; see n. 19.

[5] Here and elsewhere, my thanks to Mark Baker for many conversations.

'boiled$_T$ the soup' and 'caused the soup to boil$_I$', suggesting that 'boiled$_T$' is the result of combining 'boiled$_I$' with a covert morpheme semantically like '**ets**'. It may be hard to say what this morpheme means, using ordinary vocabulary. But this does not show that English does not have it. And we can at least begin to characterize the meaning in terms of causal/mereological notions like 'Terminater'.

In this regard, Japanese is interesting, since it provides two ways of causativizing a verb like boiled$_I$ ('wai-ta'). Sentence (24) means that Masaaki boiled$_T$ the water. But (25) means roughly that he had the water boiled$_T$—his action brought about a boiling$_T$ of the water (by someone/something).

(24) Masaaki-ga oyu-o waka-**shi**-ta
       |        |   |  |  |
      Masaaki    water   boil-?-past

(25) Masaaki-ga oyu-o waka-*sase*-ta
       |        |   |  |  |
      Masaaki    water  boil-??-past

The causative morpheme in (24) seems to be the semantic analog of **ets** in Chichewa. And 'On Monday' ('Getsuyoobi-ni') interacts with the morphemes differently. While (27) is ambiguous, (26) is not.

(26) Getsuyoobi-ni, Masaaki-ga oyu-o waka-**shi**-ta
(27) Getsuyoobi-ni Masaaki-ga oyu-o waka-*sase*-ta

Thus, even though the transitive verb in (24) seems to have the corresponding intransitive verb as a part, (26) is unambiguous.[6]

---

[6] One can express the "action on Monday" meaning with the biclausal structures 'Getsuyoobi-ni Masaaki-ga oyu-ga waku genin-o tsukut-ta' and 'Getsuyoobi-ni Masaaki-ga oyu-ga waku-yooni shita', which have, roughly and respectively, the following meanings: on Monday, Masaaki *made the cause by which* the water boiled; on Monday, Masaaki *acted with the result that* the water boiled. With regard to (25), there may well be a covert subject of 'waka-*sase*-ta'. See Motamura (2004) for relevant discussion; cf. Hart and Honoré's (1959) observation that an action by a second person can "break the causal chain" between the first person's action and a subsequent effect, even if the second person's action was intuitively a result of the first person's action.

So the nonambiguity of (26) shouldn't lead us to deny that (24) has causative structure, and likewise for the English translations.

F&L's argument would still have force if we had independent reasons for thinking that in *English*, "compounding" cannot block readings. But examples like (28–9) suggest otherwise.

(28)   Groucho was hunting elephants in pajamas

(29)   Groucho was elephant-hunting in pajamas

Only (28) sets up the punchline concerning how they got in his pajamas. So it is hardly *ad hoc* to say that if English has a covert causativizing element '$v$', 'boiled$_T$' is semantically like 'waka-**shi**-ta' in (26). And any child must be prepared to acquire English or Japanese. This alone should make us suspicious of the idea that Japanese children analyze 'waka-**shi**-ta' as having semantically significant grammatical structure, while English children treat 'boiled$_T$' as semantically primitive. These observations do not erase F&L's objection. On the contrary, as they stress, we want a plausible account of the relevant *one-way* entailments and the *non*ambiguity of examples like (19) and (26). But given a Conjunctivist semantics, along with a grammar according to which verbs like 'boiled$_T$' incorporate verbs like 'boiled$_I$', we can say that 'boiled$_T$' is a complex monadic predicate whose Values have Terminaters that are Values of 'boiled$_I$'—and likewise for many other similar verbs.[7]

---

[7] We still want some explanation of why (19) cannot have the structure indicated in (19G*),

(19)    Pat boiled the soup on Monday

(19G*)  Pat [$v$ [(boiled int-(the soup)) (on Monday)]]

corresponding to the following nonexistent reading of the English sentence: Pat was the Agent of a process that Terminated in a boiling$_I$ of the soup on Monday; and the boiling$_I$ was on Monday. But temporal adverbs may need to be "higher" on the tree, perhaps for reasons associated with tense; see Cinque (1999). And if $v$ combines with something to form an incorporated unit with *morphological* unity (see Baker (1988)), then a *phrase* like 'boil the soup' cannot combine with $v$ as in (19G*); see Pietroski (2003c), Chomsky (2003). Correlatively, 'on Monday' may need to combine with an event predicate that already specifies an endpoint (by specifying a Theme), while $v$ may

## 1.4. *Functionist Rewrite*

Of course, one *can* provide a Functionist semantics for phrases like $[[\boldsymbol{v}^\wedge\text{boiled}_\Pi]_{\Pi^*}$ (the soup)$_\alpha]_\Pi$. Letting 'R' indicate the relevant causal/mereological relation, one could adopt the following proposal:

$\|\text{boiled}_\Pi\| = \lambda y \,.\, \lambda f \,.\, \textbf{t}$ iff Past-Boiling$_I$(f) & Theme(f, y); and
$\|\boldsymbol{v}\| = \lambda F \,.\, \lambda y \,.\, \lambda x \,.\, \lambda e \,.\, \textbf{t}$ iff Agent(e, x) & $\exists f\{R(e, f)$ &

   $[F(y)](f) = \textbf{t}\}$; hence,

$\|\boldsymbol{v}^\wedge\text{boiled}_\Pi\| = \lambda y \,.\, \lambda x \,.\, \lambda e \,.\, \textbf{t}$ iff Agent(e, x) & $\exists f\{R(e, f)$ &

   Past-Boiling$_I$(f) & Theme(f, y)$\}$.

Now suppose that if R(e, f), the Theme of f is the Theme of e. It follows that $\|\boldsymbol{v}^\wedge\text{boiled}_\Pi\| = \lambda y \,.\, \lambda x \,.\, \lambda e \,.\, \textbf{t}$ iff Agent(e, x) & $\exists f\{R(e, f)$ & Past-Boiling$_I$(f) & Theme(f, y)$\}$ & Theme(e, y). But this just recodes the entire Conjunctivist proposal, in a Functionist idiom, as a claim about the meaning of '$\boldsymbol{v}$'. The work is done (not by function-application, but rather) by the ampersands, existential closure, and thematic relations.

This might be acceptable *given* a Functionist account of quantification and plurality. If one adopts a mixed view about the significance of concatenation, one might regard the proposal above as a relatively minor concession to Conjunctivists: external arguments of causative verbs are more like adjuncts than one might have initially thought; cf. Kratzer (1996). There is something right about

---

need to combine with an event predicate that does not yet specify a Theme. I have alluded several times to the idea of derivational "phases" (Chomsky, 2000*b*); and it is widely agreed that, if there are such things, $\boldsymbol{v}$ marks one. This invites the speculation, which I have also alluded to several times, that existential closure of a variable may reflect a phase of a derivation. Finally, it is worth noting that Spanish—a language like English in having causative verbs with no overt causative morpheme, but unlike English in having a rich system of clitics—provides evidence of covert syntactic structure; see Uriagereka and Pietroski (2001).

this. Examples like (3–4) may not tell against the mixed view if verbs like 'boiled$_T$' are not truly transitive.

(3)    Pat boiled the soup
(4)    The soup boiled

But at this point, we are asking whether cases of combining verbs with two arguments reveal *virtues* of the hypothesis that combining a predicate with an argument signifies function-application. The question is not whether this hypothesis is *sustainable* in light of causative constructions. And if the explanatory scope of Functionism keeps shrinking as investigation proceeds, that is suggestive.

There are some reasons for thinking that at least *many* transitive verbs are products of combining an intransitive verb with a covert element; see Hale and Keyser (1993), Chomsky (1995). But even if this is wrong, an important point remains. One cannot concede that external arguments of verbs like 'boiled$_T$' are interpreted as thematically separate conjuncts, yet insist that it is *ad hoc* to treat external arguments more generally as thematically separate conjuncts. *Perhaps* a Functionist approach to noncausative transitive verbs will prove superior to the best Conjunctivist treatment, and this will tip the balance in favor of the mixed view. But that needs showing. Given a viable alternative, one cannot just assume that concatenating predicates with external arguments signifies function-application. Moreover, if Functionism is not the default option with regard to external arguments, one cannot insist that it is the default option with regard to internal arguments. Absent reason for thinking that combining an argument with *v*-boiled$_\Pi$ signifies function-application, why think that combining an argument with boiled$_\Pi$ signifies function-application? And once we stop viewing Functionism as the null hypothesis, it becomes significant that Conjunctivists can handle examples like (3–4) pretty easily, while Functionists need to mimic a Conjunctivist account with regard to the external argument in (4).

## 2. Covert Verbs and Explanation

If verbs like 'boiled$_T$' include a covert causative element, examples like (3–4) support Conjunctivism. So perhaps Functionists should deny the antecedent of this conditional. F&L articulate a kind of skepticism that Functionists could adopt, perhaps supplemented with claims (that F&L would reject) about lexical decomposition. After considering this possibility, I review some considerations that tell against it, focusing on data that also support other arguments for Conjunctivism.

### 2.1. *A Possible Alternative*

F&L deny that (3) semantically implies (4). This is radical. Prima facie, (4) gets the Value **t** if (3) does, and this is no accident. The obvious hypothesis, which F&L reject, is that (3) and (4) are related in this way because: every part of (4) is a part of (3); and the compositional semantics for natural language ensures that if sentences share parts in this way, the more complex sentence implies the simpler one. Still, the hypothesis is not obviously true. And as we'll see, one can reject it without denying that (3) semantically implies (4).

F&L rightly warn against the glib assumption that some semantic account of causative implications *must* be right, by reminding us of the risk-free claim that anything red is colored. It is not clear that a *semantic* theory should explain why this claim is sure to be true. Prima facie, the word 'red' is not synonymous with 'colored and Φ' for any 'Φ', apart perhaps from 'red'. We certainly have no plausible analysis of 'x is red, so x is colored' that reveals such inferences as instances of conjunction-reduction. Likewise, it is a substantive hypothesis that the meaning of 'boiled$_T$' can be specified in terms of 'boiled$_I$' and something else. It is useful, in this regard, to consider an inverse strategy for explaining the implication.

Instead of saying that 'boil$_I$' is a constituent of (3), one might say that (4) has a covert external argument: [$e$ [boiled$_T$ [the soup]]], meaning roughly that 'someone/something boiled$_T$ the soup', on analogy with the passive construction 'The soup was boiled$_T$ (by someone/something)'. This view faces many difficulties, even setting aside concerns about the required syntax. For example, one can say—apparently without contradiction—that while the soup boiled, nothing boiled it. Even if nothing has in fact ever boiled spontaneously, this doesn't seem to be a *semantic* truth. It makes sense to say that ice (or a witch) can just melt, without cause, much as uranium can just decay. Something that is unbroken now might break for no reason; etc. Given a transitive analysis of (4), one also needs to explain why 'The soup boiled on Tuesday' *is clearly true* if Pat did something on Monday that caused the soup to boil on Tuesday. For in that case, 'Someone boiled the soup on Tuesday' is false, or at least not clearly true. And it is hard to even describe the apparent ambiguity of (30) if 'boiled' is always transitive.

(30)    Pat boiled the soup again

For (30) has a reading on which it is true if Pat boiled the soup once, but the soup boiled once before.

One does not rebut these objections by saying that a semantic account of causative implications must be right. And one can read F&L as making the following claim: analyzing (3) in terms of (4) and a covert verb is no more plausible, all things considered, than analyzing (4) as $[e \ [\text{boiled}_T \ [\text{the soup}]]]$.[8] In my view, this claim is false. But the apparent pattern of implication does not itself force us to adopt a "transitive plus covert-subject analysis" of (4) any more than it forces us to adopt an "intransitive plus covert-verb analysis"

---

[8] Moreover, we would be unimpressed if a theorist introduced the technical term 'Something*', saying that 'y boiled$_I$' has the Value **t** iff Something* boiled$_T$ y; where 'Something* boiled$_T$ the soup' does *not* imply 'something boiled$_T$ the soup'. The posited quantifier is not just covert, it is *new*; its alleged meaning is not that of any familiar quantifier. Without independent defense, this proposal just encodes (without yet explaining) the apparent implications in terms of the alleged meaning of 'Something*'. So we should be equally unimpressed with theories that modify traditional causative analyses simply by replacing 'cause' with 'cause*'.

of (3). Functionists impressed by this point might adopt a view according to which there are two homophonous verbs whose meanings are correctly specified as follows, suppressing covert quantification over events: $\|\text{boiled}_I\| = \lambda y$ . $\mathbf{t}$ iff y boiled$_I$, and $\|\text{boiled}_T\| = \lambda y$ . $\lambda x$ . $\mathbf{t}$ iff x boiled$_T$ y.

Without supplementation, this theory implies that the relation between boiled$_T$ and boiled$_I$ is semantically no different than the relation between boiled$_T$ and fell$_I$. F&L seem willing to accept this, since they think the alternatives are worse. Given a viable alternative, this seems like a refusal to deal with explananda. But one might follow F&L in rejecting accounts that posit extra syntax, while allowing for other kinds of semantic explanation. If the *grammatical* structures of (3–4) are as simple as they appear, they present no difficulty for Functionism. But maybe there is further *lexical* structure.

Adapting proposals due to Chierchia (1989) and Reinhart (1983), Levin and Rappaport Hovav (1995)—henceforth, L&R—argue that the meaning of 'boiled$_T$' should be represented as follows:

> an event of [x doing something] caused* an event of
> [y becoming boiled$_s$];

where 'x' and 'y' are placeholders for external and internal arguments, and 'boiled$_s$' describes a certain kind of *state*. On this view, x boiled$_T$ y only if y underwent a certain change of state. And in light of §1.2, one could reformulate this account—replacing 'caused*' with a causal/mereological notion—without affecting L&R's other claims. In explicitly Functionist terms, the idea would be that

> $\|\text{boiled}_T\| = \lambda y$ . $\lambda x$ . $\lambda e$ . $\mathbf{t}$ iff e was a process of
> [x doing something] & e Terminated in an event of
> [y becoming boiled$_s$].

L&R propose a mechanism for how certain verbs can be "detransitivized" under certain conditions. Since the details are not crucial for present purposes, let's assume that these conditions are met.

L&R go on to say that 'boiled$_I$' has a lexical meaning we can represent as follows: something boiled$_T$ y; where we allow that something boiled$_T$ y even if the cause of y boiling$_I$ was some (intuitively non-Agentive) change of state internal to y. One wonders if, on this view, *every* cause of a boiling$_I$ will end up being an event that Initiates a boiling$_T$—in which case, one of Fodor's original objections returns. Moreover, to repeat an earlier point, it still seems possible that something could boil$_I$ without cause. So we should be suspicious of semantic theories that preclude this possibility. One could, however, modify this aspect of L&R's view by adopting the following hypothesis:

$$\|\text{boiled}_I\| = \lambda y . \lambda f . \textbf{t} \text{ iff } f \text{ was an event of } [y \text{ becoming boiled}_s].$$

This would fail to explain some facts for which L&R offer an account. And this would raise questions about the independent motivation for the requisite lexical semantic structure. But since this may be the best Functionist proposal, let's explore it.[9]

Any such view avoids concerns about ambiguity. If the relevant grammatical structure of 'x boiled$_T$ y' is simply [x [boiled$_T$ y]], this explains why 'x boiled$_T$ y' seems not to have the syntactic structure of 'x caused y to become boiled$_s$'. The lexicalist hypothesis is rather that 'boil$_T$' and 'boil$_I$' have structurally related meanings: if there was a process of x doing something that Terminated in y becoming boiled$_s$, then y became boiled$_s$.[10] On this view, the meanings of

---

[9] Let me stress that I am not arguing, as Fodor and Lepore do, that lexical items are semantically atomic. While Conjunctivism is compatible with this view, it is also compatible with much of what L&R say about lexical semantics. My point is simply that, with regard to causative constructions, Conjunctivism is preferable to Functionism; though if I am correct, one should not assume Functionism when arguing for lexical semantic structure.

[10] Similarly, with regard to the overt causative morpheme in languages like Chichewa. Functionists could say that the causative implications should be explained in lexicalist terms, thus avoiding the need to assign a suitably specified function (from unary functions to binary functions) as the Value of a causative morpheme. Instead of saying that $\|\textbf{ets}\| = \lambda F . \lambda y . \lambda x . \lambda e . \textbf{t}$ iff Agent(e, x) & $\exists f\{$Terminater(e, f) & $[F(y)](f) = \textbf{t}\}$, and that $\|\textbf{gw}\| = \lambda y . \lambda f . \textbf{t}$ iff f was an event of y falling, one could adopt

'boil$_T$' and 'boil$_I$' share a part—the meaning of 'become boiled$_s$'—even though sentences like (3) and (4) do not share a part governed by grammatical principles that apply to sentential syntax.

I have no a priori objections to such hypotheses. The question here concerns which *package* of views about causative constructions is best: a relatively spare syntax and a Functionist compositional semantics, supplemented with some assumptions about lexical semantic structure; or a richer syntax, involving a covert morpheme for languages like English, together with a Conjunctivist semantics. Once the question is posed this way, Baker's (1988, 1996, 1997) work becomes directly relevant. For as noted above, and below, Baker argues that sentential syntax can be recruited to explain various "incorporation" phenomena that initially seem to motivate lex-icalist hypotheses. Put another way, if there is independent evidence for the idea that 'boil$_T$' is the result of incorporating 'boil$_I$' with a covert verb, that indirectly supports theories that diagnose causative implications in these terms. (If F&L's arguments against this idea were sound, that would support lexical decomposition, *pace* F&L. But the arguments are not sound.)

If this makes the issue seem complex, so it should. But cases of predicate–argument combination are supposed to be the cases that motivate Functionism. In so far as this motivation relies on auxiliary hypotheses about lexical semantics, one might wonder how much Functionism really explains about how the meanings of complex expressions are compositionally determined. And in so far as Functionism suggests a relatively spare syntax for causative constructions, one should consider evidence that indicates a richer syntax of the sort required by a Conjunctivist semantics. This illustrates a general point: if grammatical structure is more elaborate than Functionism predicts, but elaborate enough for Conjunctivism, then the latter (more restrictive) conception of compositional semantics may well be part of the simplest overall theory that accommodates the facts.

---

the following view: $|\text{gw-}\textbf{ets}| = \lambda y . \lambda x . \lambda e . \textbf{t}$ iff Agent(e, x) & ∃f{Terminater(e, f) & f was an event of y becoming fallen}, $|\text{gw}| = \lambda y . \lambda f . \textbf{t}$ iff f was an event of y becoming fallen.

## 2.2. *An Argument from UTAH*

In this subsection, I want to consider an argument with the following form: certain negative facts call for explanation, in terms of a constraint on how natural languages associate signals with meanings; and given this constraint, along with some other facts, English causative constructions involve covert morphology. More simply, those who don't posit the covert morpheme inherit the burden of providing an alternative explanation for certain negative facts.

In Chapter 1, I noted that natural languages do not have "thematic inverses" of transitive action verbs. At least initially, this is something of an embarrassment for Functionists. If the Value of 'pushed' is the function $\lambda y . [\lambda x . \mathbf{t}$ iff x pushed y], why is there no verb whose Value is the function $\lambda y . \lambda x . \mathbf{t}$ iff y pushed x? An event-friendly Functionist can say that $\|\text{melted}_T\| = \lambda y . \lambda x . \lambda e . \mathbf{t}$ iff e was a melting$_T$ by x of y—perhaps elaborating further, by saying that e was a melting$_T$ by x of y iff e was a process in which x did something that Terminated in an event of y becoming melted. But one still wants to know why natural languages have no expressions like the following: 'grelted', a verb whose Value is $\lambda y . \lambda x . \lambda e . \mathbf{t}$ iff e was a melting$_T$ by y of x, with 'Dorothy grelted the witch' meaning that the witch melted Dorothy. Given thematic decomposition, one can posit a constraint that effectively filters out expressions with such "thematically inverted" meanings. But this pushes the question back: if natural languages have a Functionist semantics, why should expressions like 'grelted' be filtered out?

Compare the discussion of conservativity in §4 of Chapter 2. There, the relevant negative facts concerned the absence of determiners that express certain kinds of relations between extensions. As we saw, Conjunctivists can and should describe these facts in terms of a constraint on the significance of certain grammatical relations, as opposed to a constraint on which second-order functions can be Values of determiners. This matters. If we needed a Functionist semantics for determiners, and thus had to posit a constraint on which functions can be the Values of determiners, it might be reasonable to adopt a similar view with regard to action verbs. But given a Conjunctivist semantics that accounts for conservativity, we should be suspicious of attempts to diagnose an apparent constraint on how grammatical structure contributes to meaning in terms of a constraint on lexical meanings. Indeed, the account of conservativity was an analog of Baker's (1988, 1997) proposal for how to think about the negative thematic facts illustrated with 'grelted'.

Baker defends a Uniformity of Thematic Assignment Hypothesis (UTAH), according to which grammatical relations determine— and are determined by—thematic role. On this view, only one grammatical relation signifies Agency, and any argument bearing that relation to a predicate is interpreted as an Agent-representer; likewise for other grammatical relations associated with thematical roles. Pesetsky (1995) defends a slightly weaker hypothesis, according to which there is a hierarchy of thematic roles that must be respected by the order of arguments in any given sentence. In particular, the external argument of a verb cannot be interpreted as a Theme-representer while the internal argument of the verb is interpeted as an Agent-representer.[11] For present purposes, we can ignore the differences between these views. Given either conception of how thematic roles are related to grammatical relations, English has an unpronounced causative morpheme.

Initially, it might seem that Baker's constraint is too strong. Given UTAH, 'the witch melted' and 'the witch danced' must differ grammatically if 'the witch' represents a Theme in the first sentence and an Agent in the second. (Likewise, 'Pat fell' must differ grammatically from 'Pat counted'.) But it is independently plausible that Theme-representing subjects, unlike Agent-representing subjects, are displaced *internal* arguments; see Burzio (1986), Belletti (1988), Baker (1997).[12] If the subject of 'Pat fell' is indeed a displaced

---

[11] *Why* this should be so is another question, and a very hard one. Why doesn't the mapping go the other way in natural languages? For discussion, see Uriagereka and Pietroski (2001).

[12] Burzio discusses the general fact that verbs without external arguments fail to assign accusative case; correlatively, verbs that do not assign accusative case do

internal argument—[[Pat$_{\alpha 1}$ [ . . . [fell$_\Pi$ *int*-t$_1$]]]—that tells in favor of the hypothesized constraint on the thematic significance of certain grammatical relations. And if there is such a constraint, those grammatical relations must have thematic significance, as predicted by Conjunctivism; see Chapter 1.

One might think that in a sentence like 'The rock broke the window', the rock is *not* represented as an Agent. But recall that 'Agent' is being used as a term of art in a compositional semantic theory for natural language. The Conjunctivist hypothesis is that certain verbs inflect certain grammatical relations—like *being the external argument of*—with certain thematic significance, as opposed to merely formal significance. On this view, the meaning of 'pushed' imposes the following constraint (not imposed by predicates of ordered pairs): given a Value of 'pushed'—i.e. a past event of pushing—its external participant is its Agent, and its internal participant is its Theme. But it remains an empirical question just what this commitment amounts to. And it need not correspond perfectly with any intuitive notion of Agency, or the notion(s) relevant to theories of human action. Following Dowty (1979, 1991), Baker (1997) argues that, for purposes of thinking about how grammatical relations are related to thematic roles, notions like 'Agent' should be viewed as indicators of relations characterized prototypically. A rock may not share intentional properties with paradigmatic Agents. But it may be the most Agent-like participant in a given event—say, an event in which a window is broken by the rock. (Or if you prefer, an event in which a window was broken when a rock undergoing a change of motion intersected with it.)

---

not assign an external thematic role. For example, the Italian verbs 'telefonare' and 'arrivare' both take a single argument (like 'telephone' and 'arrive' in English). But only 'telefonare' assigns accusative case, and only with 'arrivare' is the single argument the *complement* of the verb. This is evidenced by a variety of linguistic phenomena, like the distributions of auxiliary verbs and the clitic 'ne'. An attractive idea is that accusative case assignment depends on the presence of a covert verb, and that this allows for a unified treatment of causatives and Burzio's generalization; see e.g. Raposo and Uriagareka (1996), Chomsky (1995, 2000*b*).

There are, however, more interesting potential counterexamples to UTAH. Consider (31–2).

(31)  Bill was angry at the article
(32)  The article angered Bill

It seems that 'Bill' is the subject of '(be) angry' in (31) and the object of 'anger' in (32), while 'the article' is the subject of 'anger' in (32) and the object of 'angry (at)' in (31). If natural language allows for this kind of nonuniform mapping between grammatical and thematic relations, it is hard to see how natural language could be governed by a constraint that precludes the kind of mapping required by logically possible expressions like 'grelted'. So examples like (31–2) threaten the idea that the significance of grammatical relations is subject to a Baker-style constraint that precludes certain signal–meaning associations. And at this point, hypotheses about thematic hierarchies and causative verbs meet.

Pesetsky (1995) argues that, in (32), 'Bill' is indeed the subject of 'angry', which has adjoined to a covert verb whose external argument is 'the article'. The idea is that the underyling combinatorial structures are roughly as shown below.

[Bill [be-angry [(at) [the article]]]][the article [[make-angry][Bill __ ]]]
                                                                      |_____|

If this is correct, (31–2) *confirm* the hypothesis that natural language is governed by a Baker-style constraint. Pesetsky's analysis also helps explain why the article is represented as the "target" of Bill's anger in (31) and the cause of Bill's anger in (32). Pesetsky discusses the similar contrast in (33–4).

(33)  The detective worried about the TV
(34)  The TV worried the detective

In (33), the TV is represented as what the detective worried about; whereas in (34), it is represented as the cause of the detective's worrying, which may have been about (say) the suspect's alibi.

Pesetsky notes (citing Kuroda (1966) and Akatsuka (1976)) that the hypothesized structure of (32) is overt in Japanese, as indicated below:

> Tanaka-ga  sono  sirase-o    yorokon-da
> Tanka      that  news        be pleased-past
> (Tanaka was pleased at that news)

> Sono sirase-ga  Tanaka-o   yoronkob-ase-ta
> That news       Tanaka     be pleased-causative-past
> (That news pleased Tanaka)

Pesetsky then shows that a hidden English causative morpheme would explain a range of related facts.[13] And he draws an analogy with Latinate roots like 'ceive' and 'fer' that occur only with certain prefixes—like 're', 'in', 'per', and 'pre'—suggesting that the causative morpheme can attach to stems that do not occur alone as pronounced verbs. It is also worth noting that the most natural interpretation of (35)—I did something that led to Bill's being angry for weeks—seems to be unavailable for (36), which seems to require repeated episodes of me angering Bill. And while (37) is fine grammatically, (38) is not.

(35)   I made Bill angry for weeks
(36)   I angered Bill for weeks
(37)   I made Bill angry at himself
(38)   *I angered Bill at himself

The main point, though, is that positing the covert morpheme lets us preserve the attractive idea that English is governed by a constraint (on the significance of grammatical relations) that precludes "thematically inverted" sentence meanings. Absent covert morphology and the kind of syntax that Conjunctivists need, there

---

[13] For example, *the book's annoyance of Bill* (which implies that the book caused Bill to be annoyed) is much worse than *Bill's annoyance at the book* (which implies only that Bill is annoyed at the book). This semantic difference is apparently correlated with a structural difference: 'annoyance' is homophonous as between [[[annoy] **v**] ance] and [[annoy] ance].

are apparent counterexamples to generalizations like UTAH. And if one takes them to be genuine counterexamples, one needs some other account of the negative facts predicted by the constraint. Of course, if UTAH is a real constraint, the next question is why natural languages conform to it. (And if it isn't learned, one wants to know if it follows from more basic principles of universal grammar.) But if UTAH is false, then we need to explain why humans consistently acquire languages that conform to it in so many respects.

## 2.3. *Related Arguments*

UTAH also figures in the explanation of detailed linguistic facts; see Baker (1997). For example, with regard to (39–42),

(39)   Pat sprayed paint on the walls
(40)   Pat sprayed walls with the paint
(41)   Pat sprayed the paint on walls
(42)   Pat sprayed the walls with paint

UTAH predicts that (39) and (41) differ thematically from (40) and (42). The claim is that the *direct object* of 'sprayed' is the Theme-representer in each case. By contrast, without linguistic constraints on how grammatical relations (to internal/external arguments) are related to thematic roles, one would not expect a thematic asymmetry here. Why should either event participant—paint or walls— be represented as the most saliently "affected" participant that determines when the relevant event is over? Why should the direct object determine the relevant Terminater for a process of spraying in which some paint ends up on some walls (and some walls end up with some paint on them)? But UTAH's prediction is correct.

   While the sentences have closely related meanings, (41) describes a process that isn't over until the relevant quantity of paint was on walls, while (42) is true once the walls are sprayed with some paint. Moreover, as many authors have noted, one can add the modifier 'for an hour' to each of (39–42); but adding 'in an hour' to (39–40) is noticeably worse than adding 'for an hour' to (41–2). So there is *some* asymmetry here. And it is independently plausible that such asymmetries turn on whether or not the corresponding event description specifies an endpoint for the event described. To say that someone ran is not (yet) to specify an endpoint of the running. Correspondingly, one can run for an hour, but not in an hour. But one can run to the store in an hour; and 'running to the store' describes an endpoint for the event of running. In terms of Vendler's (1967) updating of observations dating back to Aristotle, one can classify event descriptions as "atelic" or "telic"; where atelic descriptions cannot be extended by adding 'in an hour', since this modifier (unlike 'for an hour') presupposes an endpoint for the event described.

It is also independently plausible that Theme-representers can determine the telicity of event descriptions. As Higginbotham notes, one can drink beer (or beers) for an hour, but not in an hour. Yet one can drink *the* beer—*a* beer, *three* beers—in an hour (and also for an hour). One can build *houses* for a year, but not in a year. Though one can build *a house* in a year; see Tenny (1994), Levin and Rappaport Hovav (1995). There are various ways to state the generalization. But a first approximation is that generic Theme-representers (as in 'drink beer') are atelic event descriptions, whereas specific Theme-representers (as in 'drink the beer') are telic; and a complex event description is telic if one of its conjuncts is telic. This suggests that '(the) paint' is indeed the Theme-representer in (39) and (41), while '(the) walls' is the Theme-representer in (40) and (42), as indicated in (39M–42M).

(39M)    ∃O[Agent(O, Pat) & Spraying(O) &
         Theme(O, paint) & On(O, the walls)]

(40M)    ∃O[Agent(O, Pat) & Spraying(O) &
         Theme(O, walls) & With(O, the paint)]

(41M)    ∃O[Agent(O, Pat) & Spraying(O) &
         Theme(O, the paint) & On(O, walls)]

(42M)    ∃O[Agent(O, Pat) & Spraying(O) &
         Theme(O, the walls) & With(O, paint)]

One can add 'in an hour' to (41) and (42), which have telic Theme-representers.

If this is correct, then UTAH helps explain some puzzling facts about examples like (39–42). So if UTAH requires covert causative morphemes in English, resisting appeal to such morphemes carries an explanatory cost. Note that (39–42) also provide further support for thematic separation. Replacing (39M) and (41M) with '∃O[Spray(O, Pat, paint)]' and '∃O[Spray(O, Pat, the paint)]' fails to represent the relevance of Theme-representers and the correlation with direct objects. Similarly, semantic representations like '∃O[Spray(O, Pat, the paint)]' and '∃O[Run(O, Pat) & To(O, the store)]' fail to reflect the fact that 'To(O, the store)' is like 'Theme(O, the paint)' with regard to telicity.[14]

Contrasts between (39–42) and the superficially similiar alterations in (43–46) are also relevant.

(43)   Pat read stories to the kids
(44)   Pat read kids the stories
(45)   Pat read the stories to kids
(46)   Pat read the kids stories

One can easily add 'in an hour' to (44) and (45); whereas adding 'in an hour' to (43) and (46) seems worse. This suggests that, in each case, '(the) stories' is understood as specifying the Theme, with '(the) kids' specifying event participants of some other kind; see the discussion of ditransitive verbs in chapter 2. Given UTAH, this makes a further prediction, as Baker (1997) notes: (43–6) illustrate a genuine *alternation*, in which one surface order is basic and the other obtained by transformation; but (39–42) do not reflect a true alternation in this sense. If this is correct, there should be symptoms of this difference. And this expectation is confirmed; see also Larson (1988).

As Baker observes, while each of (43–6) implies that there was a reading of some stories, none implies that there was a reading of

---

[14] If one analyzes 'Pat ran to the store' as '∃x[Run-to(x, Pat, the store)]', hypothesizing that 'Run-to(x, Pat, the store)' is relevantly like 'Spray(x, Pat, the paint)', one has to *stipulate* that 'Pat ran to the store' implies 'Pat ran', instead of *explaining* this implication by conjunction-reduction.

some kids. But each of (39–42) implies that there was a spraying of walls and a spraying of paint. Given (43–6), there was some story-reading but no child-reading; given (39–42), there was some wall-spraying *and* paint-spraying.[15] The verbs 'give' and 'read' generally pattern together in these respects, as do 'spray' and 'load'. Williams (1980) notes contrasts like those in (47–54),

(47)   Pat loaded *the meat* into the freezer *raw*

(48)   Pat gave *the meat* to the dog *raw*

(49)   *Pat loaded the meat into *the freezer full*

(50)   *Pat gave the meat to *the dog hungry*

(51)   *Pat loaded the freezer with *the meat raw*

(52)   Pat gave the dog *the meat raw*

(53)   Pat loaded *the freezer full* with the meat

(54)   *Pat gave *the dog hungry* the meat

concerning secondary predications. Making use of UTAH, Baker assimilates such facts to Larson's (1988) account of ditransitive verbs; (52) is a transform of (48), while (51) is not a transform of (47).[16]
So if one says that examples like (31–2) falsify UTAH,

(31)   Bill was angry at the article

(32)   The article angered Bill

---

[15] Baker also notes that one gets Theme-compounding but not Goal-compounding, even in languages where the only possible overt order for a ditransitive construction is Verb–IndirectObject–DirectObject; and this raises the question of why Goal-compounding is excluded, unless Universal Grammar ensures that (i) all languages conform to UTAH, and (ii) compounding with the IndirectObject is illicit.

[16] In Pietroski (2003*d*), I review some theoretical considerations—in particular, recent work aimed at theoretical reduction of the sort urged in Chomsky's (1995, 2000*b*) "minimalist program"—that favor appeal to a covert element that assigns a thematic role to the external argument. One would like to show how complex grammatical structures arise from concatenation of simpler elements, without assuming that natural language grammars employ "templates" for complex expressions; cf. Jackendoff (1977), Chomsky (1957, 1965, 1981). For this raises the question of why certain templates but not others are employed. One hypothesis is that English transitive and ditransitive constructions arise by somehow combining intransitive verbs with covert elements that allow for introduction of further arguments; see Larson (1988), Chomsky (2000*b*). For related discussion see Lasnik (1999), Epstein and Hornstein (1999), Uriagereka (2002), Hornstein (2001).

one has a *lot* of explanatory work to do. And it is hard to see how such examples wouldn't falsify UTAH, absent covert causative morphemes. This bears on debates about the significance of concatenation, because given UTAH and the grammatical structure it requires, a Conjunctivist account of causative implications is more economical than Functionist-lexicalist accounts. (Why adopt Functionism and lexical structure that reproduces grammatical structure interpreted in Conjunctivist fashion? And without a constraint like UTAH, a lexical account must be supplemented with a "filter" that excludes thematically inverted lexical meanings.) Summarizing the chapter thus far, Functionists face a dilemma: posit the covert morpheme *v* and reproduce a Conjunctivist semantics of causatives as a claim about the Value of *v*; or pay the costs of not positing the covert morpheme. I have tried to develop this argument in some detail, using data familiar to linguists, because it highlights a question that we should bear in mind when thinking about compositional semantics. Given certain *constraints* on how signals are associated with meanings (via grammatical forms), which conception of semantic composition figures in the simplest overall conception of signal–meaning associations (in natural language) and the relevant constraints?

# 3. Serializers

In this section, I show how the proposed Conjunctivist semantics for English causatives can be extended to account for some otherwise puzzling phenomena concerning serial verb constructions in languages like Edo, given the kind of syntax defended by Baker and Stewart (1999, 2002).[17] Functionism does not provide an equally unified account. On the contrary, in order to describe the facts about these theoretically interesting examples of predicate–argument combination, Functionists need to invoke various kinds of type-shifting that effectively mimic a Conjunctivist semantics.

---

[17] I am indebted to Mark Baker for many conversations about serial verbs.

## 3.1. *Doing Two Things with One Theme*

Sentences (55) and (56) differ in meaning. While (56) means that Ozo will cook the food and (then) eat that very food, (55) implies this and something more. The further implication is not easily specified. But roughly, the cooking and the eating must somehow figure in a "unified process" in which Ozo cooks the food with the plan of eating it.

(55)  Òzó ghá   lé   èvbàré ré
      |    |    |     |     |
      Ozo will cook  food   eat

(56)  Òzó ghá   lé   èvbàré ré órè
      |    |    |     |     |  |
      Ozo will cook  food   eat it

For example, speakers cannot use (55) to describe a scenario in which Ozo cooked the food for a guest, but the guest never arrived, so Ozo ate the food. By contrast, this situation is compatible with (56). Similarly, if Ozo buys a book and reads it as planned when he gets home, this situation can be reported with (the Edo equivalent of) 'buy the book read'. But if he comes across a book in the store, reads it, *and then* decides to buy it, one cannot describe this situation with 'read the book buy'.

These facts are reminiscent of the distinction between boiling$_T$ the soup and merely doing something that caused it to boil$_I$, since (55) implies (56), and not conversely. But (55) does not seem to be the result of *adding* anything to (56); prima facie, (56) adds something to (55). And let me stress that (55) requires not just that the eating be intended by the Agent. (He might well form an intention, once it is clear that the guest is not coming, to eat the already cooked food.) The semantics is somehow sensitive to the distinction between executing a plan in stages and merely doing one thing after another. One might paraphrase (55) as 'Ozo will cook the food in order to eat it and then do so'. The question is how to get this meaning from the parts of (55).

Abstracting from details not germane here, Baker and Stewart argue for the grammatical structure in (55G), where '*pro*' is a covert pronoun.

(55G)   $\{Ozo_\alpha\ [[(cook\text{--}\textit{v})_{\Pi^*}\ (\underline{\quad}food_\alpha)]_\Pi\ [(eat\text{--}\textit{v})_{\Pi^*}\ (\underline{\quad}pro_\alpha)]_\Pi]\}$

The idea is that 'cook' and 'eat' (or perhaps intransitive analogs) are displaced to positions in which they incorporate with covert elements.[18] If this is on the right track, it is an embarrassment for Functionists, and not just because more transitive constructions would involve covert verbs. In (55G), two verb-phrases of the same semantic type—'cook (the) food' and 'eat *pro*'—are concatenated and then combined with a *single* external argument; and as we'll see in §3.2, treating 'eat *pro*' as an adjunct would not avoid the need for further auxiliary hypotheses. By contrast, (55G) presents no structural problem for Conjunctivism, according to which combining two verb-phrases is no different semantically than combining a noun with an adjective. As we'll see, each verb and each argument can be interpreted as a monadic predicate, conjoinable with and independent of the others. If this is correct, it is further support for thematic separation; each grammatical argument $\alpha$ makes its semantic contribution independently of any verb that takes $\alpha$ as an argument.

A striking feature of (55G) concerns the unpronounced object of the second verb, whatever one takes that covert element to be. If (55)

---

[18] Baker and Stewart (2002) supplement this basic proposal with an account of certain asymmetries between the two verbs (most notably that the first must take an overt object), in terms of the second verb-phrase being a kind of secondary predicate, in roughly Williams's (1980) sense of predication. I take no stand on these further details. But I do assume that (55) involves concatenation of two predicates prior to combination with a single subject. Initially, one might think this is no more worrisome than English sentences like 'Chris sang and danced'. But presumably, Functionists will say either of two things here: the sentence involves some kind of ellipsis; or 'and' indicates *predicate* conjunction—i.e. a function from unary functions to functions from unary functions to unary functions. Neither strategy is available for (55), since 'Ozo' appears just once, and there is no coordinating conjunction. I return to the idea that 'eat *pro*' is a kind of adjunct; though as we'll see, this does not help Functionists.

is true, the food cooked must be the food eaten, as if 'food' were the object of *both* 'eat' and 'cook'. But in (55G), 'food' is not a potential antecedent for '*pro*', given the standard assumption that the antecedent to a covert element must c-command that element. (To a first approximation, expression $\alpha$ c-commands expression $\beta$ if the smallest phrase including $\alpha$ includes $\beta$.[19]) The precise details are debatable. But on any reasonable theory of antecedence, it is hard to see how 'food' could be the antecedent of '*pro*' in (55G). This is part of the puzzle that serial-verb constructions present: mandatory cointerpretation of the covert object with the overt object, even though the former is apparently not grammatically related to the latter in the way required for antecedence. Baker and Stewart suggest, without offering a specific proposal, that the right eventish semantics will ensure that 'food' specifies the Theme of *both* the cooking *and* the eating. (So if the Value of '*pro*' is the Theme of the eating, that Value is none other than the food cooked.) This promissory note can be cashed, given Conjunctivism, at least if we don't assume that the two covert verbs make the very same semantic contribution.

Let's represent the serial verb-phrase as follows, ignoring the predisplacement positions of the overt verbs: $[[(\text{cook}-v')_{\Pi^*} \text{ food}_\alpha]_\Pi [(\text{eat}-v)_{\Pi^*} \text{ pro}_\alpha]_\Pi]_\Pi$. Given Conjunctivism, something$_\text{o}$ is a Value of this phrase iff it$_\text{o}$ is a Value of both $[(\text{cook}-v')_{\Pi^*} \text{ food}_\alpha]_\Pi$ and $[(\text{eat}_\Pi-v)_{\Pi^*} \text{ pro}_\alpha]_\Pi$. Since food$_\alpha$ and pro$_\alpha$ are internal arguments, each Value of $[(\text{cook}-v')_{\Pi^*} \text{ food}_\alpha]_\Pi$ has the relevant food as its Theme, and each Value of $[(\text{eat}-v)_{\Pi^*} \text{ pro}_\alpha]_\Pi$ has the Value of pro$_\alpha$ as its Theme.[20] Thus, something$_\text{o}$ is a Value of $[[(\text{cook}-v')_{\Pi^*} \text{ food}_\alpha]_\Pi [(\text{eat}-v)_{\Pi^*} \text{ pro}_\alpha]_\Pi]$ iff it$_\text{o}$ satisfies four conditions: it$_\text{o}$ is a Value of $(\text{cook}-v')_{\Pi^*}$, its$_\text{o}$ Theme is the food, it$_\text{o}$ is a Value of $(\text{eat}-v)_{\Pi^*}$, and its$_\text{o}$ Theme is the Value of pro$_\alpha$. So if something$_\text{o}$ is a Value of the

---

[19] For example, 'John' c-commands (and can be the antecedent of) the covert subject of 'please' in [that [John is [eager [ __ to please]]]], but not in [that [[the man next to John] is [eager [ __ to please]]]].

[20] More formally: Val(O, $[(\text{cook}_\Pi-v')_{\Pi^*} \text{ food}_\alpha]_\Pi$) iff Val[O, $(\text{cook}_\Pi-v')_{\Pi^*}$) & $\exists X\{\text{Internal}(O, X) \& \forall x[Xx \leftrightarrow \text{Val}(x, \text{food}_\alpha)]\}$; and Val(O, $[(\text{eat}_\Pi-v)_{\Pi^*} \text{ pro}_\alpha]_\Pi)]$ iff Val(O, $(\text{eat}_\Pi-v)_{\Pi^*}$) & $\exists X\{\text{Internal}(O, X) \& \forall x[Xx \leftrightarrow \text{Val}(x, \text{pro}_\alpha)]\}$.

serial verb-phrase, then its$_0$ Theme is both the food and the Value of *pro*$_\alpha$. In which case, the Value of *pro*$_\alpha$ must be the food in question.

In keeping with the account of causative constructions, let's assume that each Value of (eat–*v*)$_{\Pi*}$ is a process that Terminates in an eating. Then we get the desired result by hypothesizing that, while *v* indicates Terminaters, *v'* indicates Initiaters. That is,

$$\text{Val}(o, (\text{cook}-v')_{\Pi*}) \text{ iff } \exists o'[\text{Cooking}(o') \And \text{Initiater}(o, o')]; \text{and}$$

$$\text{Val}(o, (\text{eat}-v)_{\Pi*}) \text{ iff } \exists o'[\text{Eating}(o') \And \text{Terminater}(o, o')].$$

Recall that an Initiater is a first part of a causal process. Terminaters are final parts. I assume that Initiaters (and Terminaters) can themselves be processes. Flipping a switch can Initiate a much longer process. And this is so, even if the switch-flipping itself has a more basic Initiater, like an inner act of *trying* to flip the switch; see Pietroski (1998, 2000*a*). A complex process like preparing a meal will involve various subprocesses, each of which will have its own Initiater(s). And we can allow for complex processes like *cooking the food in order to eat it and doing so*, as indicated in the diagram. The idea is that p3 satisfies all four conditions imposed

p1 = Ozo cooking the food = |_____| |_____| = p2 = Ozo eating the food
p3 = |_____| = Ozo cook-eating the food

by $[[(\text{cook}-v')_{\Pi*} \text{ food}_\alpha]_\Pi \ [(\text{eat}-v)_{\Pi*} \ pro_\alpha]_\Pi]$: p3 starts with a cooking, its Theme is the food, it ends with an eating, and its Theme is the Value of '*pro*'. Assuming that each (nonplural) event has only one Theme, it follows that the food is the Value of '*pro*'. So we can still say that Themes are associated with Terminaters.

Initially, one might wonder how 'food' could specify the *Theme* of any process specified by the serial verb-phrase, since 'food' is the internal argument of a verb that specifies how that process *begins*. But this is another point at which thematic separation pays off. By virtue of its grammatical relation to 'cook', 'food' is interpreted as a Theme-specifier, without regard to the rest of the sentence. Similar remarks apply to '*pro*'. So if concatenation signifies predicate-conjunction, regardless of the predicates conjoined, both 'food' and '*pro*' are interpreted as Theme-specifiers. Conjunctivism thus predicts that, if a particular natural language grammar allows for the concatenation of two verb-phrases each of which has an internal argument, then the resulting serial verb-phrase will include two Theme-specifiers. Hence, a Value of the serial verb-phrase will have its Theme specified twice, making room for mandatory cointerpretation of a covert element with an overt element that is not a grammatical antecedent.[21]

My claim is *not* that this is, by itself, an adequate account of sentences like (55)—much less the family of serial constructions exhibited by languages like Edo; see Baker and Stewart (1999, 2002) for discussion. At a minimum, more needs to be said about Initiaters and Terminaters: why are they, like thematic roles, grammatically ordered in a certain way; and how are "unified" processes distinguished from mere cases of one thing happening after another? But we must address such questions given any conception of compositional semantics. The question here concerns the significance of concatenation, including concatenation of verbs with *internal* arguments in serial verb constructions. And we should not be misled into thinking that the significance is obviously more than just predicate-conjunction.

At first, Conjunctivism seems wrong in light of sentences like 'Every bottle fell' or 'Brutus stabbed six turnips'; and prima facie, one cannot preserve a semantic account of causative implications by treating 'boil$_T$' and 'boil$_I$' as monadic predicates. Likewise, it can seem clear that interpreting $[(\text{cook}-v')_{\Pi^*} \text{ food}_\alpha]_\Pi$ and $[(\text{eat}-v)_{\Pi^*} pro_\alpha]_\Pi$ conjunctively will not help explain why the covert object

---

[21] Given the right verbs, serialization can be extended. In Edo, one can say that Ozo will *buy–food–cook–eat*. On the assumption that the underlying syntax is as indicated below,

$$[[(v'\text{buy}_\Pi)_{\Pi^*} \text{ food}_\alpha]_\Pi[[(v'\text{cook}_\Pi)_{\Pi^*} pro_\alpha]_\Pi[(v \text{ eat}_\Pi)_{\Pi^*} pro_\alpha]_\Pi]_\Pi]_\Pi$$

Conjunctivists can characterize the meaning of this construction as follows: Ozo is the Agent of a process that (i) starts with a buying of the food and (ii) ends with a process that (*a*) starts with a cooking of the Theme and (*b*) ends with an eating of the Theme.

must be understood as standing for the food. But in each case, it turns out that Conjunctivist analyses are attractive. With regard to quantification/plurality and causatives, I also argued that such analyses are (all things considered) no more complicated than Functionist alternatives; indeed, the former may well be preferable to the latter, despite the fact that cases of predicate–argument combination are supposed to reveal the virtues of Functionism. So let me now turn to a brief comparison of the proposed (sketch of a) Conjunctivist treatment of (55) with Functionist accounts.

## 3.2. *Shifting Values*

One can hypothesize that $\|(\text{cook}-v') \text{ food}_\alpha\| = \lambda x . \lambda e . \mathbf{t}$ iff Agent$(e, x)$ & Past-Cooking$(e)$ & Theme$(e, \text{the food})$, that $\|(\text{eat}_\Pi-v) \text{ } pro_\alpha\| = \lambda x.$ $[\lambda e . \mathbf{t}$ iff Agent$(e, x)$ & Past-Eating$(e)$ & $\exists y\{\text{Theme}(e, y)\}]$, and that 'eat *pro*' is a kind of adjunct to 'cook food'. With regard to how concatenation contributes to meaning, the mixed view dealt explicitly with cases in which expressions of type $<\mathbf{x}, \mathbf{t}>$ were combined. But one can relax this view to accommodate combinations of expressions of type $<\mathbf{x} , <\mathbf{x}, \mathbf{t}>>$. Still, a problem remains. If $\|[(\text{cook}-v')_{\Pi^*}$ food$_\alpha]_\Pi[(\text{eat}-v)_{\Pi^*}pro_\alpha]_\Pi\| = \lambda x . \lambda e . \mathbf{t}$ iff Agent$(e, x)$ & Past-Cooking$(e)$ & Theme$(e, \text{the food})$ & Agent$(e, x)$ & Past-Eating$(e)$ & $\exists y\{\text{Theme}(e, y)\}$—or more simply, $\lambda x . \lambda e . \mathbf{t}$ iff Agent$(e, x)$ & Past-Cooking$(e)$ & Theme$(e, \text{the food})$ & Past-Eating$(e)$—then (9) implies that something is *both* a cooking and an eating.

One can avoid this problem given another covert element. For suppose the grammatical structure is as follows: $[[(\text{cook}-v')_{\Pi^*}$ food$_\alpha]_\Pi$ $[\text{F } [(\text{eat}-v)_{\Pi^*} \text{ } pro_\alpha]_\Pi]_{\text{FP}}]_\Pi$ where $\|\text{F}\|$ is a function that maps $\|(\text{eat}-v)_{\Pi^*} \text{ } pro_\alpha\|$ onto a function that maps $\|(\text{cook}-v')_{\Pi^*}$ food$_\alpha\|$ onto sentential Values in the right way. And suppose that $\|(\text{eat}-v) \text{ } pro_\alpha\| = \lambda x . \lambda e . \mathbf{t}$ iff Agent$(e, x)$ & $\exists f\{\text{Past-Eating}(f)$ & Terminater$(e, f)$ & $\exists y[\text{Theme}(f, y)]\}$, while $\|(\text{cook}-v') \text{ food}_\alpha\| =$ $\lambda x . \lambda e . \mathbf{t}$ iff Agent$(e, x)$ & $\exists f\{\text{Past-Cooking}(f)$ & Initiater$(e, f)$ & Theme$(f, \text{the food})\}$. Then one could characterize $\|\text{F}\|$ so that $\|\text{F}\|(\lambda x . \lambda e . \mathbf{t}$ iff Agent$(e, x)$ & $\exists f\{\text{Past-Eating}(f)$ & $\exists y[\text{Theme}(f, y)]\})$ is a function that maps the function $\lambda x . \lambda e . \mathbf{t}$ iff

Agent(e, x) & $\exists$f{Past-Cooking(f) & Initiater(e, f) & Theme(f, the food)} onto the following: $\lambda$x . $\lambda$e . **t** iff Agent(e, x) & $\exists$f{Past-Cooking(f) & Initiater(e, f) & Theme(f, the food)} & $\exists$f{Past-Eating(f) & Terminater(e, f) & Theme(f, the food)}. But this is just a more complicated rewrite of the Conjunctivist account.

One can adopt a simpler hypothesis about the underlying syntax, provide a Functionist semantics for it, and argue that the overall account is simpler. Of course, Baker and Stewart have reasons for their proposal. (They cite, for example, facts concerning possible placement of certain adverbs.) But suppose the grammatical structure of (55) was simply as follows: [[cook$_{\Pi*}$ food$_\alpha$]$_\Pi$ [eat$_{\Pi*}$ *pro*$_\alpha$]$_\Pi$], with a covert object for eat$_{\Pi*}$, but no covert verbs; where ∥cook$_{\Pi*}$ food$_\alpha$∥ = $\lambda$x . $\lambda$e . **t** iff Agent(e, x) & Past-Cooking(e) & Theme(e, the food). Suppose also that the *basic* semantic Value of [eat$_{\Pi*}$ *pro*$_\alpha$]$_\Pi$ is the function $\lambda$x . $\lambda$e . **t** iff Agent(e, x) & Past-Eating(e) & $\exists$y[Theme(f, y)]. Then one could hypothesize a type-shift so that in the context of a serial verb-phrase, the semantic Value of [eat$_{\Pi*}$ *pro*$_\alpha$]$_\Pi$ is a function that maps ∥cook$_{\Pi*}$ food$_\alpha$∥ to the function $\lambda$x . $\lambda$e . **t** iff Agent(e, x) & e starts with a cooking & Theme(e, the food) & e ends with an eating; cf. Bittner (1999). But again, this is just a way of encoding the following idea in a superficially Functionist idiom: concatenation signifies predicate-conjunction in serial verb-phrases; and the relevant grammatical relations signify causal/mereological relations.[22]

Moreover, if one appeals to the possibility of type-shifting in order to explain why some languages allow for expressions like [[cook$_{\Pi*}$ food$_\alpha$]$_\Pi$[eat$_{\Pi*}$ *pro*$_\alpha$]$_\Pi$]$_\Pi$, one faces the question of why the relevant type-shifting is unavailable to speakers of English. By

---

[22] Bittner (1999) discusses an interesting generalization across serial verb languages, and the details of her proposal are ingenious. But the leading motivation for her type-shifting, the main effect of which is (as Bittner notes) to convert function-application into predicate-conjunction, is to preserve a simpler syntax both for serial verb languages and English. In light of arguments for covert causative morphemes, and the availability of a Conjunctivist semantics, I think the motivation for such type-shifting is undercut. But my proposal began as a reply to hers, at a Rutgers workshop in 2000. I am grateful for Bittner's helpful response to me, and to the other participants in that workshop.

contrast, the Conjunctivist can say that the semantics of English does indeed provide the resources for understanding serial verb constructions. It is just that the syntax of English does not allow for constructions like (55G).

(55G)   Ozo$_\alpha$ [[(cook–$\boldsymbol{v}$)$_{\Pi^*}$ (__food$_\alpha$)]$_\Pi$ [(eat–$\boldsymbol{v}$)$_{\Pi^*}$ (__*pro*$_\alpha$)]$_\Pi$]$_\Pi$

It is an interesting question *why* there is this (presumably parametric) difference between English and Edo, especially given that English does allow for sentences like (57).

(57)    Pat wiped the table clean

But English doesn't allow (55G); and the Conjunctivist needs no other fact to explain the absence of serial verb constructions in English. Of course, a Functionist can say that one needs the Edo syntax *and* type-shifting to get serial-verb meanings. But this concedes the central point: *given* the right syntax, the semantic facts are best described in Conjunctivist terms.

In which case, the question is whether we should say that concatenation signifies predicate-conjunction in general, or retain Functionism and appeal to type-adjustment of some kind. If we needed Functionism for other constructions, diagnosing serial verb constructions in terms of type-adjustment might be reasonable. But our question is no longer whether Functionism can be maintained (given type-adjustment) for sentences involving transitive verbs. It is whether such sentences provide reasons for adopting Functionism.

## 4. Complementizer Phrases as Conjuncts

In this final section, I briefly discuss verbs that take sentential complements, as in (58) and (59).

(58)    Nora said that Fido barked
(59)    Nick thinks that Fido barked

Much of the huge literature on this subject is addressed to questions about the semantic contribution of 'that'-clauses and other complementizer phrases (which may have covert complementizers): what are the Values of such clauses; and how are they compositionally detemined? Like many others, I have a favored account; see Pietroski (1996, 2000*a*). But for present purposes, we can abstract away from these questions in order to focus on others: what are the Values of *verbs* that take 'that'-clauses as arguments; and what is the significance of concatenating such verbs with complementizer phrases? In particular, are there reasons for treating verbs like 'say' and their sentential arguments as conjoinable monadic predicates? If so, and cases of *recursive* predicate–argument combination favor Conjunctivism, that further undercuts the hypothesis that such combination signifies function-application.

## 4.1. *Many Ways of Encoding a Traditional View*

Let's assume, at least for purposes of illustration, that a verb-phrase of the form 'said that . . .' has the following grammatical structure: $[said_{\Pi^*} [that_C \langle \ldots \rangle]_\alpha]_\Pi$; where the verb combines with a phrasal argument consisting of the complementizer $that_C$ and a sentence. And suppose that relative to assignment **A**, the Value of $[that_C \langle \ldots \rangle]_\alpha$ is the "propositional content" of the embedded sentence (relative to **A**). This presupposes that sentences have contents, at least relative to assignments, while leaving it open what contents are: Fregean senses of sentences; Russellian propositions; sets of possible worlds, as in Stalnaker (1984); classes of utterances (or sentence-context pairs) that "samesay", as suggested by Davidson (1968); interpreted logical forms, as in Larson and Ludlow (1993); or any other remotely plausible candidates for the Values of 'that'-clauses. One can think about the complementizer $that_C$ as marking a sentential clause as an expression being used to indicate a content.[23]

---

[23] Compare the allusion to phases in §3.4 of Ch 2, in the context of relative clauses. See Pietroski (1996) for elaboration in terms of Fregean senses. In languages that

Functionists can capture this view as indicated below, ignoring context-sensitivity for simplicity.

$$\|\ldots_{\Pi^*}[\text{that}_C\langle\ldots\rangle]_\alpha\| = \|\ldots_{\Pi^*}\|(\|\text{that}_C\langle\ldots\rangle\|)$$
$$\|\text{that}_C\langle\ldots\rangle\| = \text{Content}(\langle\ldots\rangle)$$
$$\|\text{said}_{\Pi^*}\| = [\lambda y \ . \ \lambda x \ . \ \mathbf{t} \text{ iff x said y}]$$

On this view, $\|\text{said}_{\Pi^*}[\text{that}_C\langle\text{Fido barked}\rangle]_\alpha\| = \lambda x \ . \ \mathbf{t}$ iff x said Content($\langle$Fido barked$\rangle$). This treats verbs like said$_{\Pi^*}$ as expressions of type $<\mathbf{x}, \ <\mathbf{x}, \mathbf{t}>>$, akin to stabbed$_\Pi$* in this respect—though unlike stabbed$_{\Pi^*}$, said$_{\Pi^*}$ can combine with a complementizer phrase. An event-friendly Functionist can also maintain that $\|\text{said}_{\Pi^*}\| = \lambda y \ . \ \lambda x \ . \ \lambda e \ . \ \mathbf{t}$ iff e was a saying by x of (the content) y. In which case, $\|\text{said}_{\Pi^*}[\text{that}_C\langle\text{Fido barked}\rangle]_\alpha\| = \lambda x \ . \ \lambda e \ . \ \mathbf{t}$ iff e was a saying by x of Content($\langle$Fido barked$\rangle$).

Given any such view, one cannot add the following principle: $\|\text{that}_C\langle\ldots\rangle\| = \|\text{that}_C\|(\|\langle\ldots\rangle\|)$. This would have the absurd implication that whenever sentences S1 and S2 have the same Value (**t** or **f**), the corresponding 'that'-clauses have the same Content; in which case for any verb V, something$_x$ would be a Value of 'V that S1' iff it$_x$ is a Value of 'V that S2'. Recognizing this, Frege held that in a natural language, the Value (*Bedeutung*) of a sentence S appearing as the complement of a verb like 'said' is the sense (*Sinn*) of S appearing as a matrix sentence. So on Frege's view, the Value of an expression depends in part on its grammatical context. In a good formal language, designed to make semantic structure explicit, each word would have the same Value wherever it appears. But the idea was that natural languages are not ideal in this respect; they allow speakers to use a sentence, when embedded within a larger expression, as a device for referring to its content.

This raises hard questions about what contents are and how they are compositionally determined. In hypothesizing that

---

employ special complementizers (as opposed to quotation marks) for direct speech reports, the embedded sentential clause is presumably marked as an expression being used to indicate the sentence spoken. See Pietroski (1999).

$\|\text{that}_C \langle \ldots \rangle\| = \text{Content}(\langle \ldots \rangle)$, one assumes that sentences have semantically relevant properties apart from their Values, and that these properties somehow determine plausible Values for complementizer phrases.[24] But given this assumption, Functionists are not alone in being able to provide a semantics for verbs that take sentential complements. One can hypothesize that a phrase like 'said that Fido barked' is interpreted as a conjunction of monadic predicates: Past-Saying(O) & Import(O, that Fido barked); where 'Import' indicates a thematic relation that can hold between certain events and the Values of 'that'-clauses, whatever they turn out to be.[25]

---

[24] Famously, this leads to difficulties; although there are many well-studied strategies for dealing with these difficulties. One might reject the hypothesis that there are just two sentential Values, in favor of the following: sentential Values are individuated finely enough so that it is plausible to identify sentential Values with propositional contents. But not only does this abandon the spare Fregean framework we began with, it is unlikely to help show that sentential complements favor Functionism. One would need to say what contents *are*, in order to say what sentential Values are and thereby preserve the initially attractive account of sentences like 'Fido barked' and 'Every dog saw a cat'; and existing proposals about contents are controversial enough, without insisting that they also serve as proposals about sentential Values. To take one much discussed example, suppose that contents are sets of possible worlds, with worlds individuated (and names interpreted) so that the following conditional is true: if Fido is identical with Rex, then the content of 'Fido barked' is also the content of 'Rex barked'. Then one is forced to say that, if Fido is identical with Rex, the Value of 'Nora thinks that Fido barked' is also the Value of 'Nora thinks that Rex barked'. In which case, Conjunctivists have an obvious reply. On the other hand, anyone who says that the Value of 'Fido barked' differs from that of 'Rex barked', even if Fido is Rex, owes an account of relevant implications; see §2.2 of the Introduction. Soames (1987, 1995, 2003) has developed an idea that can be expressed (roughly) as follows: the content of sentence S is the information that S conveys, invariantly, across possible contexts; all that remains constant across contexts in the case of a name is its bearer; so if Fido is Rex, the content of 'Fido' is the content of 'Rex'. But given the current state of inquiry, it is far from clear that *sentences* really have informational content in any robust sense. Soames may have a theory in search of phenomena. In any case, there seem to be explananda concerning how speakers *understand* sentences. And in my view, there are no good reasons for thinking that these *psychological* facts, can be redescribed and explained in terms of facts about the information carried by sentences.

[25] The term 'Import' is intended to suggest Frege's (1892*b*) idea of "cognitive significance", the "gist" (as opposed to exact details) of a speech act, and the idea of something "brought in from abroad". This invites a possible response to an old puzzle

The idea is that 'said' bears a semantically significant grammatical relation to its sentential complements; where this relation differs from the one that 'stabbed' bears to its internal arguments. More specifically, Conjunctivists can treat sentential complements as Import-specifiers, as opposed to Theme-specifiers. Let's use '*par-*' (intimating 'paratactic') to indicate the grammatical relation that a verb like 'said' bears to a sentential complement, distinguishing '*par-*' from '*int-*'. Then some events$_O$ are Values of the verb-phrase [said$_{\Pi*}$ *par-*[that$_C$ ⟨Fido barked⟩]$_\alpha$]$_\Pi$ iff they$_O$ are Values of both said$_{\Pi*}$ and *par-*[that$_C$ ⟨Fido barked⟩]$_\alpha$; where some events$_O$ are Values of *par-*[that$_C$ ⟨Fido barked⟩]$_\alpha$ iff they$_O$ are events with the Import specified by the complementizer phrase. (See Blair (2004) for articulation of a closely related view within a grammatically plausible Davidsonian framework.) Abbreviating,

Val(O, [said$_{\Pi*}$ *par-*[that$_C$ ⟨Fido barked⟩]$_\alpha$]$_\Pi$) iff
Past-Saying(O) & Import(O, Content(⟨Fido barked⟩)).

That is, some events$_O$ are Values of the complex verb-phrase iff they$_O$ were events of saying whose Import was the Content of the embedded sentence. This leaves room for elaboration and modification of various sorts; see Richard (1990) for illuminating discussion. For example, one need not *identify* Imports and Contents. And perhaps some events$_O$ are Values of the complex verb-phrase iff they$_O$ were events of saying whose Import was suitably related, in the relevant context, to Content(⟨Fido barked⟩); where Contents are context-invariant properties of linguistic expressions. For present purposes, we can leave such details unsettled.

I do think that second-order/plural quantification is wanted here, since there can be cases in which many speech events are reported

concerning "purposive" adverbs. Since 'Ed married Jo intentionally' implies 'Ed married Jo', one expects a conjunction-reduction explanation, with 'intentionally' treated as a predicate of events. But if Jo is Ed's mom, then any event of Ed marrying Jo is an event of Ed marrying his mom. Yet it doesn't follow that Ed married Jo intentionally iff Ed married his mom intentionally. So how can 'intentionally' be a predicate of events? For this reason, Davidson abandoned the conjunction-reduction model for such cases. But perhaps a *process* o is intentional iff: o was Initiated by an event of trying whose Import "matches" the content of the modified sentence.

with one sentence, even though the summarizing sentence would be a bad report of any one of the speech events. An entire interview might be correctly summarized by a reporter who says, 'The candidate said that his opponent was a lout'. But let's set this aside, and pretend that for each true report of the form 'x said that p', there was a single speech event that was an event of x saying that p. Then we can continue with this chapter's pretense, friendly to Functionists, that there is no substantive difference between my upper- and lower-case variables.

Given this simplification, one might prefer a Functionist account that does not rely on the idea that verbs like 'said' bear a special (semantically significant) grammatical relation to sentential complements. Of course, a theory according to which $\|\text{that}_C \langle \ldots \rangle\| = \text{Content}(\langle \ldots \rangle)$ is a theory according to which 'that'-clauses specify contents; one preserves the idea that concatenating 'said' with a 'that'-clause signifies function-application by hypothesizing, with Frege, that the complements of such verbs are somehow semantically special. Given the empirical facts, this is perfectly reasonable. But it is not obviously simpler than the Conjunctivist alternative, which makes explicit the specialness of the relation between a verb like 'said' and its sentential complement. Still, one might argue that Functionists need only the auxiliary hypothesis about 'that'-clauses, while Conjunctivists need a further assumption about (the significance of) the grammatical relation indicated with '*par-*'.

Put another way, one might think that Functionists need not associate complementizer phrases with thematic roles, or distinguish Theme-specifiers from Import-specifiers, since sentential complements can be treated as cases in which the Themes happen to be contents. (And without such a distinction, why interpret complementizer phrases via thematic roles?) I don't object to the idea that contents can be Themes. It seems clear that Themes can be abstracta; think of sentences like 'This weighs ten pounds' and 'She counted to a hundred in a minute'. But the distinction between Theme-specifiers and Import-specifiers is independently motivated.

## 4.2. *Explaining That*

Consider (60–2).

(60)    Nora explained that Fido barked
(61)    Nora explained the fact that Fido barked
(62)    Nora explained why Fido barked

Sentence (60) can be used to describe a situation in which Nora uttered 'Fido barked' in response to a question: Nick asked why the burglar ran off, and Nora explained that Fido barked. In such cases, *that Fido barked* is not the explanandum—the thing explained; it is *what Nora said* in explaining something else—namely, that the burglar ran off. So (60) can be true while (61) is false, and (61) can be true while (60) is false. In this respect, 'the fact that . . .' is unlike 'that . . .', and more like 'why . . .'; (61) is a paraphrase of (62), not (60). This is a striking phenomenon that a semantic theory should account for. We can describe the contrast, in Conjunctivist terms, by specifying the meanings of (60) and (61) as in (60M) and (61M).

(60M)    $\exists O$[Agent(O, Nora) & Past-Explaining(O) & Import(O, that Fido barked)]

(61M)    $\exists O$[Agent(O, Nora) & Past-Explaining(O) & Theme(O, the fact that Fido barked)]

I return to some grammatical details. But the idea is that as in (60), 'explained' can combine with a bare complemetizer phrase, which is interpreted as an Import-specifier; though as in (61), 'explained' can also combine with a real internal argument—like a phrase headed by (the determiner or definite article) 'the'—which is interpreted as a Theme-specifier. Events of explaining can have facts as Themes. If an Agent explained some fact, the explanandum is the Theme of the explaining.[26] Events of explaining can also have Imports, since explainers often utter meaningful sentences in the course of

---

[26] Themes *measure* events (see Tenny (1994)); they need not be *things affected*. If x is the Agent of an event whose Theme is an abstract entity y, then perhaps x manipulates some concrete *representation of* y. But I take no stand on this issue here. For simplicity,

explaining certain facts. But the Import of an explaining is not the explanandum. It is more typically the explanans.

In the imagined situation, Nora explained the fact that the burglar ran off by noting that Fido barked. One can describe this episode of explaining with a sentence like (60) that explicitly mentions the explanandum, or a sentence like (61) that explicitly mentions the explanans. There is an asymmetry, in that (60) feels somehow "incomplete" if an explanandum/Theme is not determined contextually; while (61) does not require, at least not in the same way, that an explanans/Import be specified contextually. Correlatively, there may be a sense in which 'that'-clause complements are more adjunct-like than 'the fact that'-clause complements; see Munro (1982). But the important point here is simply that Conjunctivists can draw an Import/Theme distinction and use this distinction to diagnose the semantic difference between (60) and (61).

By contrast, examples like (60) present difficulties for theories according to which the Value of 'explained' is a function from contents to functions. This is especially clear if one assumes that the Value of 'that Fido barked' just *is* the Value of 'the fact that Fido barked', at least if (it is a fact that) Fido barked. For in that case, (60) and (61) are semantically equivalent, given a theory according to which $\|\text{explained}_{\Pi^*}\|$ is the function $\lambda y . \lambda x . \mathbf{t}$ iff x explained y— or $\lambda y . \lambda x . \lambda e . \mathbf{t}$ iff e was an explaining by x of y. Moreover, a puzzle remains even if the Values of 'that Fido barked' and 'the fact that Fido barked' are distinct. If 'explained' expresses any relation R, then presumably, Nora bears R to something iff she explained that thing. And merely distinguishing the fact that Fido barked from (the content that is) the Value of 'that Fido barked' does not explain how Nora could bear R to exactly one of these. One can't, for example, be near the dog Fido without being near Fido. One can reject this analogy and insist that 'explains' expresses a relation sensitive to the

---

I assume that the events of explaining in question have unique Themes. This is *not*, however, to assume that *facts* have unique explanations. If a single fact can be twice explained, so be it; see Pietroski (2000c) for related discussion.

alleged distinction between facts and contents. But then one owes an account of the relation and the distinction. And in the present context, the important point is that Functionists owe an account of the distinction that does not effectively reproduce the Conjunctivist account in terms of Theme-specifiers and Import-specifiers. In particular, it won't do to say that $\|$explained$_{\Pi*}\| = \lambda y \,.\, \lambda x \,.\, \lambda e \,.\, \mathbf{t}$ iff Agent(e, x) & Past-Explaining(e) & Theme(e, y) if y is a fact & Import(e, y) if y is a content. This is no way to defend the idea that combining verbs with complementizer phrases signifies function-application. The challenge is to specify $\|$explained$_{\Pi*}\|$, without *ad hoc* devices, in a way that does justice to both (60) and (61).

Here is another way of highlighting the relevant contrast. Following Davidson (1968), one might find it initially plausible that an utterance of (58) is understood as an utterance of (58D);

(58)   Nora said that Fido barked
(58D)   Nora said that

where the demonstrative in (58D) is used to denote (the relevant utterance of) 'Fido barked'. But a parallel analysis of (60) in terms of (60D) is grossly implausible.

(60)   Nora explained that Fido barked
(60D)   Nora explained that

For (60D) is true only if the demonstrative is used to denote what Nora explained—an explanandum. By contrast, (60) is true only if the 'that'-clause is used to refer to something Nora said in the course of explaining something else. Conjunctivists can account for this by saying that the demonstrative in (60D) is an internal argument, and so a Theme-representer (given UTAH), while the 'that'-clause in (60) is an Import-specifier. Functionists, like paratactic theorists who follow Davidson (1968) too closely, have a problem; see Pietroski (2000*b*).

If the demonstrative in (60D) is used to denote the Value of the 'that'-clause in (60), then given Functionism, (uses of) these sentences should be semantically equivalent. Each should get the Value **t** iff [||explained||(||that Fido barked||)](Nora) = **t**. If 'explained' expresses a relation, between explainers and things explained, then it should not matter whether the explanandum is specified with a demonstrative or a 'that'-clause. But evidently, this grammatical difference makes a semantic difference, as predicted by the Conjunctivist account. In this regard, it is also relevant that the extraposed construction (63) is equivalent to (61), not (60).

(63)   Nora explained it, that Fido barked
(61)   Nora explained the fact that Fido barked

In (63), 'that Fido barked' is used to specify (via the pronoun 'it') the explanandum. And in (63), 'it' is presumably a Theme-specifier. So there is no prohibition against using a bare complementizer phrase to specify a content that gets represented as a Theme. This confirms the Conjunctivist account, according to which the distinction between (63) and (60) lies with the grammatical relation between 'explained' and its complement; in (63), 'it' is a real internal argument; while in (60), 'that Fido barked' is not. These examples also suggest that the Value of 'that Fido barked' may well be the fact that Fido barked, at least if (it is a fact that) Fido barked, much as the Value of 'Fido' may well be the Value of 'the dog Fido'. Otherwise, one needs a special explanation for why (61) is equivalent to (63) and (64).

(64)   Nora explained it, the fact that Fido barked

## 4.3. *Other Illustrations of the Theme/Import Distinction*

The crucial point is that 'explained' is used to characterize *speech acts* that (qua speech) have an Import and also (qua act of rendering something comprehensible) have a Theme. As (60) and (61) illustrate, this verb can combine with a Theme-specifier corresponding to the explanandum, or an Import-specifier (typically) corresponding to the explanans.

The interest of this point would be limited if 'explained' was the only speech-act verb with this semantic character. But as many authors have noted, in different contexts, replacing 'VERB that P' with 'VERB the fact that P' does not always preserve meaning and grammaticality.[27] In the present context, verbs like 'misremember', 'elaborate', and 'protest' are especially interesting. One can mis-remember that P (i.e. have the feeling of remembering that P despite it being false that P) without misremembering the fact that P (which would be to have a distorted memory of the truth that P). Similarly, one can misstate that P without misstating the fact that P, and vice versa. If Smith says that Chomsky is a linguist, Jones might *elaborate that* Chomsky is a very famous linguist, but not *elaborate the fact that* Chomsky is a very famous linguist. One can elaborate that P without "embroidering" the fact that P. If Smith replies that Chomsky is overrated, Jones might *protest that* Chomsky is a great linguist without *protesting the fact that* Chomsky is a great linguist. Likewise, one can protest the fact that P without ever protesting that P. Note that in these examples, the thing misremembered/elaborated/protested is specified as the fact that P, while the gist of the protest/elaboration/mistaken-memory is specified with a bare 'that'-clause.

There are, to be sure, verbs which take 'that'-clauses but not 'the fact that'-clauses. And the Conjunctivist proposal does not imply otherwise. For example, (65*) is somehow ill-formed, even though (65a) and (65b) are acceptable.

(65*)  Nora said the fact that Fido barked
(65a)  Nora said truly that Fido barked
(65b)  Nora said that Fido barked, and what she said is true

Similarly, one can grumble that there are too many lawyers, or grumble at the fact that there are too many lawyers. But one cannot grumble the fact that there are too many lawyers. Still, many verbs can take both kinds of complements, at least if we take account of

---

[27] See Moltmann (2004) for interesting discussion and extensive references.

perverse (though still grammatical) readings. While (66) is fine, there is something decidedly odd about (67).

(66)   The jury found that the defendant was negligent
(67)   The jury found the fact that the defendant was negligent

Nonetheless, (67) has a comprehensible interpretation which implies that facts (like missing socks) are things one can find. This highlights the point that (67) isn't a paraphrase of (66). Semanticists need to say why (67) has the meaning it does have, even if it involves some kind of "category" mistake.

Conjunctivists have a ready proposal: the verb 'found' can be combined with a Theme-specifier, as in 'found the sock'; and in (67) 'the fact that the defendant was negligent' is a Theme-specifier. This suggests that when 'the ...' appears as a direct object, it is interpreted as a Theme-specifier, as opposed to an Import-specifier. Similarly, one can fear that civil liberties are under attack (or fear a particular government official) without fearing facts *per se*; cf. Vendler (1967) and n. 27. But we can imagine committed ontologists of a certain bent suffering from "factaphobia", or perhaps a more restricted fear of facts concerning (say) numbers. With respect to such people, who may not fear that seven is a prime number, (68) might be true.

(68)   They fear the fact that seven is a prime number

Such people might know that (and even be happy that) seven is a prime number, but worry that certain facts (like certain officials) are dangerous.

There may also be morphological correlates of the Theme/Import distinction. Motamura (2003), taking Pietroski (2000b) as a point of departure, observes that the Japanese translations of 'explained that P' and 'explained the fact that P' differ interestingly. With regard to the former, the embedded sentence is marked with the case morpheme 'to'. With regard to the latter, the embedded sentence is marked with the case morpheme 'o', and the matrix verb of the embedded sentence is combined with 'koto' (a kind of complementizer or nominalizer). The translations of 'explained that Kenji killed Mariko' and 'explained the fact that Kenji killed Mariko' are shown below, indicating nominative and accusative case markers.

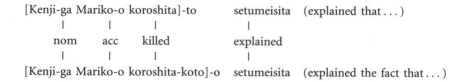

Moreover, this point extends to Japanese verbs whose English translations do not reveal a Theme/Import distinction. If you doubt the claim (or the fact) that P, then you doubt that P; and if you doubt that P, then so long as P is true, you doubt the fact that P. So if Kenji killed Mariko, but the detective doubts this, then the detective doubts (the true proposition) that Kenji killed Mariko. Sentence (69) does *not* have a meaning parallel to that of (70).

(69)   The detective doubted that Kenji killed Mariko

(70)   The detective explained that Kenji killed Mariko

That is, (69) does not mean that the detective *doubted something else* by saying (or thinking) that Kenji killed Mariko. So in English, it is hard to tell the difference between a doubt whose Import is that P and a doubt whose Theme is that P. This does not refute the Conjunctivist hypothesis. For one can say that the significance of paratactic arguments differs from that of internal arguments, while granting that in *some* cases, this difference is truth-conditionally inert; a doubt, unlike an explaining, might be such that its Import is also its Theme. Still, one wants some independent confirmation that the distinction is genuine. So it is significant that Japanese provides two sentences corresponding to (69), one with the morpheme 'to', and one with the morpheme 'o' (along with 'koto').

The two correlates of 'doubted that Kenji killed Mariko' are indicated below.

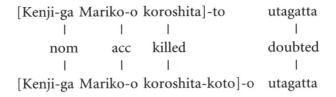

Exact translation is difficult, as Motamura's discussion reveals. But she reports that the second construction is roughly equivalent to 'doubted (the proposition) that Kenji killed Mariko', while the former can be used to convey the meaning that (69) cannot: doubted something else—say, that Mariko committed suicide—*by thinking* (or at least considering the possibility) that Kenji killed Mariko. Suppose Kenji had told the detective that Mariko committed suicide, but the detective doubted this, thinking instead that Kenji did it. Then one could describe the detective's state of mind by using '[Kenji-ga Mariko-o koroshita]-to utagatta' *but not* '[Kenji-ga Mariko-o koroshita-koto]-o utagatta'. In this case, (the proposition) that Kenji killled Mariko *is not* something that the detective doubted; it is, on the contrary, that which the detective suspects. Similar remarks apply to Japanese verbs like 'hiteishita' (denied) and 'koukaishita' (regretted).[28]

This presents a serious difficulty for any theory according to which the Value of 'utagatta' is a function from things doubted to functions. If there is any relation R such that $\|\text{utagatta}\| = [\lambda y \,.\, [\lambda x \,.\, t \text{ iff } x \text{ R } y]]$, it is hard to see how both Japanese constructions can be accommodated without *ad hoc* devices. Distinguishing contents from facts, and insisting that $\|[\text{Kenji-ga Mariko-o koroshita}]\text{-to}\| \neq \|[\text{Kenji-ga Mariko-o koroshita-koto}]\text{-o}\|$, is not enough. Functionists

---

[28] Other languages, like Korean, exhibit similar contrasts. Motamura discusses other facts that tell against the simple idea that 'to' and 'koto-o' are always indicators of Imports and Themes, respectively. But there certainly seems to be an important semantic distinction across a significant range of examples.

still need to ensure that ‖utagatta‖(‖[Kenji-ga Mariko-o koroshita]-to‖) is some function like

$\lambda x$ . **t** iff x doubted something (else) by thinking that
    Kenji killed Mariko,

while ‖utagatta‖(‖[Kenji-ga Mariko-o koroshita-koto]-o‖) =

    $\lambda x$ . **t** iff x doubted that Kenji killed Mariko.

And this evidently requires a stipulation of that which calls for explanation. One can specify ‖utagatta‖ disjunctively: $\lambda y$ . $\lambda x$ . $\lambda e$ . **t** iff Agent(e, x) & Past-Doubting(e) & Import(e, y) if y is a content & Theme(e, y) if y is a fact. But this effectively concedes that many cases of verbs combining with sentential arguments should be described in Conjunctivist terms. Moreover, if 'explained' and 'utagatta' are best dealt with in these terms, then it is hardly *ad hoc* to deal with 'doubted' in the same way, even if this particular verb does not make the Theme/Import distinction obvious.

    Likewise, Conjunctivists can grant that in (71),

    (71)   Nora said that

the Value of the demonstrative internal argument is represented as a Theme, as suggested by UTAH. But (71) can still be used to express whatever 'Nora said that P' can be used to express. Evidently, if an event of saying has a certain Import, it also has (the content that is) this Import as its Theme. Again, the hypothesis is that the grammatical distinction between paratactic arguments and internal arguments *can* be truth-conditionally significant, not that it always is. Without independent confirmation, like Japanese case-marking, this might seem like a stretch. Though absent a better account of the "explains that" phenomenon, it is hard to know what else to say about (60–72).

    Put another way, for a verb like 'say' ('doubt', 'reject'), it may be part of the verb's meaning that its complement must specify something that can be an Import. For a verb like 'push', it may be part of the verb's meaning that its complement must specify something that can be a Theme; see Grimshaw (1979, 1990), Pesetsky (1982, 1995). But this does not *preclude* combining 'say' with a demonstrative, or a phrase like 'the first thing that occurs to you'. Even if such complements always specify Themes, some Themes can also be Imports, as the proposed Conjunctivist account suggests.[29]

## 4.4. *Varieties of Covert Syntax*

One might suggest that (60) has a lot of covert syntactic structure, along the lines suggested by its paraphrase (72).

(60)   Nora explained that Fido barked

(72)   Nora explained something by saying that Fido barked

Functionists can perhaps account for the meaning of (72) in terms of the hypothesis that $\|$explained$\| = [\lambda y . [\lambda x . \textbf{t}$ iff x explained y]], with 'y' corresponding to explananda. But Motamura's observations remain. One would have to hold that '[Kenji-ga Mariko-o koroshita]-to utagatta' has similar covert structure, in addition to the already overt morpheme 'to'. Even putting this aside, it isn't independently plausible that (60) is (72) in disguise. And it's worth seeing why, if only to be clear that, in some cases, Conjunctivism can help avoid implausible appeals to covert syntax.

I have been assuming that every part of (60) is a part of (61).

(61)   Nora explained the fact that Fido barked

I concluded that 'the fact that'-clauses are Theme-specifiers, when they appear as internal arguments, while 'that'-clauses are Import-specifiers. By contrast, the suggestion now under consideration is

---

[29] The idea would be that $\forall o \forall o' \{$Val(o, say$_{\Pi^*}) \rightarrow$ [Theme(o, o') $\leftrightarrow$ Import(o, o')]$\}$. Thus, we should be wary of drawing nonlinguistic consequences from the grammatical parallels between 'She said it' and 'She kicked it'. We need not think of saying (or believing) as something *done to* a content. Compare "measurement analogies" for belief ascriptions, as discussed in Matthews (1994).

that the verb-phrase in (60) has parts that (61) does not:

$$[[\text{explained}_{\Pi*}\ \textit{something}_{\Delta P}]_\Pi\ [by\ [\textit{saying}_{\Pi*}\ [\text{that}_C\langle \text{Fido} \\ \text{barked}\rangle]_\alpha]_\Pi]_\Pi];$$

where the italicized items are unpronounced, any covert subject of '*say*' is ignored (for simplicity), and '*by*' serves to combine predicates. On this view, 'that Fido barked' is the internal argument of an unspoken verb, which is part of an adverbial phrase modifying 'explained *something*'. And one might specify the meaning of the complex verb-phrase as follows: $\lambda e$ . t iff $\exists x[\text{Explaining}(e, \text{Nora}, x)$ & $\exists f[\text{By}(e, f)$ & $\text{Saying}(f, \text{Nora}, \text{that Fido barked})]\}$. This won't help with 'Three candidates explained to five reporters that their opponents were louts'. But put this aside.

I don't know of any independent grammatical evidence for a covert '*by*'-phrase in (60). And note, in the spirit of Fodorian observations discussed above, that the meaning of (73) is compatible with the explaining being quick; yet (74) implies that the explaining was slow.

(73) Nora explained something by slowly asserting that Fido barked

(74) Nora explained slowly that Fido barked

Likewise, (75) does not have a reading equivalent to (76).

(75) Nora quickly explained slowly that Fido barked

(76) Nora quickly explained something by saying, slowly, that Fido barked

One strains to find a coherent interpretation of (75); and prima facie, there should be no such strain if (75) has 'by saying' as a part.

One might reply that the verb-phrase in (60) involves a ditransitive verb, formed by a kind of incorporation, and a covert object: $[[[\text{explained}_{\Pi*}\ \textit{by saying}]_{\Pi**}\ [\text{that Fido barked}]_\alpha]_{\Pi*}\ \textit{something}]_\Pi$. The idea would be that: $\|\text{explained } \textit{by saying}\| = \lambda c$ . $[\lambda y$ . $[\lambda x$ . $[\lambda e$ . t iff e is an explaining by x of y & $\exists f\{\text{By}(e, f)$ & f is a saying by x of c}]]]; and expected but nonexistent ambiguities are blocked for grammatical reasons, as discussed in §2. Of course, a Functionist who takes this line can hardly object if Conjunctivists take the similar (but simpler) line with respect to the hypothesized covert syntax of causative constructions. But in any case, treating verbs that apparently take two arguments as covert ditransitives runs against the thrust of recent work stemming from Larson's (1988) reduction of ditransitives to transitives. And if the verb in (60) has the verb in (61) *as a part*, why isn't this structure manifested in the corresponding Japanese constructions? Recall that in the Japanese translation of (60), the embedded sentence is marked with the morpheme 'to'; while in the translation of (61), the embedded sentence is marked with 'o' and the embedded verb combines with 'koto'. This is hardly what one would expect if (60) involved *adding* structure to (61).

It is also worth noting that 'explained', like 'said' and 'replied', can be used to report direct speech. Consider the novelistic (77),

(77)   Nora explained, 'Fido barked'

which might be a reply to the question 'What did Nora say when Nick asked why the burglar ran off'. Prima facie, (77) does not have the grammatical structure of (78).

(78)   Nora explained something by uttering 'Fido barked'

We don't need to posit covert structure in order to say that events of explaining are speech acts in which one says something in an "explainy" way—much as an event of grumbling (or mumbling) that there are too many lawyers is a speech act in which one says something in a particular way. And 'Nora grumbled that Fido barked' does not mean that Nora grumbled something else by saying that Fido barked.

To be sure, an event isn't an event of *explanation* unless something gets explained. So if Nora did any explaining, there had to be an explanandum—hence, a Theme of the explaining—whether this gets mentioned or not. But it doesn't follow that the verb 'explained' is always accompanied by a (perhaps covert) Theme-specifier, much less a covert modifying phrase. This is not to say that 'explained' *never* combines with a covert object. But an explaining can have a theme that goes unrepresented if we talk about the event by using properties that go unrepresented if we use 'explained' in reporting the speech-act, either directly or indirectly (via its gist). Reports like (77) and (79)

(79)  Nora replied with 'Fido barked'

focus on the words used in an episode of explaining or replying. And prima facie (79) does not include a covert Theme-representer; indeed, one cannot reply the fact that Fido barked. Rather, (79) says something about the form of words used by a certain replier. Likewise, (77) says something about the form of words used by a certain explainer. But while (77) presupposes that something was explained, it need not say anything about this explanandum. And while (60) also presupposes that something was explained, it may also just report what the explainer said in the course of offering the explanation.

In stylized contexts, one can even use 'explained' to report speech in which the explainer was *not* asserting an explanans. Consider the following passage from Ring Lardner's story, "The Young Immigrunts", told from the perspective of a child whose father is having a bad day.

The lease said about my and my father's trip from the Bureau of Manhattan to our new home the soonest mended. In some way ether I or he got balled up on the grand concorpse and next thing you show we was thretning to swoop down on Pittsfield.
Are you lost daddy I arsked tenderly.
Shut up he explained.

In my view,

(80)  'Shut up,' he explained

does not *mean* that he explained something (or a contextually salient thing) by uttering 'Shut up'. This builds too much into the linguistic meaning of (80). A speech report can, without covertly quantifying over potential explananda, contain a verb that indicates something about why the speech was made. And while (81) wouldn't have been as funny, it could serve as an equivalent report of the father's speech.

(81)   He explained that I should shut up

## 4.5. *Two Kinds of Explainers*

There are, of course, many more facts to account for in this vicinity. In particular, one wants to know how the current proposal bears on indirect questions and 'why'-clauses, which have their own interesting features; see Higginbotham (1993), Lahiri (2002). I cannot address these topics in any detail. But let me conclude by providing some sense of how a Conjunctivist account might be extended to "stative" verbs like 'knows' ('thinks', 'believes'). For this further confirms the need for a Theme/Import distinction.

Consider (82), which does not involve reference to any speech act.

(82)   The fact that Fido saw the burglar explains the
       fact that Fido barked

If one fact explains another, this is not because one fact *does* something that renders the other fact comprehensible. In light of (82), one might be tempted to say that the Value of 'explains' is the function $\lambda y \,.\, \lambda x \,.\, \mathbf{t}$ iff (the fact) x explains (the fact) y. But then one must say more about the tensed speech-act verb that appears in (61).

(61)   Nora explained the fact that Fido barked

Similarly, if the Value of 'explains' is the function $\lambda y \,.\, \lambda x \,.\, \mathbf{t}$ iff (the person) x explained (the fact) y, more needs to be said about 'explains' in (82). An obvious hypothesis is that 'explain' has—in addition to its eventive form, which we have been discussing—a *stative* form that appears in constructions like (82). Given sentences like (83–5),

(83)   Nora knows that Fido barked
(84)   The proposition that Fido barked implies that
       something barked

(85)  The fact that Fido barked precludes the possibility
that nothing barked

we presumably need to posit stative predicates, as in Parsons (1990);
though see the discussion of 'precedes' in Chapter 1. Using sub-
scripts, let 'explain$_\varepsilon$' be a predicate of events, while 'explain$_\sigma$' is a
predicate of states. Then one can specify the meaning of (82) as in
(82M), using 'Subject' as a label for whatever thematic relation is
associated with the external argument of the stative verb.[30]

(82M)  ∃s[Subject(s, the fact that Fido saw the burglar) &
Explaining$_\sigma$(s) &
Theme(s, the fact that Fido barked)]

On this view, (82) gets the Value **t** iff there is a state of explaining
whose subject is the fact that Fido saw the burglar, and whose
Theme is the fact that Fido barked. If (82) is true, the fact that Fido
barked is the explanandum. And while the fact that Fido saw the
burglar does not act—it does not explain$_\varepsilon$ anything—it can explain$_\sigma$
(i.e. have the property of explaining$_\sigma$) the fact that Fido barked.
Thus, it is unsurprising that there is something wrong with (86),

(86)  The fact that Fido barked explained that the
burglar ran off

except on the perverse reading where facts are Agents who can
explain$_\varepsilon$ things. Compare the verb 'provide'. If Nora built a well, she
may have provided$_\varepsilon$ a source of water for someone; but a river can
also provide$_\sigma$ a source of water for someone, where 'provide$_\sigma$' is a

---

[30] If stative and eventive verbs differ with respect to how they are grammatically
related to external arguments (say, because the latter are formed by incorporation with
a covert transitivising verb), then *being a Subject-specifier* differs from *being an Agent-
specifier*. I take no stand here on which form of 'explain' is basic, conceptually or
grammatically. (Is explanation as a relation between facts somehow a projection of our
propensity to explain facts to one another?) But at least many episodes of explaining
are plausibly viewed as acts of reporting that some fact explains another; though
equally, if a fact F1 explains another fact F2, then a person can explain F2 (to their own
satisfaction, or to someone else) by citing F1. See Bromberger (1966), Matthews (1983),
Strawson (1985), Pietroski (2000c) for discussion.

near synonym to 'be'. Similarly, Nora can provide$_\varepsilon$ an answer to a question; and the fact that Fido barked can provide$_\sigma$ an answer.

The event/state distinction also applies to (87) and (88).

(87)    Nora explained$_\varepsilon$ why the burglar ran off

(88)    The fact that Fido barked explains$_\sigma$ why the burglar ran off

And note that (87) differs in meaning from (89),

(89)    Nora explained$_\varepsilon$ the question of why the burglar ran off

which implies that Nora rendered a certain question comprehensible. By contrast, (87) implies that Nora provided an answer to that question.[31] A paratactic theorist might hope to capture the meaning of (87)—but not (89)—with (87D).

(87D)   The burglar ran off. Nora explained why.

All of which suggests that we really do need the Theme/Import distinction. But one might think there is a difficulty lurking. For (90) differs semantically from (91).

(90)    Nick knows why the burglar ran off

(91)    Nick knows the question of why the burglar ran off

While (91) says that Nick is familiar with a certain question, (90) says that he can answer the question. And of course, (90) is different again from (92).

(92)    Nick knows that the burglar ran off.

One can know that P without knowing why P. But it is independently plausible that this twist is due to a special feature of 'know': its complements must be factive, and not just in the sense that one can

---

[31] This invites the speculation that an event of explaining is a *reporting of* a contextually relevant state of explaining. One might suggest the following: Explaining$_\varepsilon$(o) iff Saying(o) & $\exists$o'{Explaining$_\sigma$(o') & $\exists$y[Theme(o, y) & Theme(o', y)] & $\exists$p[Import(o, p) & Subject(o', p)]}. Correlatively, one might hold that 'explain$_\sigma$' combines with a covert morpheme to form 'explain$_\varepsilon$'; cf. Pietroski (2003*b*,*c*).

know that P only if P; complements of 'know' are grammatically distinctive.

As illustrated in (93) and (94), 'know' exhibits a contrast with 'think' with respect to certain displacements; see Cattell (1978).

(93)  How do you think Nick went home?

(94)  How do you know Nick went home?

A possible answer to (93), whose natural interpretation is something like 'what manner of transport is such that you think Nick went home in that manner', is 'by bus'. Not so for (94), which can only be interpreted as a question about how you have acquired a certain piece of (alleged) knowledge. Similarly, 'Why did you ask if Bill left' cannot mean: for which reason, did you ask if *Bill left for that reason.*[32] This invites the hypothesis that (94) involves covert grammatical structure, as indicated below (leaving the details open), that blocks extraction of an adjunct.

How$_i$ do you think (that) [Nick got home t$_i$]?

*How$_i$ do you know [. . . (that) [Nick got home t$_i$]]?

If 'knows that P' contains covert material, this might explain why (95) is not a natural paraphrase of (96).

(95)  Nick knows the fact that the burglar ran off

(96)  Nick knows that the burglar ran off

If a 'the fact that'-clause is a Theme-specifier, (95) implies that Nick knows a certain fact in the way he knows the dog Fido—as an object of acquaintance. By contrast, (96) implies that a certain content is the Import of a knowledge state. This invites a similar diagnosis of (91), which means that Nick knows *an answer to* the question of why the burglar ran off. Perhaps as Higginbotham (1993) suggests, (90)

---

[32] There also seems to be a 'say/explain' asymmetry: when$_i$ did Nora say/*explain that [Fido barked t$_i$]? I cannot hear 'Nora explained that *Fido barked at 3 p.m.*' as an answer. But on my view, 'explain' does not take a determiner phrase ('*the fact that* Fido barked') as its complement. So another diagnosis of the asymmetry is needed.

involves covert factive structure: Nick [knows$_\sigma$ [... [why Fido barked]]].[33]

One difference between 'know' and 'explain', recall, is this: one can know the fact that P without knowing why P; but one cannot explain the fact that P without explaining why P. Correlatively, in explaining why P, one does not explain *an answer to* (the question of) why P; rather, one explains the fact that P. So perhaps the underlying syntax of (62) is as indicated in (62G).

>   (62)   Nora explained why Fido barked
>   (62G)   Nora [explained$_\varepsilon$ [... [why Fido barked]$_{CP}$]$_{\Delta P}$]$_{\Pi P}$

with the indirect question embedded in a (Theme-specifying) determiner phrase, and similarly for (82).

>   (82)   The fact that Fido saw the burglar explains$_\sigma$
>   the fact that Fido barked

If *states* of explaining cannot have Imports (unlike states of knowledge and speech acts of explaining), and so 'explain$_\sigma$' must take a determiner phrase as its direct object, then (82) provides independent reason for some such syntax. By contrast, if 'explains$_\sigma$' could take a bare complementizer phrase, one would need to account for the anomalousness of 'The fact that Fido saw the burglar explains that Fido barked'. These are speculations. But they are, I think, suggestive.

## 4.6. *Summary*

My aim in this section has not been to provide a theory of 'that'-clauses, or even a detailed compositional account of verbs that combine with such clauses. But I have tried to argue that,

---

[33] If there is a semantic restriction on 'know', to the effect that states of knowledge cannot have interrogative contents, perhaps 'know' (unlike 'ask') cannot take a bare 'why'-clause as its direct object. I assume that an answer to the question of why Q is some true claim of the form 'Q because R'. (To know why Q is not merely to know that R, where 'Q because R' is true.) If the inference from 'N knows that Q because R' to 'N knows why Q' is *valid*, more needs to be said here.

whatever we say about the Values of 'that'-clauses, we can and should adopt the following Conjunctivist view: in a phrase of the form 'VERB that P', the verb and 'that'-clause are interpreted as conjoinable monadic predicates, and 'that P' is an Import-specifier (as opposed to a Theme-specifier).

# Tentative Conclusions and Promissory Notes

I have tried to articulate and defend several related theses of varying strength.

## 1. Review

First, one *can* maintain that concatenation signifies predicate-conjunction, even for cases of predicate–argument concatenation. For one can hypothesize that certain grammatical relations have semantic significance, and that sentences reflect existential closure of a variable. Appeals to thematic relations can be viewed as a paradigm instance of this strategy, which is compatible with an essentially Fregean compositional semantics. One can generalize from the idea that (i) the subject of an action verb is understood as an expression that specifies the Agent of an event, to the idea that (ii) the external argument of a predicate is understood as an expression that specifies the external participant of a Value of that predicate. By extending this strategy, Conjunctivists can handle the usual range of textbook cases, including quantificational examples like 'Every dog saw a cat'.

Second, the resulting accounts are no more complicated than standard Functionist alternatives. There are also things to be said in favor of the idea that predicate–argument relations, as opposed to predicate–adjunct relations, carry special semantic significance. At various points, I discussed the relevance of constraints on how thematic roles are mapped to grammatical positions. Indeed, the significance of relations like *being the external argument of* might be viewed as a way of dealing with predicate–argument combinations in a system that treats concatenation as a sign of predicate-conjunction.

Third, if Conjunctivist analyses are combined (as they should be) with a Boolos-style conception of second-order quantification, they avoid various "conceptual" difficulties associated with the idea that natural language predicates have extensions. Considerations of vagueness and Russell's Paradox tell against the idea that the Value of a predicate is a function. This is not news. But the point remains. It seems that some things can be Values of a predicate without there being any set whose members are all and only the Values of the predicate. Conjunctivism also lets us start to develop an attractive conception of how semantics is related to Frege's (second-order) logic.

Fourth, it turns out that Conjunctivist accounts have various empirical and explanatory virtues, even in cases of predicate–argument combination. In Chapter 2, I focused on quantification and plurality. In Chapter 3, I discussed causal verbs that take two arguments, and verbs that take sentential complements. The idea was that these should be among the best cases for Functionism. But, I argued, even these cases reveal symptoms of an underlyingly Conjunctivist semantic architecture.

With regard to quantificational constructions, I stressed the conservativity of determiners and the restricted character of natural language quantification. With regard to plural arguments, I stressed Schein's work, especially concerning ditransitive constructions (like 'Three linguists taught five students four theories') and collective readings without implications of cooperation (as in 'They wrote ten articles'). Conjunctivists can better account for examples that illustrate "essential plurality". These virtues also interact. This becomes evident once we start thinking about the relations among quantification, plurality, the second-order character of natural language meanings, and the interpretation of second-order variables in our metalanguage.

Given a Conjunctivist semantics for quantification and plurality, and setting aside ditransitive verbs, transitive verbs presumably become quite important for Functionists. In this context, I noted that Functionists can at best mimic a Conjunctivist account of causative constructions. Then I used a serial verb construction in Edo to further illustrate how combining Conjunctivism with covert syntax can yield desirable results that Functionists must stipulate, even in a case that initially seems to tell against the hypothesis that concatenation signifies predicate-conjunction. Finally, I argued that phrases like 'explained that Fido barked' support the hypothesis that complementizer phrases (and the verbs that take them as arguments) are understood as conjoinable monadic predicates.

My tentative conclusion is twofold: while Functionism provides a convenient way of initially gesturing at some facts that call for explanation, it is false if taken as an actual hypothesis about the significance of concatenation in natural language; and while Conjunctivism is far from established, it is the better hypothesis, even as an account of predicate–argument combination. Of course, it might turn out that the real virtues of Functionism are revealed in cases not discussed here. But the trend seems to be that the scope of Functionism recedes as investigation proceeds.

## 2. Cautions

That said, I have barely begun to survey all the options concerning the significance of grammatical combination. In particular, one could propose that (i) combining predicates with adjuncts at least often signifies predicate-conjunction, (ii) combining verbs with arguments signifies something else, but not function-application, (iii) combining a determiner like 'every' with its predicative arguments signifies something else. And, perhaps, so on. Several times, I alluded to Higginbotham's distinction between theta-linking and theta-binding. In Chapter 2, I also briefly mentioned the possibility of adopting a syncategorematic treatment of words like 'every'. One can imagine many versions of such pluralism about the significance of concatenation. Though I suspect that a common conjunctive character underlies the apparently diverse modes of combination in natural language.

We can regard predicate–adjunct combination as the compositionally "pure" case, diagnosing other cases as interaction effects that also reveal the significance of certain grammatical relations. Methodologically, this strikes me as the best candidate for the null hypothesis, since we have independent reasons for thinking that some grammatical relations are semantically significant. Moreover, like Higginbotham, I think the basic facts about semantic composition reflect innately specified aspects of the human language faculty. So I worry that pluralism commits us to a needlessly sophisticated conception of what Universal Grammar says about concatenation (in addition to what it says anyway about grammatical relations). And I worry that if we take Universal Grammar to be relatively permissive about what concatenation can mean, we will be unable to account for how children stabilize on specific grammars that permit *only* the signal–meaning associations that natural languages permit. But these are speculations. And the imagined debate, between Conjunctivists and pluralists who eschew function-application, would look like a minor squabble against the predominantly Functionist background.[1] So my focus was elsewhere. Though let me enter another caveat.

It may be that the literature and textbooks do not yet reflect what the field really thinks. Perhaps it is quietly understood—and sometimes expressed in conversation—that Functionism is less a hypothesis, and more a convenient descriptive tool that can always be used to give a quick and dirty description of the facts. If so, then we should recognize this and look for a real hypothesis, be it monistic or pluralistic. My suggestion has been that Conjunctivism is a far better hypothesis than one might think, and that it is good enough to warrant explicit formulation, testing, and elaboration of

---

[1] And one could adopt the view that while quantificational constructions are special, theta-binding is indeed due to the interaction of theta-linking and something else. This is compatible with Higginbotham's (1985) notation.

the auxiliary hypotheses required to maintain it. For at least some of these auxiliaries seem to be true, and we seem to get some reasonably good explanations by taking Conjunctivism seriously.

It is, however, a *very* general thesis. Showing there are no counterexamples to Conjunctivism would require nothing less than a complete semantic theory for each natural language. So conclusions must be appropriately hedged. Of course, Functionism is an equally ambitious thesis, and pluralistic views are no less general for being disjunctive. But sometimes, the idea of trying to defend any such proposal strikes me as absurd. How can one have confidence in *any* general claim about the significance of putting two expressions together? Isn't it certain that we will find counterexamples—lots of them—as soon as we look? I am vividly aware that this book is, at best, a closely cropped snapsnot of some terrain that fits my description. One wants to see Conjunctivism defended in light of far more facts (and literature) than I have addressed here. We must also remain alive to the possibility that from a theoretical perspective, what we call semantics is a hodgepodge with little or no underlying unity. Prima facie, there are many ways for a primitive expression to be meaningful; compare 'dog' with 'if'. Perhaps there are also many ways for the meaning of a complex expression to be determined, with little or no underlying unity. Maybe quick and dirty descriptions, which we can tidy up a *little*, are all we will get.

On the other hand, one must guard against overcautiousness. Claims about semantic composition can seem quite modest, compared with generalizations that apply to everything that has mass. It is hard to see how inquiry can or should proceed, except by formulating and evaluating simple general hypotheses, in order to see where they do and don't go wrong. Moreover, the linguistic facts are not too messy for kids, who regularly find (or impose) commonalities. And if we want to discover whatever semantic unity there is across expressions, we need to explore in detail more than one proposal about the significance of concatenation in natural language. Even if Conjunctivism turns out to be completely wrong, it may be useful to compare it with Functionism and more pluralistic views, for purposes of getting a fix on the empirical content of each.

Still, one wants to know whether a view has any chance of not being immediately falsified. I cannot enumerate and deal with the potential counterexamples to Conjunctivism; and this is not just due to limitations of space. But I want to conclude with some general remarks about what a counterexample would be—since this is hardly obvious—and a suggestion about what to do next. The essential point is that, since Conjunctivism is a thesis about linguistic meaning, we should ask whether facts that appear to tell against Conjunctivism are better described as facts that tell against some ancillary assumption about how meaning is related to something else (like truth or intuitions about correct usage). This may make it seem less crazy that Conjunctivism is compatible with the richness and complexity of language use.

## 3. Larger Issues

Whatever one says about the principles governing semantic composition, the data points available to us are surely massive interaction effects that reflect many factors. This is a general point, having nothing to do with language in particular. Interesting theoretical claims are typically *not* claims about anything human inquirers can observe; that is why confirming theories takes work. Though for just this reason, we should not be too quick to abandon sweeping generalizations that seem not to "fit the facts". As noted in the introduction, it is not obvious *which* facts theories should explain.

In the study of syntax, it has become a commonplace that theories should not be judged simply according to how well they describe native speakers' intuitions about which word-strings are acceptable. We know that acceptability is neither necessary nor sufficient for grammaticality. More importantly, syntacticians have discovered generalizations that serve as explananda for deeper theories. If we learn that natural language grammars preclude extraction of auxiliary verbs from relative clauses, we can ask why this is so. And theories of grammatical structure that explain such phenomena are rightly prized. In linguistics, as in other domains, the most interesting explanations concern abstract regularities that are discovered (not observed). When studying linguistic meaning, we regularly allow for the first kind of gap between theory and data. For example, pragmatic implicature may influence judgments about whether or not a given sentence provides an appropriate description of a given situation. And while investigation has so far revealed fewer deep generalizations in this domain, the conservativity of determiners and Baker's UTAH suggest that there are phenomena to be explained. Our primary data in semantics are still the facts concerning which interpretations which strings of words can(not) have. But we can and should look for theories that also account for relevant abstract regularities that are discovered as opposed to intuited.

Elsewhere, I have urged that, once we take such considerations seriously, the balance of evidence tells against the idea that an utterance of a sentence is true in a given context iff the sentence has the Value **t** relative to that context; see Pietroski (2003*d*, forthcoming), drawing on Chomsky (1977, 2000*b*), who draws on a long tradition in philosophy, including Austin (1961, 1962), Strawson (1950), and Wittgenstein (1953).[2] To take just one example, which reflects considerations stressed by Austin and Chomsky, it is hard to provide a Conjunctivist account that does justice to 'France is hexagonal, and it is also a republic'—at least without tendentious ontological assumptions. (Is there really some entity x such that x is

---

[2] Davidson and Montague, each in their own way and followed by many others, proposed that a theory of meaning (for a natural language) would be a theory of truth. But in my view, this hypothesis ends up relying on either (i) an unduly superficial conception of semantics, according to which interesting and apparently relevant discoveries are held to be irrelevant to the main goal of showing how to associate declarative sentences with truth-conditions relative to contexts, or (ii) an unduly truth-focused and implausible conception of grammar, according to which every factor relevant to the truth or falsity of a sentential utterance is tracked by some aspect of the relevant sentence. If I am right about this, semanticists can set aside many (messy) facts about the *truth-conditions of utterances*. And this might well let us set aside many apparent difficulties for simple hypotheses about semantic composition.

France, and x is hexagonal, and x is a republic? And if not, must we say utterances of the sentence are false?) The worry does not disappear if Functionists also have trouble with such examples, of which there are legions. But before concluding that the significance of concatenation is subtle, we must consider the possibility that the subtlety lies elsewhere, perhaps in the relation between linguistic meaning and our use of language to talk about the world. (It may also be that what we call meaning is "layered", with some aspects that are strictly compositional because Conjunctivism is true, and other aspects that are sensitive to more global properties of expressions.) Conjunctivism may highlight difficulties in maintaining the hypothesis that understanding a sentence just *is* a matter of knowing how to use the sentence for purposes of (truly or falsely) describing the language-independent world. But that is not obviously a point *against* Conjunctivism.

My suspicion is that any conception of compositional semantics must be defended, in the end, in part by defending an associated conception of how meaning is related to use. Correlatively, one should not expect to find straightforward *counterexamples* to any conception of semantic composition that deals with the textbook cases. Failure to "fit the facts" with regard to complex cases is the norm, and the fate of any theory that provides more than descriptive generalizations concerning observations. At least for now, in the absence of well-confirmed views about what linguistic meaning really *is*, theory evaluation depends (as one should expect) on how proposals handle relatively simple examples and such interesting phenomena as we discover and can explain. I have argued that Conjunctivism scores well on this test.

Richard Feynman famously quipped that physicists are so successful because they study the hydrogen atom, the helium ion, and then stop. Those of us who study language have not yet found our hydrogen and helium.[3] I don't suggest that Conjunctivism will point the way. But I do think it is one step in a right direction. There was a time at which it was both convenient and theoretically

---

[3] Though there may be hints of a table of elements. See Baker (2001).

fruitful to describe complex linguistic meanings in terms of functions, arguments, and values. It may still be convenient for many purposes. But in my view, the study of meaning has progressed far enough to start providing explanations that must given in different terms.

# References

Akatsuka, N. (1976) 'Reflexivization: A Transformational Approach', in M. Shibatani (ed.), *Syntax and Semantics, vi. The Grammar of Causative Constructions* (New York: Academic Press).

Anscombe, G. (1957) *Intention* (Oxford: Blackwell).

Antony, L., and Hornstein, N. (eds.) (2003) *Chomsky and his Critics* (Cambridge, Mass.: Blackwell).

Austin, J. (1961) *Philosophical Papers* (Oxford: Oxford University Press).

—— (1962) *How to Do Things with Words* (Oxford: Oxford University Press).

Baker, M. (1988) *Incorporation* (Chicago: University of Chicago).

—— (1996) *The Polysynthesis Parameter* (New York: Oxford University Press).

—— (1997) 'Thematic Roles and Grammatical Categories', in L. Haegeman (ed.), *Elements of Grammar* (Dordrecht: Kluwer), 73–137.

—— (2001) *The Atoms of Language* (New York: Basic Books).

—— (2003) *Verbs, Nouns, and Adjectives* (Cambridge: Cambridge University Press).

—— and Stewart, O. (1999) 'On Double-Headedness and the Anatomy of the clause', Rutgers University, unpublished.

—— and —— (2002) 'A Serial Verb Construction without Constructions', Rutgers University, unpublished.

Barwise J., and Cooper, R. (1981) 'Generalized Quantifiers and Natural Language', *Linguistics and Philosophy*, 4: 159–219.

Bäuerle, R., Schwarze, C., and von Stechow, A. (eds.) (1983) *Meaning, Use, and Interpretation of Language* (Berlin: de Gruyter).

Belletti, A. (1988) 'The Case of Unaccusatives', *Linguistic Inquiry*, 19: 1–34.

Benacerraf, P. (1965) 'What Numbers could Not be', *Philosophical Review*, 74: 47–73.

Bittner, M. (1999) 'Concealed Causatives', *Natural Language Semantics*, 7: 1–78.

Blair, D. (2004) 'Parataxis and Logical Form', doctoral dissertation, University of Connecticut.

Boolos, G. (1971) 'The Iterative Conception of Set', *Journal of Philosophy*, 68: 215–31. Reprinted in Boolos (1998).

—— (1975) 'On Second-Order Logic', *Journal of Philosophy*, 72: 509–27. Reprinted in Boolos (1998).

—— (1984) 'To be is to be the Value of a Variable (or the Values of Some Variables)', *Journal of Philosophy*, 81: 430–50. Reprinted in Boolos (1998).

—— (1985) 'Nominalist Platonism', *Philosophical Review*, 94: 327–44. Reprinted in Boolos (1998).

—— (1987) 'A Curious Inference', *Journal of Philosophical Logic*, 16: 1–12. Reprinted in Boolos (1998).

—— (1998) *Logic, Logic, and Logic* (Cambridge, Mass.: Harvard University Press).

Bromberger, S. (1966) 'Why Questions', in R. Colodny (ed.), *Mind and Cosmos* (Pittsburgh: University of Pittsburgh Press).

Burge, T. (1973) 'Reference and Proper Names', *Journal of Philosophy*, 70: 425–39.

—— (1974) 'Demonstrative Constructions, Reference and Truth', *Journal of Philosophy*, 71: 205–23.

Burzio, L. (1986) *Italian Syntax* (Dordrecht: Reidel).

Carlson, G. (1984) 'Thematic Roles and their Role in Semantic Interpretation', *Linguistics*, 22: 259–79.

Castañeda, H. (1967) 'Comments', in Rescher (1967).

Cattell, R. (1978) 'On the source of Interrogative Adverbs', *Language*, 54: 61–77.

Chierchia, G. (1989) 'A Semantics for Unaccusatives and its Syntactic Consequences', Cornell University, unpublished.

—— and McConnell-Ginet, S. (2000) *Meaning and Grammar* (2nd edn. Cambridge, Mass.: MIT Press).

—— and Turner, R. (1988) 'Semantics and Property Theory', *Linguistics and Philosophy*, 11: 261–302.

Chomsky, N. (1955) 'The Logical Structure of Linguistic Theory', MS, Harvard University. Revised version published in part as *The Logical Structure of Linguistic Theory* (Plenum: New York, 1975).

—— (1957) *Syntactic Structures* (The Hague: Mouton).

—— (1965) *Aspects of the Theory of Syntax* (Cambridge, Mass.: MIT Press).

—— (1966) *Cartesian Linguistics* (Lanham Md.: University Press of America).

—— (1970) 'Remarks on Nominalization', in R. Jacobs and R. Rosenbaum (eds.), *Readings in English Transformational Grammar* (Waltham Mass.: Ginn).

—— (1977) *Essays on Form and Interpretation* (New York: North Holland).

—— (1981) *Lectures on Government and Binding* (Dordrecht: Foris).

—— (1986) *Knowledge of Language* (New York: Praeger).

—— (1995) *The Minimalist Program* (Cambridge, Mass.: MIT Press).

—— (2000a) *New Horizons in the Study of Language and Mind.* (Cambridge: Cambridge University Press).

—— (2000b) 'Minimalist Inquiries', in R. Martin, D. Michaels, and J. Uriagereka (eds.), *Step by Step: Essays on Minimalist Syntax in Honor of Howard Lasnik* (Cambridge, Mass.: MIT Press).

—— (2003) 'Reply to Pietroski', in Antony and Hornstein (2003).

Cinque, G. (1999) *Adverbs and Functional Heads: A Cross-Linguistic Perspective* (Oxford: Oxford University Press).

Collins, C. (2001) 'Eliminating Labels', in Epstein and Seely (2002).

Costa, M. (1987) 'Causal Theories of Action', *Canadian Journal of Philosophy*, 17: 831–54.

Crain, S., and Pietroski, P. (2001) 'Nature, Nuture, and Universal Grammar', *Linguistics and Philosophy*, 24: 139–86.

—— and —— (2002) 'Why Language Acquisition is a Snap', *Linguistic Review*, 19: 163–83.

Davidson, D. (1963) 'Actions, Reasons, and Causes', *Journal of Philosophy*, 60: 685–99.

—— (1967a) 'Truth and Meaning', *Synthese*, 17: 304–23.

—— (1967b) 'The Logical Form of Action Sentences', in Rescher (1967).

—— (1968) 'On Saying That', *Synthese*, 19: 130–46.

—— (1980) *Essays on Actions and Events* (Oxford: Oxford University Press).

—— (1984) *Inquiries into Truth and Interpretation* (Oxford: Oxford University Press).

—— (1985) 'Adverbs of Action', in B. Vermazen and M. Hintikka, (eds.), *Essays on Davidson: Actions and Events* (Oxford: Clarendon Press).

Davies, M. (1981) *Meaning, Quantification, and Necessity* (London: Routledge).

Davies, M. (1989) 'Two Examiners Marked Six Scripts', *Linguistics and Philosophy*, 12: 293–323.

—— (1991) 'Acts and Scenes', in N. Cooper and P. Engel (eds.), *New Inquiries into Meaning and Truth* (New York: St Martin's Press).

Demopolous, W. (ed.) (1994) *Frege's Philosophy of Mathematics* (Cambridge, Mass.: Harvard University Press).

Diesing, M. (1992) *Indefinites* (Cambridge, Mass.: MIT).

Dowty, D. (1979) *Word Meaning and Montague Grammar* (Boston: Reidel).

—— (1987) *Collective Predicates, Distribute Predicates, and All: Proceedings of the Third Eastern States Conference on Linguistics* (Columbus, Ohio: Ohio State University).

—— (1991) 'Thematic proto-roles and Arguments Selection', *Language*, 67: 547–619.

Epstein, S., and Hornstein, N. (eds.) (1999) *Working Minimalism* (Cambridge, Mass.: MIT Press).

—— and Seely, T. (eds.) (2002) *Derivation and Explanation in the Minimalist program* (Cambridge, Mass.: Blackwell).

Evans, G. (1981) 'Semantic Theory and Tacit Knowledge', in S. Holtzman and C. Leich (eds.), *Wittgenstein, to Follow a Rule* (London: Routledge & Kegan Paul).

—— (1982) *Varieties of Reference* (Oxford: Oxford University Press).

Feinberg, J. (1965) 'Action and Responsibility', in M. Black (ed.), *Philosophy in America* (Ithaca, NY: Cornell University Press).

Fillmore, C. (1968) 'The Case of Case', in E. Bach and R. Harms (eds.), *Universal in Linguistic Theory* (New York: Rinehart & Wilson).

Fine, A. (1975) 'Vagueness, Truth, and Logic', *Synthese*, 30: 265–300.

Fodor, J. (1970) 'Three Reasons for Not Deriving "Kill" from "Cause to Die"', *Linguistic Inquiry*, 1: 429–38.

—— (2002) *The Compositionality Papers* (Oxford: Oxford University Press).

—— and Lepore, E. (1998) 'The Emptiness of the Lexicon', *Linguistic Inquiry*, 29: 269–88.

Frege, G. (1879) *Begriffsschrift* (Halle: Louis Nebert). English translation in J. van Heijenoort (ed.), *From Frege to Gödel: A Source Book in Mathematical Logic, 1879–1931* (Cambridge, Mass.: Harvard University Press, 1967).

—— (1884) *Die Grundlagen der Arithmetik* (Breslau: Wilhelm Koebner). English translation in J. L. Austin (tr.), *The Foundations of Arithmetic* (Oxford: Basil Blackwell, 1974).

—— (1892a) 'Function and Concept', in Geach and Black (1980).

—— (1892b) 'Sense and Reference', in Geach and Black (1980).

—— (1893, 1903) *Grundgesetze der Arithmetik, begriffsschriftlich abgeleitet*, 2 vols. (Jena: Pohle). English translation in M. Furth (tr.), *The Basic Laws of Arithmetic* (Berkeley, Calif.: University of California, 1967).

Gärdenfors, P. (ed.) (1987) *Generalized Quantifiers: Linguistic and Logical Approaches* (Dordrecht: Reidel).

Geach, P., and Black, M. (trs.) (1980) *Translations from the Philosophical Writings of Gottlob Frege* (Oxford: Blackwell).

Gillon, B. (1987) 'The Readings of Plural Noun Phrases in English', *Linguistics and Philosophy*, 102: 199–219.

Goldman, A. (1970) *A Theory of Human Action* (Princeton: Princeton University Press).

Graff, D. (2000) 'Shifting Sands', *Philosophical Topics*, 28: 45–81.

Grimshaw, J. (1979) 'Complement Selection and the Lexicon', *Linguistic Inquiry*, 10: 279–326.

—— (1990) *Argument Structure* (Cambridge, Mass.: MIT Press).

Gruber, J. (1965) 'Studies in Lexical Relations', doctoral dissertation, MIT.

—— (1976) *Lexical Structure in Syntax and Semantics* (New York; North Holland).

Haegeman, L. (1994) *Introduction to Government and Binding* (2nd edn. Oxford: Blackwell).

Hale, K., and Keyser, S. J. (1993) 'On Argument Structure and the Lexical Expression of Syntactic Relations', in K. Hale and S. J. Keyser (eds.) *The View From Building* 20 (Cambridge, Mass.: MIT Press).

Harman, G. (1972) 'Logical Form', *Foundations of Language*, 9: 38–65.

Hart, H., and Honoré, A. (1959) *Causation and the Law* (Oxford: Oxford University Press).

Hazen, A. (1997) 'Relations in Monadic Third-Order Logic', *Journal of Philosophical Logic*, 26: 619–28.

Heck, R. (1993) 'The Development of Arithmetic in Frege's Grundgesetze der Arithmetik', *Journal of Symbolic Logic*, 58: 579–601. Reprinted with a postscript in Demopolous (1994).

Heim, I. (1982) 'The Semantics of Definite and Indefinite Noun Phrases', doctoral dissertation, University of Massachusetts, Amherst.

Heim, I. (1983) 'On the Projection Problem for Presuppositions', in M. Barlow, D. Flickinger, and M. Wescoat (eds.), *WCCFL* 2, 114–25. Reprinted in Portner and Partee (2002).

—— and Kratzer, A. (1998) *Semantics in Generative Grammar* (Oxford: Blackwell).

Herburger, E. (2001) *What Counts* (Cambridge, Mass.: MIT Press).

Higginbotham, J. (1983) 'The Logical form of Perceptual Reports', *Journal of Philosophy*, 80: 100–27.

—— (1985) 'On Semantics', *Linguistic Inquiry*, 16: 547–93.

—— (1986) 'Davidson's Program in Semantics', in E. Lepore (ed.), *Perspectives on the Philosophy of Donald Davidson* (Oxford: Blackwell).

—— (1989) 'Indefiniteness and Predication', in Reuland and ter Meulen (1989).

—— (1993) 'Interrogatives', in K. Hale and S. Keyser (eds), *The View from Building 20* (Cambridge, Mass.: MIT Press).

—— (1998) 'On Higher-Order Logic and Natural Language', *Proc. of the British Academy*, 95: 1–27.

—— and May, R. (1981) 'Questions, Quantifiers, and Crossing', *Linguistic Review*, 1: 47–79.

—— and Schein, B. (1989) 'Plurals'. *NELS XIX, Proceedings GSLA* (Amherst, Mass.: University of Massachusetts Press).

Higginbotham, J., Pianesi, F., and Varzi, A. (eds.) (2000) *Speaking of Events* (Oxford: Oxford University Press).

Horn, L. (1997) 'Negative Polarity and the Dynamics of Vertical Inference', in D. Forget *et al.* (eds.), *Negation and Polarity: Syntax and Semantics* (Amsterdam: John Benjamins).

Hornstein, N. (1995) *Logical Form: From GB to Minimalism* (Oxford: Blackwell).

—— (2001) *Move! A Minimalist Theory of Construal* (Cambridge: Blackwell).

—— (2002) 'A Grammatical Argument for a Neo-Davidsonian Semantics', in Preyer and Peters (2002).

—— and Lightfoot, D. (1981) *Explanation in Linguistics* (London: Longman).

—— and Uriagereka, J. (1999) 'Labels and Reprojection: A Note on the Syntax of Quantifiers', *University of Maryland Working Papers in Linguistics*, 8.

Horwich, P. (1997) 'The Composition of Meanings', *Philosophical Review*, 106: 503–32.

——— (1998) *Meaning* (Oxford: Oxford University Press).

Huang, J. (1982) 'Logical Relations in Chinese and the Theory of Grammar', doctoral dissertation, MIT.

——— (1995) 'Logical Form', in G. Webelhuth (ed.), *Government and Binding Theory and the Minimalist Program: Principles and Parameters in Syntactic Theory* (Oxford: Blackwell).

Jackendoff, R. (1972) *Semantic Interpretation and Generative Grammar* (Current Issues in Linguistics, 2; Cambridge, Mass.: MIT Press).

——— (1977) *X-bar Syntax* (Cambridge, Mass.: MIT Press).

——— (1983) *Semantics and Cognition* (Cambridge, Mass.: MIT Press).

——— (1987) 'The Status of Thematic Relations in Linguistic Theory', *Linguistic Inquiry*, 18: 369–411.

——— (1993) *Patterns in the Mind* (Brighton: Harvester-Wheatsheaf).

Kamp, H. (1975) 'Two Theories about Adjectives', in Keenan (1975).

——— (1981) 'A Theory of Truth and Semantic Representation', in J. Groenendijk, T. Janssen, and M. Stokhof (eds.), *Formal Methods in the Study of Language* (Amsterdam: Mathematische Centrum, University of Amsterdam). Reprinted in Portner and Partee (2002).

Kahneman, D., and Tversky, A. (1972) 'Subjective Probability: A Judgment of Representativeness', *Cognitive Psychology*, 3: 430–54.

Kaplan, D. (1989) 'Demonstratives', in J. Almog *et al.* (eds.), *Themes from Kaplan* (New York: Oxford University Press).

Katz, J., and Fodor, J. (1963) 'The Structure of a Semantic Theory', *Language*, 39: 170–210.

Keefe, R., and Smith, P. (eds.) (1996) *Vagueness: A Reader* (Cambridge, Mass.: MIT Press).

Keenan, E. (ed.) (1975) *Formal Semantics of Natural Language* (Cambridge: Cambridge University Press).

——— (1987) 'Unreducible N-ary Quantifiers in Natural Language', in Gärdenfors (1987).

——— (1996) 'The Semantics of Determiners', in Lappin (1996).

——— and Stavi, J. (1986) 'A Semantic Characterization of Natural Language Determiners', *Linguistics and Philosophy*, 9: 253–326.

Kenny, A. (1963) *Action, Emotion, and Will* (London: Routledge & Kegan Paul).

Kim, J. (1993) *Supervenience and Mind* (Cambridge: Cambridge University Press).

Kneale, W., and Kneale, M. (1962) *The Development of Logic* (Oxford: Oxford University Press).

Kratzer, A. (1989) 'Stage-Level and Individual-Level Predicates in English', University of Massachusetts, Amherst, unpublished.

—— (1996) 'Severing the External Argument from its Verb', in J. Rooryck and L. Zaring (eds.), *Phrase Structure and the Lexicon* (Dordrecht: Kluwer Academic Publishers).

Kripke, S. (1980) *Naming and Necessity* (Cambridge, Mass.: Harvard University Press).

Kuroda, S. (1966) 'Generative Grammatical Studies in the Japanese Language', doctoral dissertation, MIT. Published New York: Garland, 1979.

Lahiri, U. (2002) *Questions and Answers in Embedded Contexts* (New York: Oxford University Press).

Lakoff, G. (1970) *Irregularity in Syntax* (New York: Holt, Rinehart, & Winston).

—— (1987) *Women, Fire, and Dangerous Things* (Chicago: University of Chicago Press).

Landman, F. (1996) 'Plurality', in Lappin (1996).

Lappin, S. (1996) *The Handbook of Contemporary Semantic Theory* (Oxford: Blackwell).

Larson, R. (1988) 'On the Double Object Construction', *Linguistic Inquiry*, 19: 335–91.

—— and Ludlow, P. (1993) 'Interpreted Logical Forms', *Synthese*, 95: 305–55.

—— and Segal, G. (1995) *Knowledge of Meaning* (Cambridge, Mass.: MIT Press).

Lasnik, H. (1999) 'Chains of Arguments', in Epstein and Hornstein (1999).

Laurence, S., and Margolis, E. (2001) 'The Poverty of Stimulus Argument', *British Journal for the Philosophy of Science*, 52: 217–76.

Levin, B., and Rappaport Hovav, M. (1995) *Unaccusativity: At the Syntax-Semantics Interface* (Cambridge, Mass.: MIT Press).

Lewis, D. (1972) 'General Semantics', in D. Davidson and G. Harman (eds.), *Semantics of Natural Language* (Dordrecht: Reidel).

—— (1975) 'Adverbs of Quantification', in Keenan (1975).

—— (1979) 'Scorekeeping in a Language Game', *Journal of Philosophical Logic*, 8: 339–59.

—— (1991) *Parts of Classes* (Oxford: Blackwell).

Link, G. (1983) 'The Logical Analysis of Plurals and Mass Terms: A Lattice-Theoretic Approach', in R. Bauerle *et al.* (1983).

—— (1987) 'Generalized Quantifiers and Plurals', in Gärdenfors (1987).

—— (1991) 'Plural', in D. Wunderlich and A. von Stechow (eds.), *Semantics: An International Handbook of Contemporary Research* (Berlin: de Gruyter).

—— (1998) *Algebraic Semantics in Language and Philosophy* (Stanford Calif.: CSLI).

Ludlow, P. (1995) 'The Logical Form of Determiners', *Journal of Philosophical Logic*, 24: 47–69.

—— (2002) 'LF and Natural Logic', in Preyer and Peters (2002).

McCawley, J. (1968) 'Lexical Insertion in a Transformational Grammar without Deep Structure', *Papers from the Fourth Regional Meeting, Chicago Linguistics Society* (Chicago: Linguistics Department, Univ. of Chicago), 71–80.

McGilvray, J. (1999) *Chomsky: Language, Mind and Politics* (Cambridge: Polity Press/Blackwell).

Marantz, A. (1984) *On the Nature of Grammatical Relations* (Cambridge, Mass.: MIT Press).

Matthews, R. (1983) 'Explaining and Explanation', reprinted in D. Ruben (ed.), *Explanation* (Oxford: Oxford University Press, 1993).

—— (1994) 'The Measure of Mind', *Mind*, 103: 131–46.

May, R. (1985) *Logical Form: Its Structure and Derivation* (Cambridge, Mass: MIT Press).

Moltmann, F. (2004) 'Nonreferential Complements, Nominalizations, and Derived Objects', *Journal of Semantics*, 21: 1–43.

Montague, R. (1970) 'English as a Formal Language', reprinted in Montague (1974).

—— (1973) 'The Proper Treatment of Quantifiers in Ordinary English', in K. Hintikka *et al.* (eds.) *Approaches to Natural Language* (Dordrecht: Reidel). Reprinted in Montague (1974).

—— (1974) *Formal Philosophy* (New Haven: Yale University Press).

Motamura, M. (2003) 'The Thematic Roles of Sentential To/Ko Complements in Japanese/Korean', in P. Clancy (ed.), *Japanese/Korean Linguistics* (Chicago: University of Chicago Press).

—— (2004) ' "Zibun" As a Residue of Overt A-Movement,' doctoral dissertation, University of Maryland.

Munro, P. (1982) 'On the Transitivity of "Say" Verbs', *Syntax and Semantics*, 15: 301–18.

Neale, S. (1990) *Descriptions* (Cambridge, Mass.: MIT Press).

Parsons, T. (1990) *Events in the Semantics of English* (Cambridge, Mass.: MIT Press).

—— (2000) 'Underlying States and Time Travel', in Higginbotham, *et al.* (2000).

Partee, B. (1987) 'Noun Phrase Interpretation and Type-Shifting Principles', in J. Groenendijk, D. de Jongh, and M. Stokhof (eds.), *Studies in Discourse Representation Theory and the Theory of Generalized Quantifiers* (Dordrecht: Reidel), 115–44.

—— and Rooth, M. (1983) 'Generalized Conjunction and Type Ambiguity', in Bäuerle *et al.* (1983).

Pesetsky, D. (1982) 'Paths and Categories', doctoral disseration, MIT.

—— (1995) *Zero Syntax* (Cambridge, Mass.: MIT Press).

Pietroski, P. (1996) 'Fregean Innocence', *Mind and Language*, 11: 331–62.

—— (1998) 'Actions, Adjuncts, and Agency', *Mind*, 107: 73–111.

—— (1999) 'Compositional Quotation without Parataxis', in K. Murasugi and R. Stainton (eds.), *Philosophy and Linguistics* (Boulder, Colo.: Westview).

—— (2000*a*) *Causing Actions* (Oxford: Oxford University Press).

—— (2000*b*) 'On Explaining That', *Journal of Philosophy*, 97: 655–62.

—— (2000*c*) 'The Undeflated Domain of Semantics', *Sats: Nordic Journal of Philosophy*, 1: 161–76.

—— (2002) 'Function and Concatenation', in Preyer and Peters (2002).

—— (2003*a*) 'Events', in K. Ludwig (ed.), *Contemporary Philosophers in Focus: Donald Davidson* (Cambridge: Cambridge University Press).

—— (2003*b*) 'Quantification and Second-Order Monadicity', *Philosophical Perspectives*, 17: 259–98.

—— (2003*c*) 'Small Verbs, Complex Events: Analyticity without Synonymy', in Antony and Hornstein (2003).

—— (2003*d*) 'The Character of Natural Language Semantics', in A. Barber (ed.), *Epistemology of Language* (Oxford: Oxford University Press).

—— (forthcoming) 'Meaning before Truth', in G. Preyer and G. Peter (eds.), *Contextualism in Philosophy* (Oxford: Oxford University Press).

—— (in progress) *Semantics without Truth-Values* (Oxford: Oxford University Press).

—— and Hornstein, H. (2002) 'Does Every Sentence Like This Contain a Scope Ambiguity', in W. Hinzen and H. Rott (eds.), *Belief in Meaning: Essays at the Interface* (Frankfurt: Hansel-Hohenhausen).

Pollack, J. (1989) 'Verb Movement, Universal Grammar, and the Structure of IP', *Linguistic Inquiry*, 20: 365–424.

Portner, P., and Partee, B. (2002) *Formal Semantics: The Essential Readings* (Cambridge, Mass: Blackwell).

Preyer, G., and Peters, G. (eds.) (2002) *Logical Form and Language* (Oxford: Oxford University Press).

Putnam, H. (1971) *Philosophy of Logic* (New York: Harper & Row).

Pylkannen, L. (1999) 'On Stativity and Causation', in Tenny and Pustajevsky (1999).

Quine, W. V. O. (1950) *Methods of Logic* (New York: Henry Holt).

—— (1951) 'Two Dogmas of Empiricism', *Philosophical Review*, 60: 20–43.

—— (1960) *Word and Object* (Cambridge, Mass.: MIT Press).

—— (1970) *Philosophy of Logic* (Englewood Cliffs, NJ: Prentice Hall).

Radford, A. (1988) *Transformational Grammar* (Cambridge: Cambridge University Press).

Ramsey, F. (1927) 'Facts and Propositions', *Aristotelian Society Supplementary Volume VII*: 153–70.

Raposo, E., and Uriagereka, J. (1996) 'Indefinite SE', *Natural Language and Linguistic Theory*, 14: 749–810.

Reinhart, T. (1983) *Anaphora and Semantic Interpretation* (Chicago: University of Chicago Press).

Rescher, N. (1962) 'Plurality Quantification', *Journal of Symbolic Logic*, 27: 373–4.

—— (ed.) (1967) *The Logic of Decision and Action* (Pittsburgh: University of Pittsburgh Press).

Reuland, E., and ter Meulen, A. (eds.) (1989) *The Representation of (In)definiteness* (Cambridge, Mass.: MIT Press).

Rey, G. (1998) 'A Naturalistic A Priori', *Philosophical Studies*, 92: 25–43.

Richard, M. (1990) *Propositional Attitudes* (Cambridge: Cambridge University Press).

Ross, J. (1967) 'Constraints on Variables in Syntax', doctoral dissertation, MIT.

Russell, B. (1905) 'On Denoting', *Mind*, 14: 479–93.

—— (1918) *The Philosophy of Logical Atomism* (LaSalle, Ind.: Open Court).

Russell, B. (1919) *Introduction to Mathematical Philosophy* (London: George Allen & Unwin).

Sainsbury, M. (1990) 'Concepts without Boundaries', King's College London, Inaugural lecture. Reprinted in Keefe and Smith (1996).

Scha, R. (1981) 'Distributive, Collective, and Cumulative Quantification', in J. Groenendijk *et. al.* (eds.), *Formal Methods in the Study of Language* (Amsterdam: Mathematisch Centrum).

Schein, B. (1993) *Plurals* (Cambridge, Mass.: MIT Press).

—— (2001) 'Adverbial, Descriptive Reciprocals', in R. Hastings *et al.*, *Proceedings of Semantics and Linguistic Theory XI* (Ithaca, NY: CLC Publications).

—— (2002) 'Events and the Semantic Content of Thematic Relations', in Preyer and Peters (2002).

—— (forthcoming), *Conjunction Reduction Redux* (Cambridge, Mass.: MIT Press).

Schwarzschild, R. (1996) *Pluralities* (Dordrecht: Kluwer).

Soames, S. (1987) 'Direct Reference, Propositional Attitititudes, and Semantic Content', *Philosophical Topics*, 15: 47–87.

—— (1995) 'Beyond Singular Propositions', *Canadian Journal of Philosophy*, 25: 515–50.

—— (2003) *Beyond Rigidity* (Oxford: Oxford University Press).

Stalnaker, R. (1974) 'Pragmatic Presuppositions', in M. Munitz and P. Unger (eds.), *Semantics and Philosophy* (New York: University Press), 197–213.

—— (1978) 'Assertion', *Syntax and Semantics*, 9: 315–22.

—— (1984) *Inquiry* (Cambridge, Mass.: MIT Press).

Strawson, P. (1950) 'On Referring', *Mind*, 59: 320–44.

—— (1985) 'Causation and Explanation', in Vermazen and Hintikka (1985).

Szabolsci, A. (ed.) (1997) *Ways of Scope Taking* (Dordrecht: Kluwer).

Tarski, A. (1933) 'The Concept of Truth in Formalized Languages'; reprinted in Tarski (1983).

—— (1984) 'The Semantic Conception of Truth', *Philosophy and Phenomenological Research*, 4: 341–75.

—— (1983) *Logic, Semantics, Metamathematics*, tr. J. H. Woodger, 2nd ed., ed. J. Corcoran (Indianapolis: Hackett).

Taylor, B. (1985) *Modes of Occurrence* (Oxford: Blackwell).

Tenny, C. (1994) *Aspectual Roles and the Syntax–Semantics Interface* (Dordrecht: Kluwer).

—— and Pustajevsky, J. (eds.) (1999) *Events as Grammatical Objects* (Stanford, Calif.: CSLI Publications).

Thalberg, I. (1972) *Enigmas of Agency* (London: Allen & Unwin).

Thomson, J. (1971) 'Individuating Actions', *Journal of Philosophy*, 68: 771–81.

—— (1977) *Acts and Other Events* (Ithaca NY.: Cornell University Press).

Traugott, E. (1972) *A History of English Syntax* (New York: Holt, Rinehart, & Winston).

Travis, L. (1984) '*Parameters and the Effects of Word-Order Variation*', doctoral dissertation, MIT.

Uriagereka, J. (1999) 'Multiple Spell-Out', in S. Epstein and N. Hornstein (eds.), *Working Minimalism* (Cambridge, Mass.: MIT Press).

—— (2002) *Derivations: Exploring the Dynamics of Syntax* (London: Routledge).

—— and Pietroski, P. (2001) 'Dimensions of Natural Language', *University of Maryland Working Papers in Linguistics*, (2001): 192–219. Reprinted in Uriagereka (2002).

van Bentham, J. (1984) *Essays in Logical Semantics* (Dordrecht: Reidel).

Vendler, Z. (1967) *Linguistics in Philosophy* (Ithaca, NY: Cornell University Press).

Vermazen, B., and Hintikka, M. (eds.) (1995) *Essays on Davidson: Actions and Events* (Oxford: Clarendon Press).

Vlach, F. (1983) 'On Situation Semantics for Perception', *Synthese*, 54: 129–52.

Westerståhl, D. (1984) 'Some Results on Quantifiers', *Notre Dame Journal of Formal Logic*, 25: 152–70.

Wiggins, D. (1980) ' "Most" and "All": Some Comments on a Familiar Programme and on the Logical Form of Quantified Sentences', in M. Platts (ed.), *Reference, Truth, and Reality* (London: Routledge & Kegan Paul).

Williams, E. (1980) 'Predication', *Linguistic Inquiry*, 11: 203–38.

—— (1981) 'Argument Structure and Morphology', *Linguistic Review*, 1: 81–114.

—— (1995) *Thematic Structure in Syntax* (Cambridge, Mass.: MIT Press).

Williamson, T. (1994) *Vagueness* (London: Routledge).

—— (2004) 'Everything', *Philosophical Perspectives*, 17: 415–66.

Wilson, G. (1989) *The Intentionality of Human Action* (revised and enlarged edn. Stanford, Calif.: Stanford University Press).

Wittgenstein, G. (1921) *Tractatus Logico-Philosophicus*, tr. D. Pears and B. McGuinness (London: Routledge & Kegan Paul).

—— (1953) *Philosophical Investigations* (New York: Macmillan).

Wright, C. (1975) 'On the Coherence of Vague Predicates', Synthèse, 30: 325–65.

—— (1983) *Frege's Conception of Numbers as Objects* (Scots Philosophical Monographs, 2: Aberdeen: Aberdeen University Press).

Yi, B. (1999) 'Is Two a Property?', *Journal of Philosophy*, 96: 163–90.

Zalta, E. (2003) 'Frege (logic, theorem, and foundations for arithmetic)', *Stanford Encyclopedia of Philosophy* (Fall 2003 edn.), ed. Edward N. Zalta, http://plato.stanford.edu/archives/fall2003/entries/frege-logic.

# Index